AF661761

TOURISM AND HOTEL INDUSTRY

TOURISM AND HOTEL INDUSTRY

Vinod Nair

CYBER TECH PUBLICATIONS
4264/3, Ansari Road, Daryaganj, New Delhi-110002 (India)
Ph.: 011-23244078, 011-43559448 Fax: 011-23280028
E-Mail: cyberpublicationsdelhi@yahoo.com
Website: www.cybertechpublications.com

TOURISM AND HOTEL INDUSTRY

Vinod Nair

© Reserved

First Edition 2010

All rights reserved. No part of this publication may be reproduced, stored in a retrieval system or transmitted, in any form or by any means, electronic, mechanical, photo copying, recording or otherwise, without the prior permission of the publisher.

Asian Offset Printers

Published by :

G.S. Rawat for **Cyber Tech Publications**
4264/3, Ansari Road, Daryaganj, New Delhi-110002 (India)
Ph.: 011-23244078, 011-43559448 Fax: 011-23280028
E-Mail: cyberpublicationsdelhi@yahoo.com
Website: www.cybertechpublications.com

Preface

Tourism and Hotel Industry is one of the world's most rapidly growing industries and it has emerged as a fast growing sector in terms of employment and income generation. Its contribution to the world economy is very significant. World Travel and Tourism Council has identified tourism as the world's most rapidly developing industry and its contribution to the world economy has almost doubled from 1990s. Besides employment generation, tourism sector has played a pivotal role in poverty alleviation and sustainable human development.

The concept of tourism is very complex to define though several attempts have been made by renowned writers to explain it. The international dictionary of tourism points out that 'tour' in English and in French means a journey, a circulative trip. The 19 century dictionary defines 'tourists' "as people who travel for pleasure of travelling out of curiosity and because they have nothing better to do," and even "for the joy of boasting about it afterwards." Conceptually tourism arises from the movement of people to, and their stay in, different destinations. The 'journey' is the dynamic element in it and the 'stay' static.

Against this background this collection of papers contributed by renowned writers, academicians and experienced administrators in the field of hospitality management embodies critical analysis of various aspects of tourism industry, both in theoretical and practical terms and makes concrete suggestions for revamping the tourism industry in India. The volume has been divided into three broad categories. The introductory part examines the global, national and regional evolution of tourism sector.

The second part unfolds the recent issues and facets in tourism viz., geographical information system, strategic management, health, marketing strategies, sustainable development, service quality, personalization, natural environment, eco tourism and the impact of terrorism on tourism industry. The concluding part presents a few micro level studies from an experimental perspective.

This book explores the entire industry from an international perspective to provide a better understanding of the effective decision-making process commonly used by managers regardless of location. Issues such as employee management, placement of hotel location, marketing decisions, yield management, and others are discussed in detail. Textbooks on the hotel industry are often limited in scope to only one discipline, perspective, or geographic area.

—*Author*

CONTENTS

1

Introduction

NATURE OF THE INDUSTRY

People travel for a variety of reasons, including for vacations, business, and visits to friends and relatives. For many of these travelers, hotels and other accommodations will be where they stay while out of town. For others, hotels may be more than just a place to stay, but destinations in themselves. Resort hotels and casino hotels, for example, offer a variety of activities to keep travelers and families occupied for much of their stay.

Goods and services. Hotels and other accommodations are as different as the many family and business travelers they accommodate. The industry includes all types of lodging, from luxurious 5-star hotels to youth hostels and RV parks. While many provide simply a place to spend the night, others cater to longer stays by providing food service, recreational activities, and meeting rooms. In 2006, approximately 62,000 establishments provided overnight accommodations to suit many different needs and budgets.

Hotels and motels comprise the majority of establishments in this industry and are generally classified as offering either full-service or limited service. Full-service properties offer a variety of services for their guests, but they almost always include at least one or more restaurant and beverage service options—from coffee bars and lunch counters to cocktail lounges and formal restaurants. They also usually provide room service. Larger full-service properties usually have a variety of retail shops on the premises, such as gift boutiques, newsstands, and drug and cosmetics counters, some of which may be geared to an exclusive clientele. Additionally, a number of full-service hotels offer guests access to laundry and valet services, swimming pools, beauty salons, and fitness centers or health spas. A small, but growing, number of luxury hotel chains also manage condominium units in combination with their transient rooms, providing both hotel guests and condominium owners with access to the same services and amenities.

The largest hotels often have banquet rooms, exhibit halls, and spacious ballrooms to accommodate conventions, business meetings, wedding receptions, and other social gatherings. Conventions and business meetings are major sources of revenue for these properties. Some commercial hotels are known as conference hotels—fully self-contained entities specifically designed for large-scale meetings. They provide physical fitness and recreational facilities for meeting attendees, in addition to state-of-the-art audiovisual and technical equipment, a business center, and banquet services.

Limited-service hotels are free-standing properties that do not have on-site restaurants or most other amenities that must be provided by a staff other than the front desk or housekeeping. They usually offer continental breakfasts, vending machines or small packaged items, Internet access, and sometimes unattended game rooms or swimming pools in addition to daily housekeeping services. The numbers of limited-service properties have been growing. These properties are not as costly to build and maintain. They appeal to budget-conscious family vacationers and travelers who are willing to sacrifice amenities for lower room prices.

Hotels can also be categorized based on a distinguishing feature or service provided by the hotel. *Conference hotels* provide meeting and banquet rooms, and usually food service, to large groups of people. *Resort hotels* offer luxurious surroundings with a variety of recreational facilities, such as swimming pools, golf courses, tennis courts, game rooms, and health spas, as well as planned social activities and entertainment. Resorts typically are located in vacation destinations or near natural settings, such as mountains, seashores, theme parks, or other attractions. As a result, the business of many resorts fluctuates with the season. Some resort hotels and motels provide additional convention and conference facilities to encourage customers to combine business with pleasure. During the off season, many of these establishments solicit conventions, sales meetings, and incentive tours to fill their otherwise empty rooms; some resorts even close for the off-season.

Extended-stay hotels typically provide rooms or suites with fully equipped kitchens, entertainment systems, office space with computer and telephone lines, fitness centers, and other amenities. Typically, guests use these hotels for a minimum of 5 consecutive nights often while on an extended work assignment or lengthy vacation or family visit. *All-suite hotels* offer a living room or sitting room in addition to a bedroom.

Casino hotels combine both lodging and legalized gaming on the same premises. Along with the typical services provided by most full-service hotels, casino hotels also contain casinos where patrons can wager at table games, play slot machines, and make other bets. Some casino hotels also contain conference and convention facilities.

In addition to hotels, *bed-and-breakfast inns, recreational vehicle (RV) parks, campgrounds*, and *rooming and boarding houses* provide lodging for overnight guests and are included in this industry. *Bed-and-breakfast inns* provide short-term lodging in private homes or small buildings converted for this purpose and are characterized by highly personalized service and inclusion of breakfast in the room rate. Their appeal is quaintness, with unusual service and decor.

RV parks and campgrounds cater to people who enjoy recreational camping at moderate prices. Some parks and campgrounds provide service stations, general stores, shower and toilet facilities, and coin-operated laundries. While some are designed for overnight travelers only, others are for vacationers who stay longer. Some camps provide accommodations, such as cabins and fixed campsites, and other amenities, such as food services, recreational facilities and equipment, and organized recreational activities. Examples of these overnight camps include children's camps, family vacation camps, hunting and fishing camps, and outdoor adventure retreats that offer trail riding, white-water rafting, hiking, fishing, game hunting, and similar activities.

Other short-term lodging facilities in this industry include *guesthouses*, or small cottages located on the same property as a main residence, and *youth hostels*—dormitory-style hotels with few frills, occupied mainly by students traveling on limited budgets. Also included are *rooming and boarding houses*, such as fraternity houses, sorority houses, off-campus dormitories, and workers' camps. These establishments provide temporary or longer term accommodations that may serve as a principal residence for the period of occupancy. These establishments also may provide services such as housekeeping, meals, and laundry services.

Industry organization. In recent years, the hotel industry has become dominated by a few large national hotel chains. To the traveler, familiar chain establishments represent dependability and quality at predictable rates. Many chains recognize the importance of brand loyalty to guests and have expanded the range of lodging options offered under one corporate name to include a full range of hotels from limited-service, economy-type hotels to luxury inns. While these national corporations own some of the hotels, many properties are independently owned but affiliated with a chain through a franchise agreement or management contract. As part of a chain, individual hotels can participate in the company's national reservations service or incentive program, thereby appearing to belong to a larger enterprise. For those who prefer more personalized service and a unique experience, *boutique hotels* are becoming more popular. These smaller hotels are generally found in urban locations and provide patrons good service and more distinctive décor and food selection.

While there are nationwide RV parks and campgrounds, most small lodging establishments are individually owned and operated by a single owner, who may employ a small staff to help operate the business.

Recent developments. The lodging industry is moving towards more limited-service properties mostly in suburban, residential, or commercial neighborhoods, often siting hotels near popular restaurants. Many full-service properties are limiting or quitting the food service business altogether, choosing to contract out their food service operations to third party restaurateurs, including long-term arrangements with chain restaurant operators. Urban business and entertainment districts are providing a greater mix of lodging options to appeal to a wider range of travelers.

Increased competition among establishments in this industry has spurred many independently owned and operated hotels and other lodging places to join national or international reservation systems. This allows travelers to make multiple reservations for lodging, airlines, and car rentals with one telephone call or Internet search. Nearly all hotel chains and many independent lodging facilities operate online reservation systems through the Internet or maintain websites that allow individuals to book rooms. Online marketing of properties is so popular with guests that many hotels promote themselves with elaborate websites and allow people to investigate availability and rates.

WORKING CONDITIONS

Hours. Because hotels are open around the clock, employees frequently work varying shifts or variable schedules. Employees who work the late shift generally receive additional compensation. Many employees enjoy the opportunity to work part-time, nights or evenings, or other schedules that fit their availability for work and the hotel's needs. Hotel managers and many department supervisors may work regularly assigned schedules, but they also routinely work longer hours than scheduled, especially during peak travel times or when multiple events are scheduled. Also, they may be called in to work on short notice in the event of an emergency or to cover a position. Those who are self-employed, often owner-operators of small inns, camp sites, or RV parks, tend to work long hours and often live at the establishment or nearby.

Office and administrative support workers generally work scheduled hours in an office setting, meeting with guests, clients, and hotel staff. Their work can become hectic processing orders and invoices, dealing with demanding guests, or servicing requests that require a quick turnaround, but job hazards typically are limited to muscle and eye strain common to working with computers and office equipment.

Computer specialists, information technology and audiovisual technicians who are employed mostly by larger convention hotels typically maintain standard hours servicing the property's websites and computer and communications networks. However, they often work long hours setting up and testing equipment for events that require their services.

Work environment. Work in hotels and other accommodations can be demanding and hectic. Hotel staffs provide a variety of services to guests and must do so efficiently, courteously, and accurately.

They must maintain a pleasant demeanor even during times of stress or when dealing with an impatient or irate guest. Alternately, work at slower times, such as the off-season or overnight periods, can seem slow and tiresome. Still, hotel workers must be ready to provide guests and visitors with gracious customer service at any hour.

Food preparation and food service workers in hotels must withstand the strain of working during busy periods and being on their feet for many hours. Kitchen workers lift heavy pots and kettles and work near hot ovens and grills. Job hazards include slips and falls, cuts, and burns, but injuries are seldom serious. Food service workers often carry heavy trays of food, dishes, and glassware. Many of these workers work part time, including evenings, weekends, and holidays.

In 2006, work-related injuries and illnesses averaged 5.8 for every 100 full-time workers in hotels and other accommodations, compared with 4.4 for workers throughout private industry. Work hazards include burns from hot equipment, sprained muscles and wrenched backs from heavy lifting, and falls on wet floors.

EMPLOYMENT

Hotels and other accommodations provided 1.8 million wage and salary jobs in 2006. In addition, there were about 40,000 self-employed and unpaid family workers in the industry, who worked in bed-and-breakfast inns, camps, and small inns and hotels.

Employment is concentrated in cities and resort areas. Compared with establishments in other industries, hotels and other accommodations tend to be small. About 75 percent employed fewer than 20 workers and 55 percent employed fewer than 10 (chart). As a result, lodging establishments offer opportunities for those who are interested in owning and running their own business. Although establishments tend to be small, the majority of jobs are in larger hotels with more than 100 employees.

Hotels and other lodging places often provide first jobs to many new entrants to the labor force. In 2006, about 17 percent of the workers were younger than age 25, compared with about 14 percent across all industries.

OCCUPATIONS IN THE INDUSTRY

The vast majority of workers in this industry—more than 4 out of 5 in 2006—were employed in service and office and administrative support occupations. Workers in these occupations usually learn their skills on the job. Postsecondary education is not required for most entry-level positions; however, college training may be helpful for advancement in some of the occupations. For those in administrative support—mainly hotel desk clerks—and service occupations, positive personality traits and a customer-service orientation may be more important than formal schooling. Traits most important for success in the hotels and other accommodations industry are good communication skills; the ability to get along with people in stressful situations; a neat, clean appearance; and a pleasant manner.

Service occupations. Service workers are by far the largest occupational group in the industry, accounting for 65 percent of the industry's employment. Most service jobs are in housekeeping occupations—including *building cleaning workers*, *maids and housekeeping cleaners*, and *janitors and cleaners*—and in food preparation and serving jobs—including *chefs and head cooks*, *waiters and waitresses*, *bartenders*, *fast food and counter workers*, and various other kitchen and dining room workers. The industry also employs many *baggage porters and bellhops*, *gaming services workers*, and *grounds maintenance workers*.

Workers in cleaning and housekeeping occupations ensure that the lodging facility is clean and in good condition for the comfort and safety of guests. *Maids and housekeeping cleaners* clean lobbies, halls, guestrooms, and bathrooms. They make sure that guests not only have clean rooms, but have all the necessary furnishings and supplies. They change sheets and towels, vacuum carpets, dust furniture, empty wastebaskets, and mop bathroom floors. In larger hotels, the housekeeping staff may include assistant housekeepers, floor supervisors, housekeepers, and executive housekeepers. *Janitors* help with the cleaning of the public areas of the facility, empty trash, and perform minor maintenance work.

Workers in the various *food preparation and serving* occupations deal with customers in the dining room or at a service counter. *Waiters and waitresses* take customers' orders, serve meals, and prepare checks. In smaller establishments, they often set tables, escort guests to their seats, accept payment, and clear tables. In larger restaurants, some of these tasks are assigned to other workers.

Hosts and hostesses welcome guests, show them to their tables, and give them menus. *Bartenders* fill beverage orders for customers seated at the bar or from waiters and waitresses who serve patrons at tables. *Dining room and cafeteria attendants* and *bartender helpers* assist waiters, waitresses, and bartenders by clearing, cleaning, and setting up tables, replenishing supplies at the bar, and keeping the serving areas stocked with linens, tableware, and other supplies. *Fast food and counter workers* take orders and serve food at fast-food counters and in coffee shops; they also may operate the cash register.

Chefs, cooks and food preparation workers prepare food in the kitchen. Larger hotels employ chefs and cooks who specialize in the preparation of many different kinds of food. They may have titles such as salad chef, grill chef, or pastry chef. Individual chefs may oversee the day-to-day operations of different kitchens in a hotel, such as a fine-dining full-service restaurant, a casual or counter-service establishment, or banquet operations. Chef positions generally are attained after years of experience and, sometimes, formal training, including apprenticeships. Larger establishments also employ *executive chefs* and *food and beverage directors* who plan menus, purchase food, and supervise kitchen personnel for all of the kitchens in the property. *Food preparation workers* shred lettuce for salads, cut up food for cooking, and perform simple cooking steps under the direction of the chef or head cook. Beginners may advance to more skilled food preparation jobs with experience or specialized culinary training.

Many full-service hotels employ a uniformed staff to assist arriving and departing guests. *Baggage porters and bellhops* carry bags and escort guests to their rooms. *Concierges* arrange special or personal services for guests. They may take messages, arrange for babysitting, make restaurant reservations, provide directions, arrange for or give advice on entertainment and local attractions, and monitor requests for housekeeping and maintenance. *Doorkeepers* help guests into and out of their cars, summon taxis, and carry baggage into the hotel lobby.

Hotels also employ the largest percentage of *gaming services* workers because much of gaming takes place in casino hotels. Some gaming services positions are associated with oversight and direction—supervision, surveillance, and investigation—while others involve working with the games or patrons themselves, by tending the slot machines, handling money, writing and running tickets, dealing cards, and performing related duties.

The industry also employs a large number of *recreation and fitness workers*. At resort hotels and at vacation and recreational camps, recreation workers organize and conduct recreation activities for guests and campers. *Camp counselors* lead and instruct children and teenagers in outdoor-oriented forms of recreation, such as swimming, hiking, horseback riding, and camping. In addition, counselors at vacation and resident camps also provide guidance and supervise daily living and general socialization. Other types of campgrounds may employ trail guides for activities such as hiking, hunting, and fishing.

Office and administrative support occupations. These positions accounted for 19 percent of the jobs in hotels and other accommodations in 2006. Hotel desk clerks, bookkeeping and accounting clerks, and switchboard operators ensure that the front office operates smoothly. *Hotel, motel, and resort desk clerks* process reservations and guests' registrations and checkouts, monitor arrivals and departures, handle complaints, and receive and forward mail. The duties of hotel desk clerks depend on the size of the facility. In smaller lodging places, one clerk or a manager may do everything. In larger hotels, a larger staff divides the duties among several types of clerks.

Management, business, and financial operations occupations. Hotels and other lodging places employ many different types of managers to direct and coordinate the activities of the front office, kitchen, dining room, and other departments, such as housekeeping, accounting, personnel, purchasing, publicity, sales, security and maintenance. *Lodging managers*, typically the general manager and assistant managers, make decisions that affect the general operations of the hotel, including setting room rates, establishing credit policy, and having ultimate responsibility for resolving problems. In smaller establishments, lodging managers also may perform many of the front-office clerical tasks. In the smallest establishments, the owners—sometimes a family team—do all the work necessary to operate the business.

Other managers are responsible for different phases of hotel operations. For example, *food and beverage managers* oversee restaurants, lounges, and catering or banquet operations. *Rooms managers* look after reservations and occupancy levels to ensure proper room assignments and authorize discounts, special rates, or promotions. Large hotels, especially those with conference centers, use an executive committee structure to improve departmental communications and coordinate activities. Other managers who may serve on a hotel's executive committee include *public relations* or *sales managers, human resource directors, executive housekeepers*, and *heads of hotel security*.

Other occupations. Hotels and other accommodations employ a variety of workers found in many other industries. *General maintenance and repair workers* fix leaky faucets, do some painting and carpentry, make sure that heating and air-conditioning equipment works properly, mow lawns, and exterminate pests. The industry also employs cashiers, accountants, personnel workers, and entertainers. As properties acquire and use more sophisticated computer systems, they employ more *computer specialists* to help maintain these systems as well as the hotel's website, and computer connections for guests. Also, many additional workers inside a hotel may work for other companies under contract to the hotel or may provide personal or retail services directly to hotel guests from space rented by the hotel. This group includes guards and security officers, barbers, cosmetologists, fitness trainers and aerobics instructors, valets, gardeners, and parking attendants.

Table 1. Employment of wage and salary workers in hotels and other accommodations by occupation, 2006 and projected change, 2006-2016.(Employment in thousands)

Occupation	Employment, 2006		Percent change, 2006-16
	Number	Percent	
All occupations	1,833	100.0	13.9
Management, business, and financial occupations	94	5.1	17.1
General and operations managers	12	0.7	4.0
Lodging managers	29	1.6	26.6
Meeting and convention planners	8	0.5	15.8
Accountants and auditors	8	0.4	16.0
Service occupations	1,184	64.6	13.5
Security guards	30	1.7	9.5

Chefs and head cooks	13	0.7	10.2
First-line supervisors/managers of food preparation and serving workers	23	1.3	16.2
Cooks, restaurant	57	3.1	12.8
Food preparation workers	21	1.1	16.1
Bartenders	36	2.0	16.3
Fast food and counter workers	28	1.5	23.9
Waiters and waitresses	133	7.2	6.9
Food servers, nonrestaurant	41	2.3	9.5
Dining room and cafeteria attendants and bartender helpers	46	2.5	7.9
Dishwashers	33	1.8	7.1
Hosts and hostesses, restaurant, lounge, and coffee shop	19	1.0	6.7
First-line supervisors/managers of housekeeping and janitorial workers	32	1.7	16.4
Janitors and cleaners, except maids and housekeeping cleaners	52	2.9	18.9
Maids and housekeeping cleaners	424	23.1	15.8
Landscaping and groundskeeping workers	22	1.2	16.1
Gaming supervisors	11	0.6	18.8
Gaming dealers	34	1.9	18.8
Amusement and recreation attendants	12	0.6	15.9
Baggage porters and bellhops	25	1.4	6.2
Concierges	8	0.4	4.9
Recreation workers	10	0.5	9.7
Sales and related occupations	52	2.9	12.0
Cashiers, except gaming	15	0.8	5.1
Gaming change persons and booth cashiers	7	0.4	-5.0
Sales representatives, services	12	0.7	27.2

Office and administrative support occupations	345	18.8	13.8
First-line supervisors/managers of office and administrative support workers	25	1.3	8.0
Switchboard operators, including answering service	9	0.5	-7.1
Bookkeeping, accounting, and auditing clerks	23	1.3	16.0
Hotel, motel, and resort desk clerks	207	11.3	17.2
Reservation and transportation ticket agents and travel clerks	13	0.7	4.6
Secretaries and administrative assistants	16	0.9	10.0
Installation, maintenance, and repair occupations	82	4.5	15.5
Maintenance and repair workers, general	70	3.8	15.7
Production occupations	38	2.1	18.2
Laundry and dry-cleaning workers	31	1.7	18.9
Transportation and material moving occupations	24	1.3	9.3
Taxi drivers and chauffeurs	8	0.4	14.2
Parking lot attendants	8	0.5	5.2

Note: Columns may not add to totals due to omission of occupations with small employment

Training and Advancement

Most large hotel properties employ persons in occupations that require a wide range of skills and experience. Most entry-level jobs require little or no previous training; basic tasks usually can be learned in a short time. Lodging managers and many department heads conversely usually require some formal training or years of hospitality industry experience, or both. All positions though require employees to maintain a customer-service orientation. Yet, almost all workers in the hotel and other accommodations industry undergo some on-the-job training provided under the supervision of an experienced employee or manager to acclimate new employees to any unique characteristics of the property or the local area.

Hotel managers and owners recognize the importance of personal service and attention to guests; so they look for persons with positive personality traits and good communication skills when filling many guest services positions, such as desk clerk and host and hostess positions. Many hotel managers place a greater emphasis on customer service skills while providing specialized training in other skill areas, such as computer technology and software. Vocational courses and apprenticeship programs in food preparation, catering, and hotel and restaurant management, offered through restaurant and lodging associations and trade unions, provide training opportunities. Programs range in length from a few months to several years.

Service workers. Most service workers need only a high school diploma or equivalent to get hired, but some can be hired with even less. Some entry-level jobs are filled by students looking for part-time or seasonal work. Most hotels, particularly the chain hotels, have some formal training sessions for new employees that may include video or on-line training. Advancement opportunities for service workers in the hotel industry vary widely. Some workers, such as housekeepers and janitors, generally have few opportunities for advancement. In large properties, some may advance to supervisory positions. Advancement opportunities for chefs and cooks are better than those for most other service occupations. Cooks often advance to chef or to supervisory and management positions, such as executive chef, restaurant manager, or food service manager. Hotel desk clerks sometimes advance to supervisory or managerial front-office positions.

Promotional opportunities often are greatest for those who are willing to take on a new assignment in a different department. Advancement for those who excel at customer service and demonstrate a willingness to learn front-office jobs can serve as a steppingstone to jobs in public relations, advertising, sales, and management.

Management, business, and financial operations occupations. Many hotels fill first-level manager positions by promoting staff from within—particularly those with good communication skills, a solid educational background, tact, loyalty, and a capacity to endure hard work and long hours. People with these qualities still advance to manager jobs but, more recently, lodging chains have primarily been hiring persons with 4-year college degrees in the liberal arts or other fields and starting them in assistant manager or management trainee positions. Bachelor's and Master's degree programs in hotel, restaurant, and hospitality management provide the strongest background for a career as a hotel manager, with nearly 150 colleges and universities offering such programs. Graduates of these programs are highly sought by employers in this industry, because of their familiarity with technical issues and their ability to learn related skills quickly. Eventually, they may advance to a top management position in a hotel or a corporate management position in a large chain operation. Upper management positions, such as general manager, food service manager, or sales manager, generally require considerable formal training and job experience. Some department managers, executive housekeepers, and executive chefs, generally require some specialized training and extensive on-the-job experience. To advance to positions with more responsibilities, lodging managers frequently change employers or relocate within a chain to a property in another area.

Office and administrative support occupations. For office and administrative support workers, advancement opportunities in the hotel industry vary widely. These occupations offer excellent entry-level job prospects and can serve as a steppingstone to jobs in hospitality, public relations, advertising, sales, and management.

Outlook

The hotels and other accommodations industry is expected to provide many new jobs over the 2006-16 period. New hotel construction and steady strength in the business and international travel segments will create job opportunities in an array of occupations in this industry.

Employment change. Wage and salary employment in hotels and other accommodations is expected to increase by 14 percent, compared with 11 percent growth projected for all industries combined. Travel and tourism, having rebounded since the recession following 9/11, is expected to continue growing and result in a greater need for transient rooms. All segments of the hotel market are expected to see increases in the number of rooms, but the greatest number of rooms coming on line will be in limited service hotels that do not provide food service. Many of these newer hotels are being built in the suburbs where a growing population is increasingly based and a base of business establishments is being developed.

Employment outlook varies somewhat by service class of hotel and occupation. Growth of full-service hotels, casino hotels, and the small, but burgeoning, luxury hotel market that specializes in personal service will cause employment of lodging managers to grow much faster than the average. The accelerating trend toward chain-affiliated hotels should provide managers with opportunities for advancement into general manager positions, manager jobs at larger and busier properties, and corporate administrative jobs.

Opportunities should be more limited for self-employed managers or owners of small lodging places, such as bed-and-breakfast inns, because of the competition from long-established chains as they move into new markets once friendly to the quainter properties. Job opportunities at outdoor recreation and RV parks should grow as RVs and driving vacations gain popularity in the United States. Also, gaming services and gaming manager occupations should grow as more casino hotels are built.

Employment of hotel, motel, and resort desk clerks is expected to grow faster than some other occupations in the industry in part because the growing numbers of limited-service hotels still require desk clerks. Employment of waiters and waitresses will grow more slowly—reflecting the increasing number of hotels and other accommodations that either do not offer full-service restaurants or contract them out to other food service establishments.

Job prospects. Although most of the hotels opening over the next decade will be limited service hotels, most of the job openings will arise in full-service hotels, including convention, casino, and resort hotels, because they employ the most workers. Limited-service properties do not operate restaurants, or lounges; therefore, these establishments offer a narrower range of employment opportunities; however, the streamlined organizational structure offers a faster route to the general manager level for those more interested in running or owning their own hotel. Job opportunities will be concentrated in the largest hotel occupations, such as building cleaning workers and hotel, motel, and resort desk clerks. These workers are found in all types of hotels and accommodations, from the limited service economy hotels to posh casino hotels. They also are important to the growing luxury hotel segment that emphasizes personal service.

Some occupations in this industry have relatively high numbers of workers who leave their jobs and must be replaced. Many young people and those looking only for seasonal or part-time work, and not a career, take food service and clerical jobs that require little or no previous training. To attract and retain workers, the hotel and other accommodations industry is placing more emphasis on training and retaining employees. Therefore, job opportunities in this industry should be plentiful for first-time jobseekers and people with limited skills.

Earnings

Industry earnings. Earnings in hotels and other accommodations generally are much lower than the average for all industries. In 2006, average earnings for all nonsupervisory workers in this industry were $353 a week, compared with $533 a week, for workers throughout private industry. Many workers in this industry earn the Federal minimum wage of $5.85 an hour or less, if tips are included as a substantial part of earnings. Workers in these lower paying occupations will see their future earnings increase on a phased-in basis to $7.25 per hour by 2009. Some States have laws that establish a higher minimum wage.

Food and beverage service workers, as well as hosts and hostesses, maids and housekeeping cleaners, concierges, and baggage porters and bellhops, derive their earnings from a combination of hourly earnings and customer tips. Waiters and waitresses often derive the majority of their earnings from tips, which vary greatly depending on menu prices and the volume of customers served. Many employers also provide free meals and furnish uniforms. Food service personnel may receive extra pay for working at banquets and on other special occasions. In general, workers with the greatest skills, such as restaurant cooks, have the highest earnings, and workers who receive tips have the lowest.

Salaries of lodging managers are dependent upon the size and sales volume of the establishment and their specific duties and responsibilities. Managers may earn bonuses ranging up to 50 percent of their basic salary. In addition, they may be furnished with meals, parking, laundry, and other services, and sometimes on-site lodging for themselves and their families. Some hotels offer profit-sharing plans, tuition reimbursement, and other benefits to their employees.

Benefits and union membership. About 10 percent of the workers in hotels and other accommodations are union members or are covered by union contracts, compared with 13 percent of workers in all industries combined.

2

The Hotel Tourism

Tourism is travel for recreational or leisure purposes. The World Tourism Organization defines **tourists** as people who "travel to and stay in places outside their usual environment for more than twenty-four (24) hours and not more than one consecutive year for leisure, business and other purposes not related to the exercise of an activity remunerated from within the place visited". Tourism has become a popular global leisure activity. In 2007, there were over 903 million international tourist arrivals, with a growth of 6.6% as compared to 2006. International tourist receipts were USD 856 billion in 2007.

Despite the uncertainties in the global economy, international tourist arrivals during the first four months of 2008 followed a similar growth trend than the same period in 2007. However, as a result of the economic crisis of 2008, international travel demand suffered a strong slowdown beginning in June 2008, with growth in international tourism arrivals worldwide falling to 2% during the boreal summer months, while growth from January to April 2008 had reached an average 5.7% compared to its 2007 level. Growth from 2006 to 2007 was only 3.7%, as total international tourism arrivals from January to August were 641 million tourists, up from 618 million in the same period in 2007.

Tourism is vital for many countries, such as the U.A.E, Egypt, Greece and Thailand, and many island nations, such as The Bahamas, Fiji, Maldives and the Seychelles, due to the large intake of money for businesses with their goods and services and the opportunity for employment in the service industries associated with tourism. These service industries include transportation services, such as airlines, cruise ships and taxis, hospitality services, such as accommodations, including hotels and resorts, and entertainment venues, such as amusement parks, casinos, shopping malls, the various music venues and the theatre.

Definition

Hunziker and Krapf, in 1941, defined tourism as people who travel "the sum of the phenomena and relationships arising from the travel and stay of non-residents, insofar as they do not lead to permanent residence and are not connected with any earning activity." In 1976, the Tourism Society of England's definition was: "Tourism is the temporary, short-term movement of people to destination outside the places where they normally live and work and their activities during the stay at each destination. It includes movements for all purposes." In 1981, the International Association of Scientific Experts in Tourism defined tourism in terms of particular activities selected by choice and undertaken outside the home.

The United Nations classified three forms of tourism in 1994, in its "Recommendations on Tourism Statistics: Domestic tourism", which involves residents of the given country traveling only within this country; Inbound tourism, involving non-residents traveling in the given country; and Outbound tourism, involving residents traveling in another country. The UN also derived different categories of tourism by combining the three basic forms of tourism: Internal tourism, which comprises domestic tourism and inbound tourism; National tourism, which comprises domestic tourism and outbound tourism; and International tourism, which consists of inbound tourism and outbound tourism. *Intrabound tourism* is a term coined by the Korea Tourism Organization and widely accepted in Korea. Intrabound tourism differs from domestic tourism in that the former encompasses policymaking and implementation of national tourism policies.

Recently, the tourism industry has shifted from the promotion of inbound tourism to the promotion of intrabound tourism, because many countries are experiencing tough competition for inbound tourists. Some national policymakers have shifted their priority to the promotion of intrabound tourism to contribute to the local economy. Examples of such campaigns include: "See America" in the United States; "Truly Asia" in Malaysia; "Get Going Canada" in Canada; "Peru. Live the Legend" in Peru; "Wow Philippines" in the Philippines; "Uniquely Singapore" in Singapore; "100% Pure New Zealand" in New Zealand; "Amazing Thailand" in Thailand; "Incredible India" in India; and "The Hidden Charm" in Vietnam.

WORLD TOURISM STATISTICS AND RANKINGS

Most Visited Countries

The World Tourism Organization reports the following ten countries as the most visited in 2007 by number of international travelers. When compared to 2006, Ukraine entered the top ten list, surpassing Russia, Austria and Mexico. Most of the top visited countries continue to be on the European continent.

Rank	Country	UNWTO Regional Market	International tourist arrivals (2007)	International tourist arrivals (2006)
1	France	Europe	81.9 million	79.1 million
2	Spain	Europe	59.2 million	58.5 million
3	United States	North America	56.0 million	51.1 million
4	China	Asia	54.7 million	49.6 million
5	Italy	Europe	43.7 million	41.1 million
6	United Kingdom	Europe	30.7 million	30.7 million
7	Germany	Europe	24.4 million	23.6 million
8	Ukraine	Europe	23.1 million	18.9 million
9	Turkey	Europe	22.2 million	18.9 million
10	Mexico	North America	21.4 million	21.4 million

International Tourism Receipts

International tourist receipts were USD 96.7 billion in 2007, up from USD 85.7 billion in 2006. When the export value of international passenger travel receipts is accounted for, total receipts in 2007 reached a record of USD 1.02 trillion or 3 billion a day. The World Tourism Organization reports the following countries as the top ten tourism earners for the year 2007. It is noticeable that most of them are on the European continent, but the United States continues to be the top earner.

Rank	Country	UNWTO Regional Market	International Tourism Receipts (2007)	International Tourism Receipts (2006)
1	United States	North America	$96.7 billion	$85.7 billion
2	Spain	Europe	$57.8 billion	$51.1 billion
3	France	Europe	$54.2 billion	$46.3 billion
4	Italy	Europe	$42.7 billion	$38.1 billion
5	China	Asia	$41.9 billion	$33,9 billion
6	United Kingdom	Europe	$37.6 billion	$33.7 billion
7	Germany	Europe	$36.0 billion	$32.8 billion
8	Australia	Oceania	$22.2 billion	$17.8 billion
9	Austria	Europe	$18.9 billion	$16.6 billion
10	Turkey	Europe	$18.5 billion	$16.9 billion

International Tourism Top Spenders

The World Tourism Organization reports the following countries as the top ten biggest spenders on international tourism for the year 2007. For the fifth year in a row, German tourists continue as the top spenders. A study by Dresdner Bank forecasts that for 2008, Germans and Europeans, in general, will continue to be the top spenders, because of the strength of the Euro against the United States dollar, with strong demand for the U.S. in favor of other destinations.

Rank	Country	UNWTO Regional Market	International Tourism Expenditures (2007)	International Tourism Expenditures (2006)
1	Germany	Europe	$82.9 billion	$73.9 billion
2	United States	North America	$76.2 billion	$72.1 billion
3	United Kingdom	Europe	$72.3 billion	$63.1 billion
4	France	Europe	$36.7 billion	$31.2 billion
5	China	Asia	$29.8 billion	$24.3 billion
6	Italy	Europe	$27.3 billion	$23.1 billion
7	Japan	Asia	$26.5 billion	$26.9 billion
8	Canada	North America	$24.8 billion	$20.5 billion
9	Russia	Europe	$22.3 billion	$18.2 billion
10	South Korea	Asia	$20.9 billion	$18.9 billion

History

Wealthy people have always traveled to distant parts of the world, to see great buildings, works of art, learn new languages, experience new cultures and to taste different cuisines. Long ago, at the time of the Roman Republic, places such as Baiae, were popular coastal resorts for the rich. The word *tourism* was used by 1811 and *tourist* by 1840. In 1936, the League of Nations defined *foreign tourist* as "someone travelling abroad for at least twenty-four hours". Its successor, the United Nations, amended this definition in 1945, by including a maximum stay of six months.

Leisure Travel

Leisure travel was associated with the Industrial Revolution in the United Kingdom – the first European country to promote leisure time to the increasing industrial population. Initially, this applied to the owners of the machinery of production, the economic oligarchy, the factory owners and the traders. These comprised the new middle class. Cox & Kings was the first official travel company to be formed in 1758.

The British origin of this new industry is reflected in many place names.

In Nice, France, one of the first and best-established holiday resorts on the French Riviera, the long esplanade along the seafront is known to this day as the *Promenade des Anglais*; in many other historic resorts in continental Europe, old, well-established palace hotels have names like the *Hotel Bristol*, the *Hotel Carlton* or the *Hotel Majestic* – reflecting the dominance of English customers.

Many leisure-oriented tourists travel to the tropics, both in the summer and winter. Places often visited are: Cuba, the Dominican Republic, Thailand, North Queensland in Australia and Florida in the United States.

Winter Tourism

Major ski resorts are located in the various, mainland European countries, Canada, the United States, Australia, New Zealand, Japan, Korea, Chile and Argentina.

Mass Tourism

Mass tourism could only have developed with the improvements in technology, allowing the transport of large numbers of people in a short space of time to places of leisure interest, so that greater numbers of people began to enjoy the benefits of leisure time.

In the United States, the first great seaside resort, in the European style, was Atlantic City, New Jersey and Long Island, New York. In continental Europe, early resorts included: Ostend, popularized by the people of Brussels; Boulogne-sur-Mer (Pas-de-Calais) and Deauville (Calvados) for the Parisians; and Heiligendamm, founded in 1797, as the first seaside resort at the Baltic Sea.

Adjectival Tourisms

Adjectival tourism refers to the numerous niche or specialty travel forms of tourism that have emerged over the years, each with its own adjective. Many of these have come into common use by the tourism industry and academics. Others are emerging concepts that may or may not gain popular usage. Examples of the more common niche tourism markets include:

1. Culinary tourism
2. Dark tourism
3. Disaster tourism
4. Ecotourism
5. Heritage tourism
6. LGBT tourism
7. Medical tourism
8. Nautical tourism
9. Sex tourism
10. Space tourism
11. War tourism

Recent Developments

There has been an upmarket trend in the tourism over the last few decades, especially in Europe, where international travel for short breaks is common. Tourists have higher levels of disposable income and greater leisure time and they are also better-educated and have more sophisticated tastes. There is now a demand for a better quality products, which has resulted in a fragmenting of the mass market for beach vacations; people want more specialised versions, such as Club 18-30, quieter resorts, family-oriented holidays or niche market-targeted destination hotels.

The developments in technology and transport infrastructure, such as jumbo jets, low-cost airlines and more accessible airports have made many types of tourism more affordable. There have also been changes in lifestyle, such as retiree-age people who sustain year round tourism. This is facilitated by internet sales of tourism products. Some sites have now started to offer dynamic packaging, in which an inclusive price is quoted for a tailor-made package requested by the customer upon impulse.

There have been a few setbacks in tourism, such as the September 11 attacks and terrorist threats to tourist destinations, such as in Bali and several European cities. Also, on December 26, 2004, a tsunami, caused by the 2004 Indian Ocean earthquake, hit the Asian countries on the Indian Ocean, including the Maldives. Thousands of lives were lost and many tourists died. This, together with the vast clean-up operation in place, has stopped or severely hampered tourism to the area.

The terms *tourism* and *travel* are sometimes used interchangeably. In this context, travel has a similar definition to tourism, but implies a more purposeful journey. The terms *tourism* and *tourist* are sometimes used pejoratively, to imply a shallow interest in the cultures or locations visited by tourists.

SUSTAINABLE TOURISM

"Sustainable tourism is envisaged as leading to management of all resources in such a way that economic, social and aesthetic needs can be fulfilled while maintaining cultural integrity, essential ecological processes, biological diversity and life support systems." (World Tourism Organization)

Sustainable development implies "meeting the needs of the present without compromising the ability of future generations to meet their own needs" (World Commission on Environment and Development, 1987).

MEDICAL TOURISM

When there is a significant price difference between countries for a given medical procedure, particularly in Southeast Asia, India, Eastern Europe and where there are different regulatory regimes, in relation to particular medical procedures (e.g. dentistry), travelling to take advantage of the price or regulatory differences is often referred to as "medical tourism".

EDUCATIONAL TOURISM

Educational tourism developed, because of the growing popularity of teaching and learning of knowledge and the enhancing of technical competency outside of the classroom environment. In educational tourism, the main focus of the tour or leisure activity includes visiting another country to learn about the culture, such as in Student Exchange Programs and Study Tours, or to work and apply skills learned inside the classroom in a different environment, such as in the International Practicum Training Program.

OTHER DEVELOPMENTS

Creative Tourism

Creative tourism has existed as a form of cultural tourism, since the early beginnings of **tourism** itself. Its European roots date back to the time of the Grand Tour, which saw the sons of aristocratic families traveling for the purpose of mostly interactive, educational experiences. More recently, creative tourism has been given its own name by Crispin Raymond and Greg Richards, who as members of the Association for Tourism and Leisure Education (ATLAS), have directed a number of projects for the European Commission, including cultural and crafts tourism, known as sustainable tourism. They have defined "creative tourism" as tourism related to the active participation of travelers in the culture of the host community, through interactive workshops and informal learning experiences.

Meanwhile, the concept of creative tourism has been picked up by high-profile organizations such as UNESCO, who through the Creative Cities Network, have endorsed creative tourism as an engaged, authentic experience that promotes an active understanding of the specific cultural features of a place.

More recently, creative tourism has gained popularity as a form of cultural tourism, drawing on active participation by travelers in the culture of the host communities they visit. Several countries offer examples of this type of tourism development, including the United Kingdom, the Bahamas, Jamaica, Spain, Italy and New Zealand.

Dark Tourism

One emerging area of special interest tourism has been identified by Lennon and Foley (2000) as "dark" tourism. This type of tourism involves visits to "dark" sites, such as battlegrounds, scenes of horrific crimes or acts of genocide, for example: concentration camps. Dark tourism poses severe ethical and moral dilemmas: should these sites be available for visitation and, if so, what should the nature of the publicity involved be. Dark tourism remains a small niche market, driven by varied motivations, such as mourning, remembrance, macabre curiosity or even entertainment. Its early origins are rooted in fairgrounds and medieval fairs.

Growth

The World Tourism Organization (UNWTO) forecasts that international tourism will continue growing at the average annual rate of 4 %. By 2020 Europe will remain the most popular destination, but its share will drop from 60% in 1995 to 46%. Long-haul will grow slightly faster than intraregional travel and by 2020 its share will increase from 18% in 1995 to 24%.

With the advent of e-commerce, tourism products have become one of the most traded items on the internet. Tourism products and services have been made available through intermediaries, although tourism providers (hotels, airlines, etc.) can sell their services directly. This has put pressure on intermediaries from both on-line and traditional shops.

It has been suggested there is a strong correlation between Tourism expenditure per capita and the degree to which countries play in the global context. Not only as a result of the important economic contribution of the tourism industry, but also as an indicator of the degree of confidence with which global citizens leverage the resources of the globe for the benefit of their local economies. This is why any projections of growth in tourism may serve as an indication of the relative influence that each country will exercise in the future.

Space tourism is expected to "take off" in the first quarter of the 21st century, although compared with traditional destinations the number of tourists in orbit will remain low until technologies such as a space elevator make space travel cheap.

Technological improvement is likely to make possible air-ship hotels, based either on solar-powered airplanes or large dirigibles. Underwater hotels, such as Hydropolis, expected to open in Dubai in 2009, will be built. On the ocean, tourists will be welcomed by ever larger cruise ships and perhaps floating cities.

Latest Trends

As a result of the economic crisis of 2008, international arrivals suffered a strong slowdown beginning in June 2008. Growth from 2007 to 2008 was only 3.7% during the first eight months of 2008. The Asian and Pacific markets were affected and Europe stagnated during the boreal summer months, while the Americas performed better, reducing their expansion rate but keeping a 6% growth from January to August 2008. Only the Middle East continued its rapid growth during the same period, reaching a 17% growth as compared to the same period in 2007. This slowdown on international tourism demand was also reflected in the air transport industry, with a negative growth in September 2008 and a 3.3% growth in passenger traffic through September. The hotel industry also reports a slowdown, as room occupancy continues to decline. As the global economic situation deteriorated dramatically during September and October as a result of the global financial crisis, growth of international tourism is expected to slow even further for the remaining of 2008, and this slowdown in demand growth is forecasted to continue into 2009 as recession has already hit most of the top spender countries, with long-haul travel expected to be the most affected by the economic crisis. However, some travel destinations have experienced growth during hard economic times, drawing on low costs of living, accessibility, and friendly immigration laws permitting tourists to stay for extended periods of time. Recession tourism, a phrase coined by Matt Landau in his research about Panama, has evolved as an alternative escape option for nervous crisis-goers in 2009.

Negative Impacts

Tourism is the issue that nearly every city faces. It is worldwide and a threat to beaches, famous landmarks, holy areas and also resorts. Attracting a high volume of tourists can have negative impacts, such as the impact of 33 million tourists a year on the city of New York, or the potential to impact fragile environments negatively, or the impact of the December 26, 2004 tsunami on the tourists themselves. The environment can be affected negatively by cruise ship pollution in many ways, including ballast water discharge, and by pollution from aircraft.

3

Tourism and Hospitality

India offers myriad exciting experiences to tourists. The country boasts of the world's highest mountains, miles of coastline with excellent beaches, tropical forests and wildlife, lagoon backwaters, ancient monuments and World Heritage sites, forts and palaces, and of course, the Taj Mahal. The Indian tourism and hospitality industry has thus emerged as one of the key sectors driving the country's growth and is thriving, owing to a huge surge in both business and leisure travel by foreign and domestic tourists.

According to the latest Tourism Satellite Accounting (TSA) research, released by the World Travel and Tourism Council (WTTC) and its strategic partner Accenture, India's travel and tourism industry was estimated to generate approximately US$ 100 billion in 2008. This figure is expected to go up to almost US$ 275.5 billion by 2018, growing at an average of 9.4 per cent over the next ten years. Moreover, according to the TSA research, travel and tourism is expected to contribute 6.1 per cent to India's national gross domestic product (GDP) and provide almost 40 million jobs by 2018. Significantly, a country brand index (CBI) 2008 survey, conducted by FutureBrand—a leading global brand consultancy—in collaboration with public relations firm Weber Shandwick's Global Travel & Lifestyle Practice, has ranked India second in the value-for-money index.

The rapid growth of India's tourism industry has been instrumental in making South Asia the preferred tourist destination as noted by the UN World Tourism Organisation (UNWTO).

In fact, according to the World Travel and Trade Council, demand in tourism in India will continue to grow at a rapid pace. It estimates the demand to grow at an average of 8.8 per cent between 2004 and 2013, making India the world's third fastest-growing tourist market. The boom in the Indian tourism industry has percolated to the rural areas as well. India continues to attract tourists owing to its splendid historical architecture and rich culture along with beautiful beaches and rural tourism.

FOREIGN TOURIST ARRIVALS

Estimates of foreign tourist arrivals (FTAs) and foreign exchange earnings (FEE) (on the basis of data received from major airports) are important indicators of the tourism sector.

FTA figures for 2008 were 5.37 million against 5.08 million in 2007, showing a 6-8 per cent rise over 2007, indicating that despite the global financial meltdown and the recent terrorist attacks, the number of tourists coming to India have gone up. In fact, the Indian growth rate of 5.6 per cent for international tourist arrivals exceeded the United Nations World Tourism Organisation's (UNWTO) forecast of a growth rate of 2-3 per cent for international tourist arrivals in the world for 2008.

According to figures released by the Tourism Ministry, FEE from this sector posted a rise of 8 per cent at US$ 11.5 billion in 2008 as against US$ 10.70 billion registered in 2007.

PROMOTING TOURISM

Amidst fears of global meltdown likely to impact the tourism sector in India, the government is trying to woo tourists.

The Himachal government has launched the 'Himachal Pradesh Home Stay Scheme 2008'. Under the scheme, tourists are given the opportunity see the rural areas of Himachal, enjoying their stay in comfortable home-stay accommodations. Every Home Stay Unit owner shall get the unit registered with the state department of tourism and the owner of the Home Stay Unit would charge the rates approved by the department.

Under the 'Vibrant Gujarat' programme, the Gujarat government plans to actively market the tourism sector and is expecting an inflow of US$ 20.22 billion in the next five years as investment. The government is planning to introduce an investor tourism policy for the same.

With a 1,650-km coastline, the state has big plans of developing beaches in regions like Kutch and Mandvi on similar lines like those in Kerala and Goa.

At the Vibrant Gujarat Global Investors' Summit, memorandums of understanding (MoUs) worth US$ 9.10 billion for hotels, convention centres, resorts, and adventure tourism in the state, were signed.

Apart from various tourism destinations, the governments also plan to market festivals such as Navrathri and the International Kite Festival.

The government has singled out 37 destinations for tourism development and over the last two years, over 600 projects in 300 tourist destinations have been developed with an investment of US$ 20.22 million. Amongst them, the government is planning to promote Kutch as an aqua-tourism destination for not only bringing in leisure travellers, but also travellers in the Meeting, Incentive, Conference and Exhibition (MICE) segment.

Outbound Tourists

A booming economy and increase in disposable income has led to a massive growth in the number of Indians travelling abroad.

Indian outbound tourist flow is expected to increase at a CAGR of 13.30 per cent during 2008-2012, according to a new report titled, 'Indian Tourism Industry Analysis', by RNCOS, a leading market research and information analysis company.

Similarly, Euromonitor International estimates the outgoing tourism expenditure from India to grow to US$ 21 million by 2011, representing a growth rate of over 25.7 per cent between 2006 and 2011.

Medical Tourism

'First World treatment' at Third World prices' is how industry sources define medical tourism in India. Although

India is a recent entrant into medical tourism, it is fast catching up. According to a study by McKinsey and the Confederation of Indian Industry (CII), medical tourism in India could become a US$ 2 billion industry by 2012 (from US$ 350 million in 2006). Credit Suisse estimates medical tourism to be growing at about 25-30 per cent annually. Indian hospitals are fast becoming the first choice for an increasing number of foreign tourists, and as per a Credit Suisse estimate, nearly 180,000 medical tourists were treated in India in 2004.

The key selling points of the medical tourism industry are its cost effectiveness and its combination with the attractions of tourism. Many travel agents are now selling combined packages of treatment and vacation. India has some of the best hospitals and treatment centres which are well equipped and are at par with those in the US, UK and Europe with costs that are a fraction–only a tenth and sometimes even a sixteenth–of the cost in the West.

Hospitality

The boom in India's tourism industry and the surge in tourist inflow to the country have percolated to other associated sectors like hospitality. The revenues for the Indian hotel and restaurant industry in the year 2006-07 exceeded US$ 118.85 million, an increase of nearly 22 per cent over the previous year. The industry is poised for rapid growth and is projected to be well worth over US$ 158.49 million by the year 2010.

And with the continuing surge in tourist inflow, this sector is likely to offer tremendous opportunity for investors. For example, while the estimated number of required hotel rooms is around 240,000, the current availability is just 90,000 rooms-leaving a shortfall of 150,000 rooms to be provided. India's hospitality sector is expected to see around 40 international hotel brands by 2011, according to a report by Ma Foi Management Consultants. Moreover, the sector is expected to provide over 400,000 jobs.

Along with these large-scale expansion plans, international hotel asset management companies are also likely to enter India. Several global hotel chains see immense investment opportunities in the sector with global chains like Hilton, Marriott International, Berggruen Hotels, Cabana Hotels, Premier Travel Inn (PTI), InterContinental Hotels group and Hampshire amongst others having announced major investment plans in India with others likely to follow suit. With land prices coming down and a huge opportunity for quality hotels in India, many global hotel players are announcing new projects in India. According to Rashes Shah, analyst with brokerage firm, ICICI Direct,"International hotel majors have a long-term view of India. Most properties will become operational only around 2012 by which time the market is expected to bounce back. Most of them also have enough cash to buy land."

Emerging Trends

Hotels are no longer satisfied with the plain-vanilla room concept but are now getting ready for alternate hospitality formats such as residential hotels, destination resorts, condo hotels, vacation ownership and private residents' club.

- Four Seasons is developing a destination resort in Puthenkayal, Kerala, which will have 75 villas and also 20 branded, luxury private residences. The resort will be operational by 2012.
- Nearly 11 per cent of the hotel demand in the country is from long-stay guests. The Leela Group is looking at tapping this market. Its property in Gurgaon will have 90 apartments called 'The Residence', aimed at long-stay guests.
- India's largest real estate player, DLF, is building India's first residential hotel in Goa with the Hilton Group. DLF plans to invest US$ 2 billion to have six hotels on a similar format in the next five years.

International Recognition

India's booming tourism sector has not only witnessed international investments but also achieved international accolades with its increasing appeal as the leading global tourist destination. The government has been instrumental in making tourism a priority sector. Its efforts have borne fruits with a series of international recognition and awards.

- India has been elected to head the UN World Tourism Organisation (UNWTO), the highest policy making world tourism body represented by 150 countries.
- The world's leading travel and tourism journal, Conde Nast Traveller, has ranked India as the 'numero uno' travel destination in the world.
- India was adjudged Asia's leading destination at the regional World Travel Awards (WTA).
- India's Taj Mahal continues to figure in the Seven Wonders of the World.
- Bangalore-based Leela Palace Kempinski was voted the favourite business hotel in the world in a Readers' Choice Awards by Conde Nast Traveller in 2007.
- India bagged the World's leading Destination Marketing Award for the Incredible India campaign in 2007.
- According to the country brand index (CBI) 2008 survey, conducted by FutureBrand - a leading global brand consultancy - in conjunction with public relations firm Weber Shandwick's Global Travel & Lifestyle Practice, India ranks second in value-for-money index.

Government Initiatives

To unlock the huge potential in this sector, the government has taken various initiatives for the development of this sector.

- Launch of Incredible India campaign to promote tourism both in domestic and international markets.
- Recognition of spare rooms available with various house owners by classifying these facilities as 'Incredible India Bed and Breakfast Establishments', under 'Gold' or 'Silver' category.
- A new category of visa, 'Medical Visa' ('M'-Visa), has been introduced which can be given to foreign tourists coming into India for medical tourism.
- Ministry of Tourism has tied up with United Nations Development Programme (UNDP) to promote rural tourism.

- Companies in the hotels sector can now raise external commercial borrowings (ECBs) under the automatic route and utilise the proceeds for both foreign currency and/or rupee capital expenditure.

The Road Ahead

With India being on the global tourist map and an increasing number of people coming to India for tourism or business, hotels are looking at expansion in a major way.

- The US-based Hilton Hotels Corporation will be launching its upscale brand, Doubletree, in India. Its 182-room hotel in Gurgaon is scheduled to open in 2010.
- Global Hyatt Corporation plans to add 20 properties in India over the next four years, with a presence in Tier 2 and 3 cities as well.
- Marriott International Inc is also planning to open seven hotels in 2009, which entails 1,561 new rooms. An additional 14 (previously announced) hotels are likely to be commissioned by 2012.
- InterContinental Hotels Group will be developing 22 additional hotels to its current portfolio of 13 hotels, within the next few years. These will be built under its three brands — InterContinental Hotels & Resorts, Crowne Plaza Hotels & Resorts and Holiday Inn Hotels & Resorts.
- The Taj Hotels Resorts and Palaces, in a joint venture with CC Africa, a leading safari operator and ecotourism company from Africa - is opening two safari lodges in Madhya Pradesh at Panna and Kanha National Parks. It already has a safari lodge each at Bandhavgarh and Pench National Parks.
- EIH, which owns the Oberoi and Trident group of hotels, is looking at opening 10 hotels in India and abroad in the next three years. These include a luxury Oberoi Hotel in Gurgaon to be opened in 2009, a 320-room Trident hotel at the Bangalore International Airport to be opened in 2010, and two hotels to be opened in Hyderabad in 2010.

- Hotels in Hyderabad are on an expansion spree and 4,000 rooms will be added in the next couple of years. Around 20 major properties including that of Park Hyatt, Trident, Marriott, Leela and Taj among others will effectively double the current capacity of 4,000 rooms across all types of hotels.

The government is promoting 2009 as the 'Visit India Year'. The idea behind the scheme is that those who visit India in 2009 would subsequently experience India's rural tourism, eco tourism, adventure tourism, and wellness tourism in specially designed packages in 2010 and 2011. The reduced rates would also make India an inexpensive tourist destination.

Apart from leisure travel, the new emerging target areas would be business travel, domestic travel, medical tourism and the mid-market segment.

CULINARY TOURISM

Judging by the surge since 2001 in the number of times "culinary tourism" has appeared as a subject matter or in a session title in tourism industry conferences and programs, we can see that **Culinary Tourism** is valued by tourism industry professionals as one of the most popular niches in the world's tourism industry. This makes sense, given recent consumer focus on healthy and organic eating, culinary/food pedigrees, and the simple fact that all travelers must eat. Not every visitor goes shopping or visits museums, but all travelers eat. For anyone who doubts, look at the increase in cooking shows featured on The Travel Channel Anthony Bourdain No Reservations or travel shows featured on The Food Network Rachel Ray's $40 a Day series, as examples.

Culinary Tourism is defined as the pursuit of unique and memorable eating and drinking experiences, according to the International Culinary Tourism Association. Culinary Tourism differs from agritourism in that culinary tourism is considered a subset of cultural tourism (cuisine is a manifestation of culture) whereas agritourism is considered a subset of rural tourism, according to Culinary Tourism: The Hidden Harvest. That said, culinary tourism and agritourism are inextricably linked, as the seeds of cuisine can be found in agriculture. Culinary Tourism is not just experiences of the highest caliber - that would be gourmet tourism. This is perhaps best illustrated by the notion that Culinary Tourism is about what is "unique and memorable, not what is necessarily pretentious and exclusive". Similarly, wine tourism, beer tourism and spa tourism are also regarded as subsets of culinary tourism.

DARK TOURISM

Dark tourism (also **black tourism** or **grief tourism**) is tourism involving travel to sites associated with death and suffering. **Thanatourism**, derived from the Ancient Greek word *thanatos* for the personification of death, is associated with dark tourism but refers more specifically to violent death; it is used in fewer contexts than the terms dark tourism and grief tourism.

This includes castles and battlefields such as Culloden near Inverness, Scotland; sites of disaster, either natural or man made such as Ground Zero in New York; prisons now open to the public such as Beaumaris Prison in Anglesey, Wales; and purpose built centers such as the London Dungeon.

One of the most notorious destinations for dark tourism is the Nazi extermination camp at Auschwitz in Poland, Chernobyl site in ex USSR or Bran Castle, Poienari Castle in Romania.

DISASTER TOURISM

Disaster tourism is the act of traveling to a disaster area as a matter of curiosity. The behavior can be a nuisance if it hinders rescue, relief, and recovery operations.

If not done because of pure curiosity, it can be cataloged as disaster learning.

Hurricane Katrina

Disaster tourism took hold in the Greater New Orleans Area in the aftermath of Hurricane Katrina. There are now guided bus tours to neighborhoods that were severely damaged by storm-related flooding. Some local residents have criticized these tours as unethical, because the tour companies are profiting from the misery of their communities and families. The Army Corps of Engineers has noted that traffic from tour buses and other tourist vehicles have interfered with the movement of trucks and other cleanup equipment on single-lane residential roads. Furthermore, during the first six months after the storm, most of these neighborhoods lacked electricity, phone access, street signs, or access to emergency medical or police assistance. Simply traveling to these neighborhoods was hazardous. For these reasons, organized disaster tours are now banned from two of the most severely damaged areas in the city, the Lower 9th and St. Bernard Parish near the Industrial Canal.

On the other hand, such communities as Gentilly and Lakeview, along the 17th Street Canal, have welcomed organized tour groups as a means to publicize the scale of the destruction and attract more aid to the city. Much of the recovery effort in the New Orleans relies on out-of-state volunteers and donations. Numerous non-profit organization, including Habitat for Humanity International and Catholic Charities, have converged on the city to gut and rebuild homes. There is also a movement by local residents to bring congressmen and other national leaders to the city and view the damage in person, since recovery efforts have been hampered by the failure of many homeowners and businesses to receive claims from their insurance providers.

ECOTOURISM

Ecotourism is travel to fragile, pristine, and usually protected areas that strives to be low impact and (often) small scale. It helps educate the traveler; provides funds for conservation; directly benefits the economic development and political empowerment of local communities; and fosters respect for different cultures and for human rights. As defined by the co-founder of the Center for Responsible Travel, Martha Honey, Ph.D., in her book *Ecotourism and Sustainable Development, Second Edition: Who Owns Paradise?*. Most serious studies of ecotourism including several University programs now use this as the working definition.

Ecotourism (also known as **ecological tourism**) is a form of tourism, that appeals to ecologically and socially conscious individuals. Generally speaking, ecotourism focuses on volunteering, personal growth and learning new ways to live on the planet. It typically involves travel to destinations where flora, fauna and cultural heritage are the primary attractions. Ecotourism is a conceptual experience, enriching those who delve into researching and understanding the environment around them. It gives us insight into our impacts, as human beings and also a greater appreciation of our own natural habitats.

Responsible ecotourism includes programs that minimize the negative aspects of conventional tourism on the environment and enhance the cultural integrity of local people. Therefore, in addition to evaluating environmental and cultural factors, an integral part of ecotourism is the promotion of recycling, energy efficiency, water conservation and creation of economic opportunities for the local communities.

Criteria

Ecotourism is a form of tourism that involves traveling to tranquil and unpolluted natural areas. According to the definition and principles of ecotourism established by The International Ecotourism Society (TIES) in 1990, ecotourism is "Responsible travel to natural areas that conserves the environment and improves the well-being of local people." (TIES, 1990). Martha Honey, expands on the TIES definition by describing the seven characteristics of ecotourism, which are:

- Involves travel to natural destinations.
- Minimizes impact.
- Builds environmental awareness.
- Provides direct financial benefits for conservation.
- Provides financial benefits and empowerment for local people.
- Respects local culture.
- Supports human rights and demographic movements.

Ideally, ecotourism should satisfy several criteria, such as:

- Conservation of biological diversity and cultural diversity through ecosystem protection
- Promotion of sustainable use of biodiversity, by providing jobs to local populations
- Sharing of socio-economic benefits with local communities and indigenous peoples by having their informed consent and participation in the management of ecotourism enterprises
- Tourism to unspoiled natural resources, with minimal impact on the environment being a primary concern.
- Minimization of tourism's own environmental impact
- Affordability and lack of waste in the form of luxury
- Local culture, flora and fauna being the main attractions

For many countries, ecotourism is not simply a marginal activity to finance protection of the environment, but is a major industry of the national economy. For example, in Costa Rica, Ecuador, Nepal, Kenya, Madagascar and Antarctica, ecotourism represents a significant portion of the gross domestic product and economic activity.

The concept of ecotourism is widely misunderstood and in practice is often used as a marketing tool to promote tourism, which is related to nature. This is an especially frequent malpractice in the realm of Jungle tourism. Critics claim that these greenwashing practices, carried out in the name of ecotourism, often consist of placing a hotel in a splendid landscape, to the detriment of the ecosystem. According to them, ecotourism must above all sensitize people to the beauty and the fragility of nature. They condemn some operators as greenwashing their operations: using the labels of "green" and "eco-friendly", while behaving in environmentally irresponsible ways.

Although academics disagree about who can be classified as an ecotourist and there is precious little statistical data, some estimate that more than five million ecotourists - the majority of the ecotourist population - come from the United States, with others from Western Europe, Canada and Australia.

Currently, there are various moves to create national and international ecotourism accreditaion programs, although the process is also controversial. National ecotourism certification programs have been put in place in countries such as Costa Rica, Australia, Kenya and Sweden.

History

Ecotourism, responsible tourism, jungle tourism and sustainable development have become prevalent concepts since the late 1980s, and ecotourism has experienced arguably the fastest growth of all sub-sectors in the tourism industry. The popularity represents a change in tourist perceptions, increased environmental awareness, and a desire to explore natural environments. Such changes have become as much a statement affirming one's social identity, educational sophistication, and disposable income as it has about preserving the Amazon rainforest or the Caribbean reef for posterity.

CRITICISMS

Definitional Problems and Greenwashing

To approach an understanding of the problem, a clear definition must delineate what is, and is not, ecotourism. Ideally, ecotourism satisfies several general criteria, including the conservation of biological diversity and cultural diversity through ecosystem protection, promotion of sustainable use of biodiversity, share of socio-economic benefits with local communities through informed consent and participation, increase in environmental and cultural knowledge, affordability and reduced waste, and minimization of its own environmental impact. In such ways, it contributes to the long term benefits to both the environment and local communities.

However, in the continuum of tourism activities that stretch from conventional tourism to ecotourism proper, there has been a lot of contention to the limit at which biodiversity preservation, local socio-economic benefits, and environmental impact can be considered "ecotourism". For this reason, environmentalists, special interest groups, and governments define ecotourism differently. Environmental organizations have generally insisted that ecotourism is nature-based, sustainably managed, conservation supporting, and environmentally educated. The tourist industry and governments, however, focus more on the product aspect, treating ecotourism as equivalent to any sort of tourism based in nature. As a further complication, many terms are used under the rubric of ecotourism. Nature tourism, low impact tourism, green tourism, bio-tourism, ecologically responsible tourism, and others have been used in literature and marketing, although they are not necessary synonymous with ecotourism.

The problems associated with defining ecotourism have led to confusion among tourists and academics alike. Definitional problems are also subject of considerable public controversy and concern because of greenwashing, a trend towards the commercialization of tourism schemes disguised as sustainable, nature based, and environmentally friendly ecotourism. According to McLaren, these schemes are environmentally destructive, economically exploitative, and culturally insensitive at its worst. They are also morally disconcerting because they mislead tourists and manipulate their concerns for the environment. Despite objections, greenwashing continues to grow unabated. The Nature's Sacred Paradise, a theme park in Quintana Roo, Mexico, is responsible for displacing local Mayan communities and illegally keeping endangered species in captivity to attract visitors. The development and success of such large scale, energy intensive, and ecologically unsustainable schemes are a testament to the tremendous profits associated with being labeled as ecotourism.

NEGATIVE IMPACT OF TOURISM

Ecotourism has become one of the fastest-growing sectors of the tourism industry, growing annually by 10-15% worldwide (Miller, 2007). One definition of ecotourism is "the practice of low-impact, educational, ecologically and culturally sensitive travel that benefits local communities and host countries" (Honey, 1999). Many of the ecotourism projects are not meeting these standards. Even if some of the guidelines are being executed, the local communities are still facing other negative impacts. South Africa is one of the countries that are reaping significant economic benefits from ecotourism, but negative effects - including physical displacement of persons, gross violation of fundamental rights, and environmental hazards - far outweigh the medium-term economic benefits (Miller, 2007). A tremendous amount of money is being spent and human resources continue to be used for ecotourism despite the lack of success, and even more money is put into public relation campaigns to dilute the effects of criticism. Ecotourism channels resources away from other projects that could contribute more sustainable and realistic solutions to pressing social and environmental problems. "The money tourism can generate often ties parks and managements to eco-tourism" (Walpole et al. 2001). But there is a tension in this relationship because eco-tourism often causes conflict and changes in land-use rights, fails to deliver promises of community-level benefits, damages environments, and has plenty of other social impacts. Indeed many argue repeatedly that eco-tourism is neither ecologically nor socially beneficial, yet it persists as a strategy for conservation and development (West, 2006). While several studies are being done on ways to improve the ecotourism structure, these examples provide rationale for stopping it altogether.

The ecotourism system exercises tremendous financial and political influence. The evidence above shows that at the very least a strong case exists for restraining such activities. Funding could be used for field studies aimed at finding alternative solutions to tourism and the diverse problems Africa faces in result of urbanization, industrialization, and over exploitation of agriculture (Kamuaro, 2007). At the local level ecotourism has become a source of conflict over control of land, resources, and tourism profits. There are many problems with the idea of ecotourism. Environmental, the effects on the local people, and conflicts over profit distribution are only a few of the negative effects of ecotourism. In a perfect world more efforts would be made towards educating tourists of the environmental and social effects of their travels. Very few regulations or laws stand in place as boundaries for the investors in ecotourism.

These should be implemented to prohibit the promotion of unsustainable ecotourism projects and materials which project false images of destinations, demeaning local and indigenous cultures.

DIRECT ENVIRONMENTAL IMPACTS

Ecotourism operations occasionally fail to live up to conservation ideals. It is sometimes overlooked that ecotourism is a highly consumer-centered activity, and that environmental conservation is a means to further economic growth.

Although ecotourism is intended for small groups, even a modest increase in population, however temporary, puts extra pressure on the local environment and necessitates the development of additional infrastructure and amenities. The construction of water treatment plants, sanitation facilities, and lodges come with the exploitation of non-renewable energy sources and the utilization of already limited local resources. The conversion of natural land to such tourist infrastructure is implicated in deforestation and habitat deterioration of butterflies in Mexico and squirrel monkeys in Costa Rica. In other cases, the environment suffers because local communities are unable to meet the infrastructure demands of ecotourism. The lack of adequate sanitation facilities in many East African parks results in the disposal of campsite sewage in rivers, contaminating the wildlife, livestock, and people who draw drinking water from it.

Aside from environmental degradation with tourist infrastructure, population pressures from ecotourism also leaves behind garbage and pollution associated with the Western lifestyle. Although ecotourists claim to be educationally sophisticated and environmentally concerned, they rarely understand the ecological consequences of their visits and how their day-to-day activities append physical impacts on the environment. As one scientist observes, they "rarely acknowledge how the meals they eat, the toilets they flush, the water they drink, and so on, are all part of broader regional economic and ecological systems they are helping to reconfigure with their very activities." Nor do ecotourists recognize the great consumption of non-renewable energy required to arrive at their destination, which is typically more remote than conventional tourism destinations. For instance, an exotic journey to a place 10,000 kilometers away consumes about 700 liters of fuel per person.

Ecotourism activities are, in of itself, issues in environmental impact because they disturb fauna and flora. Ecotourists believe that because they are only taking pictures and leaving footprints, they keep ecotourism sites pristine, but even harmless sounding activities such as a nature hike can be ecologically destructive. In the Annapurna Circuit in Nepal, ecotourists have worn down the marked trails and created alternate routes, contributing to soil impaction, erosion, and plant damage. Where the ecotourism activity involves wildlife viewing, it can scare away animals, disrupt their feeding and nesting sites, or acclimate them to the presence of people. In Kenya, wildlife-observer disruption drives cheetahs off their reserves, increasing the risk of inbreeding and further endangering the species.

ENVIRONMENTAL HAZARDS

Unfortunately, industrialization, urbanization, and unsustainable agriculture practices have all had serious effects on the environment. Ecotourism is now also playing a role in this depletion. While the term ecotourism may sound relatively benign, one of its most serious impacts is its consumption of virgin territories (Kamuaro, 2007). These invasions often include deforestation, disruption of ecological life systems and various forms of pollution, all of which contribute to environmental degradation. The number of motor vehicles crossing the park increases as tour drivers search for rare species. The number of roads has disrupted the grass cover which has serious effects on plant and animal species. These areas also have a higher rate of disturbances and invasive species because of all the traffic moving off the beaten path into new undiscovered areas (Kamuaro, 2007). Ecotourism also has an effect on species through the value placed on them. "Certain species have gone from being little known or valued by local people to being highly valued commodities. The commodification of plants may erase their social value and lead to overproduction within protected areas. Local people and their images can also be turned into commodities" (West, 2006). Kamuaro brings up a relatively obvious contradiction, any commercial venture into unspoiled, pristine land with or without the "eco" prefix as a contradiction in terms. To generate revenue you have to have a high number of traffic, tourists, which inevitably means a higher pressure on the environment.

Local People

Most forms of ecotourism are owned by foreign investors and corporations that provide few benefits to local communities. An overwhelming majority of profits are put into the pockets of investors instead of reinvestment into the local economy or environmental protection. The limited numbers of local people who are employed in the economy enter at its lowest level, and are unable to live in tourist areas because of meager wages and a two market system.

In some cases, the resentment by local people results in environmental degradation. As a highly publicized case, the Maasai nomads in Kenya killed wildlife in national parks to show aversion to unfair compensation terms and displacement from traditional lands. The lack of economic opportunities for local people also constrains them to degrade the environment as a means of sustenance. The presence of affluent ecotourists encourage the development of destructive markets in wildlife souvenirs, such as the sale of coral trinkets on tropical islands and animal products in Asia, contributing to illegal harvesting and poaching from the environment. In Suriname, sea turtle reserves use a large portion of their budget to guard against these destructive activities.

Displacement of People

One of the most powerful examples of communities being moved in order to create a park is the story of the Masai. About 70% of national parks and game reserves in East Africa are on Masai land (Kamuaro, 2007). The first undesirable impact of tourism was that of the extent of land lost from the Masai culture. Local and national governments took advantage of the Masai's ignorance on the situation and robbed them of huge chunks of grazing land, putting to risk their only socio-economic livelihood. In Kenya the Masai also have not gained any economic benefits. Despite the loss of their land, employment favours better educated workers. Furthermore the investors in this area are not local and have not put profits back into local economy. In some cases game reserves can be created without informing or consulting local people, who come to find out about the situation when an eviction notice is delivered (Kamuaro, 2007). Another source of resentment is the manipulation of the local people by their government. "Eco-tourism works to create simplistic images of local people and their uses and understandings of their surroundings. Through the lens of these simplified images, officials direct policies and projects towards the local people and the local people are blamed if the projects fail" (West, 2006). Clearly tourism as a trade is not empowering the local people who make it rich and satisfying. Instead ecotourism exploits and depletes, particularly in African Masai tribes. It has to be reoriented if it is to be useful to local communities and to become sustainable (Kamuaro, 2007).

THREATS TO INDIGENOUS CULTURES

Ecotourism often claims that it preserves and "enhances" local cultures. However, evidence shows that with the establishment of protected areas local people have illegally lost their homes, and most often with no compensation (Kamuaro, 2007). Pushing people onto marginal lands with harsh climates, poor soils, lack of water, and infested with livestock and disease does little to enhance livelihoods even when a proportion of ecotourism profits are directed back into the community. The establishment of parks can create harsh survival realities and deprive the people of their traditional use of land and natural resources. Ethnic groups are increasingly being seen as a "backdrop" to the scenery and wildlife. The local people struggle for cultural survival and freedom of cultural expression while being "observed" by tourists. Local indigenous people also have strong resentment towards the change, "Tourism has been allowed to develop with virtually no controls. Too many lodges have been built, too much firewood is being used and no limits are being placed on tourism vehicles. They regularly drive off-track and harass the wildlife. Their vehicle tracks criss-cross the entire Masai Mara. Inevitably the bush is becoming eroded and degraded" (Kamuaro, 2007).

Mismanagement

While governments are typically entrusted with the administration and enforcement of environmental protection, they often lack the commitment or capability to manage ecotourism sites effectively. The regulations for environmental protection may be vaguely defined, costly to implement, hard to enforce, and uncertain in effectiveness. Government regulatory agencies, as political bodies, are susceptible to making decisions that spend budget on politically beneficial but environmentally unproductive projects. Because of prestige and conspicuousness, the construction of an attractive visitor's center at an ecotourism site may take precedence over more pressing environmental concerns like acquiring habitat, protecting endemic species, and removing invasive ones. Finally, influential groups can pressure and sway the interests of the government to their favor. The government and its regulators can become vested in the benefits of the ecotourism industry which they are supposed to regulate, causing restrictive environmental regulations and enforcement to become more lenient.

Management of ecotourism sites by private ecotourism companies offers an alternative to the cost of regulation and deficiency of government agencies. It is believed that these companies have a self interest in limited environmental degradation, because tourists will pay more for pristine environments, which translates to higher profit. However, theory indicates that this practice is not economically feasible and will fail to manage the environment.

The model of monopolistic competition states that distinctiveness will entail profits, but profits will promote imitation. A company that protects its ecotourism sites is able to charge a premium for the novel experience and pristine environment. But when other companies view the success of this approach, they also enter the market with similar practices, increasing competition and reducing demand. Eventually, the demand will be reduced until the economic profit is zero. A cost-benefit analysis shows that the company bears the cost of environmental protection without receiving the gains. Without economic incentive, the whole premise of self interest through environmental protection is quashed; instead, ecotourism companies will minimize environment related expenses and maximize tourism demand.

The tragedy of the commons offers another model for economic unsustainability from environmental protection, in ecotourism sites utilized by many companies. Although there is a communal incentive to protect the environment, maximizing the benefits in the long run, a company will conclude that it is in their best interest to utilize the ecotourism site beyond its sustainable level. By increasing the number of ecotourists, for instance, a company gains all the economic benefit while paying only a part of the environmental cost. In the same way, a company recognizes that there is no incentive to actively protect the environment; they bear all the costs, while the benefits are shared by all other companies. The result, again, is mismanagement.

Taken together, the mobility of foreign investment and lack of economic incentive for environmental protection means that ecotourism companies are disposed to establishing themselves in new sites once their existing one is sufficiently degraded.

IMPROVING SUSTAINABILITY

Regulation and Accreditation

Because the regulation of ecotourism is poorly implemented or nonexistent, ecologically destructive greenwashed operations like underwater hotels, helicopter tours, and wildlife theme parks are categorized as ecotourism along with canoeing, camping, photography, and wildlife observation. The failure to acknowledge responsible, low impact ecotourism puts these companies at a competitive disadvantage. Many environmentalists have argued for a global standard of accreditation, differentiating ecotourism companies based on their level of environmental commitment. A national or international regulatory board would enforce accreditation procedures, with representation from various groups including governments, hotels, tour operators, travel agents, guides, airlines, local authorities, conservation organizations, and non-governmental organizations.

The decisions of the board would be sanctioned by governments, so that non-compliant companies would be legally required to disassociate themselves from the use of the ecotourism brand.

Crinion suggests a Green Stars System, based on criteria including a management plan, benefit for the local community, small group interaction, education value and staff training. Ecotourists who consider their choices would be confident of a genuine ecotourism experience when they see the higher star rating.

In addition, environmental impact assessments could be used as a form of accreditation. Feasibility is evaluated from a scientific basis, and recommendations could be made to optimally plan infrastructure, set tourist capacity, and manage the ecology. This form of accreditation is more sensitive to site specific conditions.

Guidelines and Education

An environmental protection strategy must address the issue of ecotourists removed from the cause-and-effect of their actions on the environment. More initiatives should be carried out to improve their awareness, sensitize them to environmental issues, and care about the places they visit.

Tour guides are an obvious and direct medium to communicate awareness. With the confidence of ecotourists and intimate knowledge of the environment, they can actively discuss conservation issues. A tour guide training program in Costa Rica's Tortuguero National Park has helped mitigate negative environmental impacts by providing information and regulating tourists on the parks' beaches used by nesting endangered sea turtles.

SMALL SCALE, SLOW GROWTH AND LOCAL CONTROL

The underdevelopment theory of tourism describes a new form of imperialism by multinational corporations that control ecotourism resources. These corporations finance and profit from the development of large scale ecotourism that causes excessive environmental degradation, loss of traditional culture and way of life, and exploitation of local labor. In Zimbabwe and Nepal's Annapurna region, where underdevelopment is taking place, more than 90 percent of ecotourism revenues are expatriated to the parent countries, and less than 5 percent go into local communities.

The lack of sustainability highlights the need for small scale, slow growth, and locally based ecotourism. Local peoples have a vested interest in the well being of their community, and are therefore more accountable to environmental protection than multinational corporations. The lack of control, westernization, adverse impacts to the environment, loss of culture and traditions outweigh the benefits of establishing large scale ecotourism.

The increased contributions of communities to locally managed ecotourism create viable economic opportunities, including high level management positions, and reduce environmental issues associated with poverty and unemployment. Because the ecotourism experience is marketed to a different lifestyle from large scale ecotourism, the development of facilities and infrastructure does not need to conform to corporate Western tourism standards, and can be much simpler and less expensive. There is a greater multiplier effect on the economy, because local products, materials, and labor are used. Profits accrue locally and import leakages are reduced. However, even this form of tourism may require foreign investment for promotion or start up. When such investments are required, it is crucial for communities for find a company or non-governmental organization that reflects the philosophy of ecotourism; sensitive to their concerns and willing to cooperate at the expense of profit.The basic assumption of the multiplier effect is that the economy starts off with unused resources, for example, that many workers are cyclically unemployed and much of industrial capacity is sitting idle or incompletely utilized. By increasing demand in the economy it is then possible to boost production. If the economy was already at full employment, with only structural, frictional, or other supply-side types of unemployment, any attempt to boost demand would only lead to inflation. For various laissez-faire schools of economics which embrace Say's Law and deny the possibility of Keynesian inefficiency and under-employment of resources, therefore, the multiplier concept is irrelevant or wrong-headed.

As an example, consider the government increasing its expenditure on roads by $one million, without a corresponding increase in taxation. This sum would go to the road builders, who would hire more workers and distribute the money as wages and profits. The households receiving these incomes will save part of the money and spend the rest on consumer goods. These expenditures in turn will generate more jobs, wages, and profits, and so on with the income and spending circulating around the economy.

The multiplier effect arises because of the induced increases in consumer spending which occur due to the increased incomes — and because of the feedback into increasing business revenues, jobs, and income again. This process does not lead to an economic explosion not only because of the supply-side barriers at potential output (full employment) but because at each "round", the increase in consumer spending is less than the increase in consumer incomes. That is, the marginal propensity to consume (mpc) is less than one, so that each round some extra income goes into saving, leaking out of the cumulative process. Each increase in spending is thus smaller than that of the previous round, preventing an explosion.Ecotourism has to be implemented with care.

NATURAL RESOURCE MANAGEMENT

Natural resource management can be utilized as a specialized tool for the development of eco-tourism. There are several places throughout the world where the amount of natural resources are abundant. But, with human encroachment and habitats these resources are depleting. Without knowing the proper utilization of certain resources they are destroyed and floral and faunal species are becoming extinct. Ecotourism programmes can be introduced for the conservation of these resources. Several plans and proper management programmes can be introduced so that these resources remain untouched. Several organizations, NGO's, scientists are working on this field. Natural resources of hill areas like Kurseong in West Bengal are plenty in number with various flora and fauna, but tourism for business purpose poised the situation. Researcher from Jadavpur University presently working in this area for the develeopment of eco-tourism which can be utilized as a tool for natural resource management.

Tour operators, travel agencies & retailers

Some companies specialise in ecotourism, designing their trips to be environmentally, culturally and socially friendly. Companies such as Intrepid Travel, Frontier, and Marine Conservation Society, Peregrine Adventures, World Expeditions, Explore Worldwide and Exodus offer trips catering for the thoughtful traveller. Some tour operators are keenly aware of the impacts that they may have on specific areas and rotate clients around to different sites for snorkeling, bird watching, and other activities. Others are just beginning to see the advantage of "green" travel destinations.

HERITAGE TOURISM

Cultural heritage tourism (or just **heritage tourism**) is a branch of tourism oriented towards the cultural heritage of the location where tourism is occurring.

Culture has always been a major object of travel, as the development of the Grand Tour from the 16th century onwards attests. In the 20th century, some people have claimed, culture ceased to be the objective of tourism: tourism is now culture. Cultural attractions play an important role in tourism at all levels, from the global highlights of world culture to attractions that underpin local identities. (Richards, 1996)

According to the Weiler and Hall, culture, heritage and the arts have long contributed to appeal of tourist destination. However, in recent years 'culture' has been rediscovered as an important marketing tool to attract those travellers with special interests in heritage and arts. According to the Hollinshead, cultural heritage tourism defines as cultural heritage tourism is the fastest growing segment of the tourism industry because there is a trend toward an increase specialization among tourists. This trend is evident in the rise in the volume of tourists who seek adventure, culture, history, archaeology and interaction with local people.

Cultural heritage tourism is important for various reasons; it has a positive economic and social impact, it establishes and reinforces identity, it helps preserve the cultural heritage, with culture as an instrument it facilitates harmony and understanding among people, it supports culture and helps renew tourism (Richards, 1996). Putangina Cultural heritage tourism has a number of objectives that must be met within the context of sustainable development such as; the conservation of cultural resources, accurate interpretation of resources, authentic visitors experience, and the stimulation of the earned revenues of cultural resources. We can see, therefore, that cultural heritage tourism is not only concerned with identification, management and protection of the heritage values but it must also be involved in understanding the impact of tourism on communities and regions, achieving economic and social benefits, providing financial resources for protection, as well as marketing and promotion. (J. M. Fladmark, 1994)

Heritage tourism involves visiting historical or industrial sites that may include old canals, railways, battlegrounds, etc. The overall purpose is to gain an appreciation of the past. It also refers to the marketing of a location to members of a diaspora who have distant family roots there.

Decolonization and immigration form the major background of much contemporary heritage tourism. Falling travel costs have also made heritage tourism possible for more people.

Another possible form involves religious travel or pilgrimages. Many Catholics from around the world come to the Vatican and other sites such as Lourdes or Fátima. Large numbers of Jews have both visited Israel and emigrated there. Many have also gone to Holocaust sites and memorials. Islam commands its followers to take the *hajj* to Mecca, thus differentiating it somewhat from tourism in the usual sense, though the trip can also be a culturally important event for the pilgrim.

Heritage Tourism can also be attributed to historical events that have been dramatised to make them more entertaining. For example a historical tour of a town or city using a theme such as ghosts or vikings.

LGBT TOURISM

Gay tourism or **LGBT tourism** is a form of niche tourism marketed to gay, lesbian, bisexual and transgender (LGBT) people. They are usually open about their sexual orientation and gender identity but may be more or less open when traveling; for instance they may be closeted at home or if they have come out, may be more discreet in areas known for violence against LGBT people. The main components of LGBT tourism is for cities and countries wishing to attract LGBT tourists; people looking to travel to LGBT-friendly destinations; people wanting travel with other LGBT people when traveling regardless of the destination and LGBT travelers who are mainly concerned with cultural and safety issues. The slang term *gaycation* has come to imply a version of a vacation that includes a pronounced aspect of LGBT culture, either in the journey or destination. The LGBT tourism industry includes travel agents, tour companies, cruise lines and travel advertising and promotions companies who market these destinations to the gay community. Coinciding with the increased visibility of LGBT people raising children in the 1990s, an increase in family-friendly LGBT tourism has emerged in the 2000s, for instance R Family Vacations which includes activities and entertainment geared towards couples including same-sex weddings. R Family's first cruise was held aboard Norwegian Cruise Lines's *Norwegian Dawn* with 1600 passengers including 600 children.

Major companies in the travel industry have become aware of the substantial money (also known as the "pink dollar" or "pink pound") generated by this marketing niche, and have made it a point to align themselves with the gay community and gay tourism campaigns. According to a 2000 Tourism Intelligence International report 10% of international tourists were gay and lesbian accounting for more than 70 million arrivals worldwide. This market segment is expected to continue to grow as a result ongoing acceptance of LGBT people and changing attitudes towards sexual and gender minorities. The gay and lesbian segment is estimated at $55 billion annual market as of 2007. Outside larger companies, LGBT tourists are offered other traditional tourism tools, such as LGBT hospitality networks of LGBT individuals who offer each other hospitality during their travels and even home swaps where people live in each others homes. Also available are social groups for resident and visiting gay, lesbian, bisexual and transgender expatriates and friends exist worldwide.

GAY TRAVEL DESTINATIONS

Gay travel destinations are popular among practitioners of gay tourism because they usually have permissive or liberal attitudes towards gays, feature a prominent gay infrastructure (bars, businesses, restaurants, hotels, nightlife, entertainment, media, organisations, etc.), the opportunity to socialize with other gays, and the feeling that one can relax safely among other gay people.

Gay travel destinations are often large cities, although not exclusively, and often coincide with the existence of gay neighborhoods. These municipalities and their tourism bureaus often work actively to develop their reputations as places for gays to travel to, commonly by aligning themselves to local gay organisations. Travel analysts state that the existence of a core gay friendly population is often the primary catalyst for the development of a gay-friendly tourist destination.

Gay tourism might also coincide with special gay events such as annual gay pride parades, gay neighborhood festivals and such gay community gatherings as gay chorus festivals and concerts, gay square dance conventions, gay sports meets such as Gay Games, World Outgames or Eurogames and conferences of national and international gay organisations. Gay tourism blossoms during these peak periods.

Gay tourism practitioners spend $64 billion a year on gay travel, according to Community Marketing Inc. The adult GLBT community has a total economic spending power of more than $600 billion per year, according to Wietck Combs. Philadelphia and Community Marketing found that for every one dollar invested in gay tourism marketing, $153 was returned in direct economic spending in shops, hotels, restaurants and attractions. Since 2002, there has been a historic rise in gay tourism marketing. Destinations such as Philadelphia, Dallas and Ft. Lauderdale have engaged in gay tourism campaigns.

The gay cruise industry is experiencing a significant growth period. Community Marketing Inc. found in research studies that gay business travelers are 30% more likely to convert to a leisure visitor.

Philadelphia was the first destination in the world to create and air a television commercial specifically geared towards practitioners of gay tourism. Philadelphia was also the first destination to commission a research study aimed at a specific destination to learn about gay travel to a specific city.

Work is underway in conjunction with Israel's Ministry of Tourism to turn Tel Aviv into the international tourist destination for the gay-lesbian community in order to boost business in restaurants, hotels, city attraction sites and beaches. In an effort to boost gay tourism in Tel Aviv, the Gay and Lesbian Union has bid to host in Tel Aviv the 2009 Euro Pride, the largest annual gay parade in the world.

GAY TOURISM SPECIALISTS

The International Gay and Lesbian Travel Association (IGLTA) holds an annual world convention and four symposia in different tourism destinations around the world. Each symposium attracts over 100 representatives of tour agencies and travel publications that specialise in the gay and lesbian market. The association was founded in 1983, and it currently represents over 900 members. Its headquarters are in Fort Lauderdale, Florida.

The "14th International Gay & Lesbian World Travel Expo" in 2006 will visit six U.S. cities. The annual Expo series is produced by Community Marketing, a gay tourism research and travel marketing firm.

Out Traveler, from the publishers of *Out* and *The Advocate*, is a glossy magazine aimed at gay and lesbian travellers. It is published six times yearly. One of Europe's gay and lesbian travel marketing specialists is Out Now Consulting.

MEDICAL TOURISM

Medical tourism (also called **medical travel**, **health tourism** or global healthcare) is a term initially coined by travel agencies and the mass media to describe the rapidly-growing practice of traveling across international borders to obtain health care.

Such services typically include elective procedures as well as complex specialized surgeries such as joint replacement (knee/hip), cardiac surgery, dental surgery, and cosmetic surgeries. However, virtually every type of health care, including psychiatry, alternative treatments, convalescent care and even burial services are available. As a practical matter, providers and customers commonly use informal channels of communication-connection-contract, and in such cases this tends to mean less regulatory or legal oversight to assure quality and less formal recourse to reimbursement or redress, if needed.

Over 50 countries have identified medical tourism as a national industry. However, accreditation and other measures of quality vary widely across the globe, and there are risks and ethical issues that make this method of accessing medical care controversial. Also, some destinations may become hazardous or even dangerous for medical tourists to contemplate.

History

The concept of medical tourism is not a new one. The first recorded instance of medical tourism dates back thousands of years to when Greek pilgrims traveled from all over the Mediterranean to the small territory in the Saronic Gulf called Epidauria. This territory was the sanctuary of the healing god Asklepios. Epidauria became the original travel destination for medical tourism.

Spa towns and sanitariums may be considered an early form of medical tourism. In eighteenth century England, for example, medtrotters visited spas because they were places with supposedly health-giving mineral waters, treating diseases from gout to liver disorders and bronchitis.

Description

Factors that have led to the increasing popularity of medical travel include the high cost of health care, long wait times for certain procedures, the ease and affordability of international travel, and improvements in both technology and standards of care in many countries.

Medical tourists can come from anywhere in the world, including Europe, the UK, Middle East, Japan, the United States, and Canada. This is because of their large populations, comparatively high wealth, the high expense of health care or lack of health care options locally, and increasingly high expectations of their populations with respect to health care. An authority at the Harvard Business School recently stated that "medical tourism is promoted much more heavily in the United Kingdom than in the United States".

A forecast by Deloitte Consulting published in August 2008 projected that medical tourism originating in the US could jump by a factor of ten over the next decade. An estimated 750,000 Americans went abroad for health care in 2007, and the report estimated that a million and a half would seek health care outside the US in 2008. The growth in medical tourism has the potential to cost US health care providers billions of dollars in lost revenue.

A large draw to medical travel is convenience and speed. Countries that operate public health-care systems are often so taxed that it can take considerable time to get non-urgent medical care. The time spent waiting for a procedure such as a hip replacement can be a year or more in Britain and Canada; however, in New Zealand, Costa Rica, Singapore, Hong Kong, Thailand, Cuba, Colombia, Philippines or India, a patient could feasibly have an operation the day after their arrival. In Canada, the number of procedures in 2005 for which people were waiting was 782,936. Additionally, patients are finding that insurance either does not cover orthopedic surgery (such as knee/hip replacement) or imposes unreasonable restrictions on the choice of the facility, surgeon, or prosthetics to be used. Medical tourism for knee/hip replacements has emerged as one of the more widely accepted procedures because of the lower cost and minimal difficulties associated with the traveling to/from the surgery. Colombia provides a knee replacement for about $5,000 USD, including all associated fees, such as FDA-approved prosthetics and hospital stay-over expenses. However, many clinics quote prices that are not all inclusive and include only the surgeon fees associated with the procedure.

According to an article by the University of Delaware publication, UDaily:

> *"The cost of surgery in India, Thailand or South Africa can be one-tenth of what it is in the United States or Western Europe, and sometimes even less. A heart-valve replacement that would cost $200,000 or more in the US, for example, goes for $10,000 in India—and that includes round-trip airfare and a brief vacation package. Similarly, a metal-free dental bridge worth $5,500 in the US costs $500 in India, a knee replacement in Thailand with six days of physical therapy costs about one-fifth of what it would in the States, and Lasik eye surgery worth $3,700 in the US is available in many other countries for only $730. Cosmetic surgery savings are even greater: A full facelift that would cost $20,000 in the US runs about $1,250 in South Africa."*

Popular **medical travel** worldwide destinations include: Argentina, Brunei, Cuba, Colombia, Costa Rica, Hong Kong, Hungary, India, Jordan, Lithuania, Malaysia, The Philippines, Singapore, South Africa, Thailand, and recently, Saudi Arabia, UAE, Túnisia and New Zealand.

Popular **cosmetic surgery travel** destinations include: Argentina, Bolivia, Brazil, Colombia, Costa Rica, Cuba, Mexico and Turkey. In South America, countries such as Argentina, Bolivia, Brazil and Colombia lead on plastic surgery **medical skills** relying on their experienced plastic surgeons. **In Bolivia** and Colombia, plastic surgery has also become quite common. According to the "Sociedad Boliviana de Cirugia Plastica y Reconstructiva", more than 70% of middle and upper class women in the country have had some form of plastic surgery. Colombia also provides advanced care in cardiovascular and transplant surgery.

In Europe Belgium, Poland and Slovakia are also breaking into the business. South Africa is taking the term "medical tourism" very literally by promoting their "medical safaris".

A specialized subset of medical tourism is **reproductive tourism** and **reproductive outsourcing**, which is the practice of traveling abroad to undergo in-vitro fertilization, surrogate pregnancy and other assisted reproductive technology treatments including freezing embryos for retro-production.

However, perceptions of medical tourism are not always positive. In places like the US, which has high standards of quality, medical tourism is viewed as risky. In some parts of the world, wider political issues can influence where medical tourists will choose to seek out health care.

Health tourism providers have developed as intermediaries to unite potential medical tourists with provider hospitals and other organisations. Companies are beginning to offer global health care options that will enable North American and European patients to access world health care at a fraction of the cost of domestic care. Companies that focus on medical value travel typically providc nurse case managers to assist patients with pre- and post-travel medical issues. They also help provide resources for follow-up care upon the patient's return.

Process

The typical process is as follows: the person seeking medical treatment abroad contacts a medical tourism provider. The provider usually requires the patient to provide a medical report, including the nature of ailment, local doctor's opinion, medical history, and diagnosis, and may request additional information. Certified medical doctors or consultants then advise on the medical treatment.

The approximate expenditure, choice of hospitals and tourist destinations, and duration of stay, etc., is discussed. After signing consent bonds and agreements, the patient is given recommendation letters for a medical visa, to be procured from the concerned embassy. The patient travels to the destination country, where the medical tourism provider assigns a case executive, who takes care of the patient's accommodation, treatment and any other form of care. Once the treatment is done, the patient can remain in the tourist destination or return home.

International Healthcare Accreditation

Because standards are important when it comes to health care, there are parallel issues around medical tourism, international healthcare accreditation, evidence-based medicine and quality assurance.

In the United States, the best known accreditation group is the Joint Commission International (JCI). They have been inspecting and accrediting health care facilities and hospitals outside of the United States since 1999 and are a trusted source for American medical tourists. Many international hospitals today see obtaining JCI accreditation as a way to attract American patients.

In the UK and Hong Kong, the Trent International Accreditation Scheme is a key player. The different international healthcare accreditation schemes vary in quality, size, cost, intent and the skill and intensity of their marketing. They also vary in terms of cost to hospitals and healthcare institutions making use of them. A forecast by Deloitte Consulting regarding medical tourism published in August 2008 noted the value of accreditation in ensuring quality of healthcare and specifically mentioned JCI, ISQUA and Trent.

Increasingly, some hospitals are looking towards dual international accreditation, perhaps having both JCI to cover potential US clientele and Trent for potential British and European clientele. As a result of competition between clinics for American medical tourists, there have been initiatives to rank hospitals based on patient-reported metrics.

Other relevant organizations include:

- The Society for International Healthcare Accreditation (SOFIHA), a free-to-join group providing a forum for discussion and for the sharing of ideas and good practice by providers of international healthcare accreditation and users of the same. The primary role of this organisation is to promote a safe hospital environment for patients.
- HealthCare Tourism International, the first US-based non-profit to accredit the non-clinical aspects of health tourism, such as language issues, business practices, and false or misleading advertising prevention. The group provides accreditation for all major groups involved in the health tourism industry including hotels, recovery facilities, and medical tourism booking agencies.
- The United Kingdom Accreditation Forum (UKAF) is an established network of accreditation organisations with the intention of sharing experience good practice and new ideas around the methodology for accreditation programmes, covering issues such as developing healthcare quality standards, implementation of standards within healthcare organisations, assessment by peer review and exploration of the peer review techniques to include the recruitment, training, monitoring and evaluation of peer reviewers and the mechanisms for awards of accredited status to organisations.
- The International Medical Travel Association, (IMTA) is the first nonprofit association formed to help address quality standards, liability issues, continuity of care, and other issues.
- Medical Tourism Association, is the second nonprofit association in the industry which focuses on transparency in quality and pricing.

Risks

Medical tourism carries some risks that locally-provided medical care does not. Some countries, such as India, Malaysia, or Thailand have very different infectious disease-related epidemiology to Europe and North America. Exposure to diseases without having built up natural immunity can be a hazard for weakened individuals, specifically with respect to gastrointestinal diseases (e.g. Hepatitis A, amoebic dysentery, paratyphoid) which could weaken progress, mosquito-transmitted diseases, influenza, and tuberculosis. However, because in poor tropical nations diseases run the gamut, doctors seem to be more open to the possibility of considering any infectious disease, including HIV, TB, and typhoid, while there are cases in the West where patients were consistently misdiagnosed for years because such diseases are perceived to be "rare" in the West.

The quality of post-operative care can also vary dramatically, depending on the hospital and country, and may be different from US or European standards. However, JCI and Trent fulfill the role of accreditation by assessing the standards in the healthcare in the countries like India, China and Thailand. Also, traveling long distances soon after surgery can increase the risk of complications.

Long flights and decreased mobility in a cramped airline cabin are a known risk factor for developing blood clots in the legs such as venous thrombosis or pulmonary embolus economy class syndrome. Other vacation activities can be problematic as well — for example, scars may become darker and more noticeable if they sunburn while healing. To minimise these problems, medical tourism patients often combine their medical trips with vacation time set aside for rest and recovery in the destination country.

Also, health facilities treating medical tourists may lack an adequate complaints policy to deal appropriately and fairly with complaints made by dissatisfied patients.

Differences in healthcare provider standards around the world have been recognised by the World Health Organization, and in 2004 it launched the World Alliance for Patient Safety. This body assists hospitals and government around the world in setting patient safety policy and practices that can become particularly relevant when providing medical tourism services.

Legal Issues

By traveling outside their home country for medical care, medical tourists may encounter unfamiliar ethical and legal issues. The limited nature of litigation in non-US countries is one reason for the lower cost of care overseas. While some countries currently presenting themselves as attractive medical tourism destinations provide some form of legal remedies for medical malpractice, these legal avenues may be unappealing to the medical tourist. Should problems arise, patients might not be covered by adequate personal insurance or might be unable to seek compensation via malpractice lawsuits. Hospitals and/or doctors in some countries may be unable to pay the financial damages awarded by a court to a patient who has sued them, owing to the hospital and/or the doctor not possessing appropriate insurance cover and/or medical indemnity. However new insurance products are available that protect the patient should an alleged medical malpractice occur overseas.

Ethical Issues

There can be major ethical issues around medical tourism. For example, the illegal purchase of organs and tissues for transplantation has been alleged in countries such as India and China.

Medical tourism may raise broader ethical issues for the countries in which it is promoted. For example in India, some argue that a "policy of 'medical tourism for the classes and health missions for the masses' will lead to a deepening of the inequities" already embedded in the health care system. In Thailand, in 2008 it was stated that, "Doctors in Thailand have become so busy with foreigners that Thai patients are having trouble getting care".

Employer-sponsored Health care in the US

More and more U.S. employers are looking into medical travel programs as a viable healthcare benefit option for their employees. The most compelling reasons for this include its promise of offering patients more quality healthcare options at a fraction of the cost of that within the U.S., the ability to compete better globally, ability to improve employee retention and satisfaction, and because it can be seamlessly integrated into the employer's existing health benefit plan design at no cost. A few US employers have started offering incentives in their employee benefit packages, such as paying for air travel and waiving out-of-pocket expenses for care outside of the US. For example, in January 2008, Hannaford Bros., a supermarket chain based in Maine, began paying the entire medical bill for employees to travel to Singapore for hip and knee replacements, including travel for the patient and companion. Medical travel packages can integrate with all types of health insurance, including limited benefit plans, preferred provider organizations and high deductible health plans.

Insurers are beginning to establish partnerships with overseas health providers to treat their insureds as well. A 2008 article in *Fast Company* discusses the globalization of healthcare and describes how various players in the US healthcare market have begun to explore it.

Subfields

Dental

Dental tourism involves individuals seeking dental care outside of their local healthcare systems.

Fertility

Fertility tourism is the practice of traveling to another country for fertility treatments. The main reasons for fertility tourism are legal regulation of the sought procedure in the home country, or lower price. In-vitro fertilization, donor insemination and surrogacy are major procedures involved.

Destinations

Africa and Middle East

Countries in this region involved in medical tourism include Brunei, Saudi Arabia, South Africa, and Tunisia.

Israel

Israel is emerging as a popular destination for medical tourists. In 2006, 15,000 foreigners travelled to the country for medical procedures, bringing in $40 million of revenue. Medical tourists choose Israel for several reasons. Some come from European nations such as Bulgaria where certain procedures are not available. Others come to Israel, perhaps most commonly from the US, because they can receive quality health care at a fraction of the cost it would be at home, for both surgeries and in-vitro fertilization treatments. Other medical tourists come to Israel to visit the Dead Sea, a world-famous therapeutic resort. The Israel Ministry of Tourism and several professional medical services providers have set out to generate awareness of Israel's medical capabilities.

Jordan

Jordan is an emerging medical tourism destination, with related revenues exceeding one billion dollars in 2007. More 250,000 patients from other countries sought treatment in Jordan that year. This included an estimated 45,000 Iraqis and approximately 25,000 patients each from Palestine and Sudan. An estimated 1,800 US citizens, 1,200 UK citizens, and 400 Canadians also sought treatment in Jordan that year. Treatment costs can be as low as 25 percent of costs in the US. The kingdom was rated as number one in the region and fifth in the world as a medical tourism hub in a study by the World Bank.

UAE

Hospitals in Dubai and other emirates have expressed an intent to develop in medical tourism. Some have American-sourced international healthcare accreditation, while others are looking towards the UK, Australia and Canada for accreditation services.

The Americas

Countries in the Americas that are treating foreign patients include Argentina, Bolivia, Colombia, Costa Rica, and the Dominican Republic.

Brazil

Brazil has long been known as a destination for cosmetic surgery. For non-cosmetic procedures, Brazil is only now entering the global market. However, Albert Einstein Jewish Hospital in São Paulo was the first JCI-accredited facility outside of the US, and more than a dozen Brazilian medical facilities have since been similarly accredited. Brazil requires visas for Americans based on a reciprocal arrangement since Brazilians are required to obtain a visa to visit the US.

Canada

Canada has entered the medical tourism field. In comparison to US health costs, medical tourism patients can save 30 to 60 percent on health costs in Canada. Canada's quality of healthcare is cited by the World Health Organization as equal to if not better than that of the US in most categories.

Cuba

Cuba has been a popular medical tourism destination for more than 40 years. Thousands of patients travel to Cuba, particularly from Latin America and Europe, attracted by the "fine reputation of Cuban doctors, the low prices and nearby beaches on which to recuperate." In 2006, Cuba attracted nearly 20,000 health tourists.

Medical treatments included joint replacement, cancer treatment, eye surgery, cosmetic surgery and addictions rehabilitation. Costs are about 60 to 80 percent less than US costs.

Cuba has hospitals for Cuban residents and others that focus on serving foreigners and diplomats. In the 2007 American documentary film, "Sicko," which criticizes the US healthcare system, producer Michael Moore leads a group of uninsured American patients to Cuba to obtain more affordable medical treatment. "Sicko" has greatly increased foreigners' interest in Cuban healthcare. A recent Miami Herald story focused on the high quality of health care that Canadian and American medical tourism patients receive in Cuba.

The Cuban government has developed Cuban medical tourism to generate income for the country. Residents of Canada, the UK and most other countries can travel to Cuba without any difficulty; a tourist visa is generally required. For Americans, however, because of the US trade policy towards Cuba, travelers must either obtain US government approval, or, more frequently, travel to Cuba from Canada, Mexico, the Bahamas, Jamaica or the Dominican Republic. Cuban immigration authorities do not stamp the passports of US visitors so that Americans can keep their travels a private matter.

To date no Cuban facility has achieved JCI Accreditation.

Mexico

Americans, particularly those living near the Mexican border, now routinely cross to Mexico for medical care. Popular specialties include dentristry and plastic surgery. Mexican dentists often charge one-fifth to one-fourth of US prices, while other procedures typically cost a third what they would in the US.

This trend has alarmed American healthcare providers who, fearing a loss of business, warn patients away from Mexico. "The phenomenon has unsettled US-based dentists who tell horror stories of rampant infections, undetected cases of oral cancer and shoddy work south of the border", claims hotly disputed by Mexican dentists. "In Texas, legislators explored the possibility of allowing health maintenance organizations to operate on both sides of the border. However, physicians in south Texas lobbied against the changes, arguing that local doctors could not compete with the lower costs in Mexico". US doctors point out that the Mexican legal system makes it almost impossible to sue Mexican doctors for malpractice.

However, many who travel to Mexico for care report that they are satisfied. According to a report commissioned by Families U.S.A., a Washington advocacy group for health-care issues, "About 90 percent feel the care they had received in Mexico had been good or excellent. About 80 percent rated the care they had received in the United States as good or excellent".

Indeed "some U.S. dentists ... have conceded to the competition and begun a 'reverse migration' opening offices in Mexico to take advantage of lower costs". More American insurers are providing coverage for travelers, as the out-of-pocket costs to them are much lower. "With healthcare costs in the United States continuing to rise, many employers in Southern California are turning to insurance plans that send their workers to Mexico for routine care, plans that are growing by nearly 3,000 people a year".

In addition to dental and plastic surgery, Mexican hospitals are popular for bariatric surgery for weight loss, considered an elective procedure that is not covered by some US insurers. A popular bariatric procedure, lap band surgery, which was approved by the FDA in the US in 2001, has been performed for longer by Mexican surgeons.

Panama

In Panama, health and medical tourism is growing rapidly. Factors drawing medical tourists include Panama's tourist appeal, position as a hub for international travel, and use of the American dollar as the official currency. Many of Panama's doctors are bilingual, board certified, and accustomed to working with the same medical equipment and technology used in the United States and Europe. On most procedures, Panama offers savings of more than 50% compared to the US and Europe. No Panamanian hospitals currently have international healthcare accreditation, whether through US, British, Australian or Canadian sources.

United States

Much attention has been given to the growing trend of U.S. citizens seeking health care in other countries. But while the trend continues, and raises important questions about why so many Americans can't afford health care at home, a new report points out that the largest segment of medical travelers are headed stateside.

The availability of advanced medical technology and sophisticated training of physicians are cited as driving motivators for growth in foreigners traveling to the U.S. for medical care. Also, it has been noted that the decline in value of the U.S. dollar is offering additional incentive for foreign travel to the U.S. However, costs differences between the US and many locations in Asia far outweigh any currency fluctuations.

Several major medical centers and teaching hospitals offer international patient centers that cater to patients from foreign countries who seek medical treatment in the U.S. Many of these organizations offer service coordinators to assist international patients with arrangements for medical care, accommodations, finances and transportation including air ambulance services.

It should be noted that many locations in the US that offer medical care comparable in price to foreign medical facilities are not Joint Commission Accredited.

Uruguay

Uruguay recently entered the medical tourism market. A private medical tourism initiative, Uruhealth, has been created with support from the Ministries of Tourism and Public Health. The initiative involves the infrastructure, human resources and experience of two healthcare companies: MP Personalized Medicine (Montevideo) and SEMM-Mautone Hospital (Punta del Este).

Asia/Pacific

Many Asian Pacific countries are medical tourism destinations. In addition to the countries listed here, New Zealand is an emerging player.

China

Although not necessarily considered a destination for such procedures as cancer treatment, hip replacement or treatment for heart disease; China is becoming a destination for Westerners who want to take advantage of stem cell treatments that are still considered experimental or have yet to be approved in their home country for conditions such as paralysis.

Hong Kong

As of 2006, Hong Kong had 12 private hospitals and 39 public hospitals, providing 3,124 and 27,755 beds respectively. A wide range of health care services are offered. All 12 of Hong Kong's private hospitals have been surveyed and accredited by the UK's Trent Accreditation Scheme since early 2001. This has been a major factor in the ascent of standards in Hong Kong's private hospitals. The Trent scheme works closely with the hospitals it assesses to generate standards appropriate to the locality (with respect to culture, geography, public health, primary care interfaces etc.), and always uses combinations of UK-sourced and Hong Kong-sourced surveyors. Some of Hong Kong's private hospitals have now gone on to obtain dual international accreditation, with both Trent and JCI (and have therefore attained a standard surpassing some of the best hospitals in Thailand and Singapore). Others are looking towards dual international accreditation with Trent and the Australian group. Hong Kong public hospitals have yet to commit to external accreditation.

India

India's medical tourism sector is expected to experience an annual growth rate of 30%, making it a Rs. 9,500-crore industry by 2015. Estimates of the value of medical tourism to India go as high as $2 billion a year by 2012. Advantages for medical tourists include reduced costs, the availability of latest medical technologies and a growing compliance on international quality standards, as well as the fact that foreigners are less likely to face a language barriers in India. The Indian government is taking steps to address infrastructure issues that hinder the country's growth in medical tourism.

Most estimates claim treatment costs in India start at around a tenth of the price of comparable treatment in America or Britain. The most popular treatments sought in India by medical tourists are alternative medicine, bone-marrow transplant, cardiac bypass, eye surgery and hip replacement. India is known in particular for heart surgery, hip resurfacing and other areas of advanced medicine.

Ministry of Tourism India(MoT) is planning to extend its Market Development Assistance (MDA) scheme to cover Joint Commission International (JCI) and National Accreditation Board of Hospitals (NABH) certified hospitals. A policy announcement of this effect is likely soon. Hospital groups like Apollo Hospitalsand Fortis Healthcare have increased their presence in international market for medical tourism. The south Indian city of Chennai has been declared India's Health Capital, as it nets in 45% of health tourists from abroad and 30-40% of domestic health tourists.

Malaysia

Malaysia has ambitions to develop itself as a medical tourism hub. The country has excellent hospitals, English is widely spoken, and many staff have been trained to a high level in the UK or in the US.

There is a highly active Association for Private Hospitals of Malaysia working to develop medical tourism. However, while Malaysia has a national accreditation scheme (MSQH), few of Malaysia's hospitals currently hold international healthcare accreditation, whether British, American or Australian.

Philippines

The Philippines has been growing as a destination for medical tourism. The US Medical Tourism Association magazine reported that this services sub-sector grew 8.0% in 2007. The Philippines is one of a few countries that sends qualified physicians and dentists to the US, a testament to its quality of medical education.

Procedures can be performed at a fraction of the amount that a patient would spend on the same procedure in the US or Europe. Some medical centers are accredited by the American accreditation group Joint Commission International (JCI).

Singapore

Singapore has a dozen hospitals and health centers with JCI accreditation. In 1997 (published 2000), the World Health Organization ranked Singapore's health care system sixth best in the world and the highest ranked system in Asia. Singapore has close political links to the USA.

"SingaporeMedicine" is a multi-agency government-industry partnership committed to strengthening Singapore's position as a medical hub and promoting Singapore as a destination for advanced patient care. Patients come from neighboring countries, such as Indonesia and Malaysia, and patient numbers from Indochina, South Asia, the Middle East and Greater China are growing.

Patients from developed countries such as the United States and the UK are also beginning to choose Singapore as their medical travel destination for relatively affordable health care services in a clean cosmopolitan city.

Taiwan

The Taiwanese government has declared its determination for the country to become a medical tourism center. It is estimated that the government will contribute NT$44.4 million to construct a platform for the collaboration of the government and the medical sector in promoting medical tourism.

Costs for procedures remain comparatively low. Taiwan is known for liver transplants, bone marrow transplants, and reconstructive and plastic surgery.

Thailand

Medical tourism has been a growing segment of Thailand's tourism and health-care sectors. In 2005, one Bangkok hospital took in 150,000 treatment seekers from abroad. In 2006, medical tourism was projected to earn the country 36.4 billion baht.

Treatments for medical tourists in Thailand range from cosmetic, organ transplants and orthopaedic treatments to dental and cardiac surgeries. Treatments also include spa, physical and mental therapies. Thailand offers everything from cardiac surgery to organ transplants at a price much lower than the US or Europe.

Thai medicine also features a higher, more personalized level of nursing care than westerners are accustomed to receiving in hospitals at home. One patient who received a coronary artery bypass surgery at Bumrungrad International hospital in Bangkok said the operation cost him US$12,000 (8,200 euros), as opposed to the $100,000 (68,000 euros) he estimated the operation would have cost him at home. Bumrungrad treated approximately 55,000 American patients in 2005 alone, a 30% increase from the previous year.

Hospitals in Thailand are a popular destination for other Asians. Bangkok Hospital, which caters to medical tourists, has a Japanese wing, and Phyathai Hospitals Group has interpreters for over 22 languages, besides the English-speaking medical staff. When Nepal Prime Minister Girija Prasad Koirala needed medical care in 2006, he went to Bangkok.

Today many Thai physicians hold US or UK professional certification. One Thai hospital, Bumrungrad International, states that many of its doctors and staff are trained in the UK, Europe and the US. Bumrungrad International was accredited most recently in 2005 by an American group in order to ensure an international standard of medical services.

Some of the country's major hospitals also have achieved other accreditations, and some have achieved certification by the International Organization for Standardization's ISO 9001:2000 (However, ISO not an accreditation scheme).

The US consular information sheet gives the Thai health care system high marks for quality, particularly facilities in Bangkok, although the World Health Organization ranks the Thai healthcare system at number 47, below the USA's ranking at 37 and the United Kingdom's ranking at 18. The UK's Foreign and Commonwealth Office web site states "There are excellent international hospitals in Bangkok but they can be expensive".

Serious political problems during late 2008, including mass demonstrations and the complete closure of major airports, have made travel to Thailand less appealing than in the past, and the US State Department web site has expressed concerns about the country.

Europe

Countries in Europe that have active medical tourism sectors include Cyprus, Germany, Hungary, Lithuania, Malta, Poland, Portugal, Czech Republic, Slovakia, Spain, and Ukraine.

Poland

Since 2004, when Poland joined the European Union, it has become another locale for people seeking cheaper medical treatments. The quality of care in Poland must comply with EU standards. One well-known medical center in Poland is The Clinical Hospital No. 10 and Polyclinic in Bydgoszcz City.

Turkey

Turkey has attracted medical tourists from Europe and is seeking to build on its geothermal resources with expansion of therapeutic spas. German Hospital in Istanbul operates the country's first ISO-certified IVF center, while Memorial Hospital was the first private hospital to receive American JCI accreditation. Since then, over 15 hospitals have achieved Joint Commission International accreditation.

4

Promoting Tourism in Rural Areas

TOURISM DEVELOPMENT OVERVIEW

Advantages and Disadvantages of Tourism Development

The pros and cons of tourism development in rural America are varied. Tourism provides income and diversification to rural communities. Most of the dollars generated from outside visitors stay within the local economy.

In addition to gains from direct sales to visitors, many indirect benefits are realized from tourism. Visitors contribute to the tax revenues collected and can influence the quality of life by financing community facilities such as swimming pools, golf courses, restaurants, and shopping facilities. Community events intended for tourists, also attract local residents. Many potential industries prefer locations that provide high quality services and recreational resources. If the community is a pleasant place, the visitors may become a permanent resident.

Tourism offers other indirect benefits. For example, the need to provide services to tourists creates new jobs in the community. Although they may not be high paying employment opportunities, these jobs satisfy the need of students and dual-earning families for part-time or seasonal employment.

On the other hand, developing and maintaining the tourist industry in a community requires added costs and puts pressure on public services. The cost of surveys, impact analysis, promotions, insurance, fund raising, and operations are some points to consider.

Managing Resources Requires Planning

Advanced planning maximizes the advantages and minimizes the disadvantages of developing rural tourism.

Steps in Planning and Developing Tourism

1. Define Goals/Objectives
2. Identify Existing Resources/Attractions
3. Consult Outside Organizations
4. Analyze Feasibility/Impacts
5. Develop Marketing Plan
6. Identify Alternatives
7. Implement Plan
8. Monitor/Evaluate Results

Tips and Technologies

Many communities can develop tourism into a major industry using these techniques:

- Understand the potential for tourism development
- Inform and educate the community to create support
- Secure investments for public and private sources
- Manage natural, human, and financial resources
- Build an image for the community

Where to Start

Leaders must first assess the potential for tourism in the community. What businesses serve travelers and how much additional revenue will it generate? Are these enough services to satisfy the potential demands? What are the goals and objectives of the community? Talk about tourism with other members of the community. Tourism requires support, and one way to gain support is by informing and educating the citizenry.

Introduce the idea to the Chamber of Commerce, at civic clubs, at city council, or at other community organization meetings. The community and its leaders can broaden support for tourism by securing financial commitments from public and private sources.

Existing Resources

Managing natural, human and financial resources is an important component of tourism development. Most communities have existing resources and attractions that can draw visitors, such as:

Capitalize on Existing Resources

- natural settings
- scenery
- parks and recreations
- historical identity
- cultural identity
- ethnic identity
- volunteers
- students
- retirees
- events
- festivals
- fairs
- shops
- hotels
- local industries
- art galleries

What Does Your Community Have to Offer?

Conduct an inventory of the things that your community has to offer to tourists. Describe each type of attraction in terms of quality and quantity. Separate them by "core elements" (primary reasons tourist are attracted) and "secondary elements" (supporting resources; those that contribute positively to the tourists' travel experience). Look ahead at the resources that might be enhanced or used more fully.

Surveys and Models

Surveys and models are used in the process of tourism planning to determine:

- Community attitudes toward tourism
- Recreational use value and demand
- Tourism patterns
- Travel costs
- Economic impacts

Types of survey methods include telephone interviews, questionnaires, and mall interviews.

Telephone interview are low in cost, and provide a quick turn-around. In order to simplify the responses, the interviewer offers a minimum number of choices to each question in the survey. The interviewer also sends a letter before the call is made to state the date and time of the survey and ask the customer's cooperation.

Questionnaires can be used to identify the different types of tourists, or market segments. The surveyor lists responses that can be checked off by the visitor. This type of response is easy to tabulate. The survey may include questions that ask:

- Where does the visitor live?
- What attracts the visitor to the community?
- How does the visitor find out about tourist attractions?
- What type of businesses/facilities does the visitor use?
- What kinds of accommodations/services are needed?

The survey tests the questionnaire to determine the typical responses and to modify the questions.

Face-to-face interviews are useful if visual aids are necessary, for instance, in evaluating what promotional materials are pleasing to the consumer. These interviews are conducted at a central location, such as in a shopping mall.

Developing a Marketing Plan

An important step in tourism planning is determining target market segments. Experts begin by defining the market areas that will draw the most visitors. They then divide the market into trip length categories. Finally, they define the clientele that will be attracted to the community. Use the chart below as a guide:

When the expert has determined the market segments, leaders of the community are ready to make a written marketing plan. This plan helps them to see the best combination of marketing strategies, prices, places and promotions to use. Which characteristics are unique to the community? Using the plan, the leaders are able to develop a theme that ties the community's businesses and services together.

It is important to involve all facets of the community in the decision making process. Remember that everyone and everything the visitor has contact with projects and promotes something about the community.

Keep your promotional messages short and targeted to the community theme. Use your theme to promote your community:

- on brochures, billboards, posters
- on t-shirts, hats, stickers, coupons
- at demonstrations, contests, the library
- for public announcements on television, radio or community calendars

5

Hospitality Service

The concept of **Hospitality Services**, also known as "accommodation sharing", "hospitality exchange" (short "hospex"), and "home stay networks", refers to centrally organized social networks of individuals who trade accommodation without monetary exchange. While this concept could also include house swapping or even time share plans, it has come to be associated mostly with travelers and tourists staying with one another free of charge. Since the 1990s, these services have increasingly moved away from using printed catalogs and the telephone, to connecting users via the internet. As of March, 2008 over 1,000,000 people are registered users of these internet networks.

History

In 1949, Bob Luitweiler founded the first hospitality service called Servas Open Doors as a cross national, non-profit, volunteer run organization advocating interracial and international peace. The next began in 1965 when John Wilcock set up the Traveler's Directory as a listing of his friends willing to host each other when traveling. This later became the Hospitality Exchange in 1988 when Joy Lily rescued the organization from imminent shutdown. Hospitality Club is the direct successor Hospex, the first Internet-based service, operating out of Germany since 2000. CouchSurfing is the largest hospitality exchange organization and was founded in 2004. Just as all the individual services have their own individual creation stories and organizational histories (often including demise and resurrection), many also have specific niche markets that they cater to including students, activists, religious pilgrims, and even occupational groups like police officers. However, the trend in recent years points to a greater consolidation of users in networks without a specific group, value, or lifestyle affiliation.

How they Work

In essence, these systems employ reciprocity – users gain access to other users' information only by posting their own. Required fields normally include name and contact information, though newer services encourage users to include more detailed personal material, including likes and dislikes, hopes and dreams, and even photographs. Of course, more information included tends to improve the chances that someone will find them trustworthy enough to host or stay with while traveling. It is very much akin to social networking sites.

Benefits

Monetary Savings

Staying in private homes means that travelers can save lots of money on accommodation that they would usually be spending on hotels or hostels. Used over a long period of time (2 to 4 weeks), this strategy can cut overall travel budgets in half, or even more combined with hitchhiking. These savings can then be passed on towards more generously patronizing local establishments or simply staying abroad for longer periods of time.

Local Economic Sustainability

Many tourist vacations today are sold in package form, often including flights, hotels, rental cars, sightseeing tours, and coupons for chain restaurants and bars. While this makes purchasing more convenient, it also puts more money in the hands of large multinational corporations exploiting the synergy strategy of marketing their products in the context of their subsidiary companies operating in other markets.

Many years ago, this might have been termed *collusion*; today, however, it is the norm. This comes at the expense of locally owned independent businesses. Accommodation sharing helps to break apart this monopoly and hopefully redirects some of the tourist revenue back to the local or national economy.

Ecological Sustainability

While this is especially important in more rural travel venues where hotels are often built in very picturesque, though fragile environments, every night stayed at a local's home means that much less demand for such hotel rooms. Also, if accommodation sharing does in fact increase the length of average stays, it may reduce the amount of trips to and from different locations and back home again, thus reducing the overall fuel expenditures in the process.

Local Contact

Ostensibly, one of the primary reasons we travel is to experience what life is like for people living in other countries. Making interpersonal connections and fostering understanding of different cultures may in the long run also be important to international relations. However, even in our increasingly globalized world, supposedly rife with diversity, in many popular travel destinations, we find tourists milling around "tourist enclaves", where the companies they patronize back home have set up shop to cater to their desires while they are abroad. Sociologist George Ritzer has referred to this phenomenon as the "McDonaldisation of society" and the more recently, the "globalization of nothing". The location of hotels near these centers only fosters more convenient envelopment of the tourist money. During hospitality exchanges, hosts want to show off their local knowledge and exciting "off the map" venues. Not only may travelers get a distinctly different experience, but they will also get a feel for the everyday lives of local residents.

Reciprocity

These systems foster richer and more convenient travel experiences not so much on the premise of altruism, but on the basis of social exchange theory. Implicit in the agreement to host travelers is the ability to ask to be hosted by them in the future. If one enjoys having interesting guests in their home, this works out well for both parties. It works comparatively better if you are visited by travelers from a locale you find particularly attractive. Thus, hosting someone from New York City in Gainesville, Florida seems to be an unbelievable opportunity. Moreover, if you are a Westerner visiting someone in a developing country, your stay might be the only way that this individual or family could afford a trip to a rich nation. This may mean more than just a relaxing vacation for such disadvantaged parties.

Authenticity and Adventure

Tourism has always searched for these two qualities, but much like Midas and his golden touch, the reach of tourism has to a large extent destroyed the opportunity to encounter them in most places. Unluckily, the experience has been thoroughly commodified by everyone who wanted to secure their opportunity to make a profit in the process. Accommodation sharing offers a way out of this bind and a viable alternative to having one's desires manipulated by corporate conglomerates who never had the best interests of the place or the people foremost in their minds.

Drawbacks

Lack of Guarantee

There is no contractual agreement between users in these systems. Reservations are made, but if they are for some reason broken, there is no higher authority to which one could plead for a refund or other compensation. The only repercussion will be the poor rating you give that user and your only consolation will be that your warning will deter others from visiting or hosting them. For those who feel insecure unless their travel arrangements are written in stone before departure, this system will not be comforting.

POTENTIAL INTERPERSONAL CONFLICT OR AWKWARDNESS

There is a chance that guest and host will not get along. Perhaps there will be scheduling or ideological conflicts. Maybe you will find that hosts or visitors have misrepresented themselves. Perhaps the experience will not live up to your expectations. Intense interpersonal communications in advance and a flexibility once you have arrived is your best bet. These experiences require additional planning and courtesy towards the demands of your host. Thus, your living conditions, length of stay, and overall experience will be circumscribed by the living conditions you enter into.

DIGITAL DIVIDE AND DEMOGRAPHIC SEGREGATION

The average user is a young white person who speaks English and lives in a developed nation. While there are many users who do not fit this description, the more different they are, the less likely they will be involved. This is especially true for persons living in the developing world who likely do not have easy access to the fundamental prerequisite for using these services: computers and the Internet. Thus, the sample population found in searches of these databases are really much less diverse than a geographical representation of worldwide users might suggest.

Security

There is a distinct possibility that someone will abuse the system and that innocent users (especially women) will get hurt. All services include disclaimers that require users to waive their rights to hold anyone but themselves responsible for any harm that may come to them in using the system. They advise that the best defense mechanism is to only involve oneself with users that have extensive personal information and interpersonal networks within the system that have been verified by others. It does seem entirely plausible that someone clever and patient enough might be able to invent an entire group of complex user identities and build histories convincing enough to fool even more cautious patrons. Still, the difference between these systems and the other social networking platforms popular nowadays on the web (such as Facebook, MySpace, Tribe, Orkut and LiveJournal) is that any agreement reached through the accommodation sharing medium is contingent on actually meeting other people face-to-face. Other web scams are easier because interpersonal interactions rely so much on putative identities that are never actually verified in the real world. However, this does not diminish the greater risk to physical well being that this kind of traveling by definition must entertain. The best advice is to meet unknown persons in public spaces first, and try to meet some of their acquaintances in person before agreeing to a hospitality exchange.

Example Networks

There are countless websites that serve the idea of hospitality service, with new ones appearing as this phenomenon becomes more popular. While this page is not intended to be a directory listing, here is a small sample of the well-established and long-standing networks:

- CouchSurfing - A very active network with over 700 thousand members in more than 200 countries
- Hospitality Club - A very active network with over 390 thousand members in more than 200 countries
- Servas International - human rights and global peace oriented since 1949. A relatively small network now with over 15,000 members with a very long history.

HOTEL

A **hotel** is an establishment that provides paid lodging on a short-term basis. The provision of basic accommodation, in times past, consisting only of a room with a bed, a cupboard, a small table and a washstand has largely been replaced by rooms with modern facilities, including en-suite bathrooms and air conditioning or climate control. Additional common features found in hotel rooms are a telephone, an alarm clock, a television, and Internet connectivity; snack foods and drinks may be supplied in a mini-bar, and facilities for making hot drinks. Larger hotels may provide a number of additional guest facilities such as a restaurant, a swimming pool or childcare, and have conference and social function services.

Some hotels offer meals as part of a room and board arrangement. In the United Kingdom, a hotel is required by law to serve food and drinks to all guests within certain stated hours; to avoid this requirement it is not uncommon to come across *private hotels* which are not subject to this requirement.

In Japan, capsule hotels provide a minimized amount of room space and shared facilities.

In Australia and Canada, hotel may also refer to a pub or bar. In India, the word may also refer to a restaurant since the best restaurants were always situated next to a good hotel.

Etymology

The word *hotel* is derived from the French *hôtel* (coming from *hôte* meaning *host*), which referred to a French version of a townhouse or any other building seeing frequent visitors, rather than a place offering accommodation. In contemporary French usage, *hôtel* now has the same meaning as the English term, and *hôtel particulier* is used for the old meaning. The French spelling, with the circumflex, was also used in English, but is now rare. The circumflex replaces the 's' found in the earlier *hostel* spelling, which over time took on a new, but closely related meaning. Grammatically, hotels usually take the definite article - hence "The Astoria Hotel" or simply "The Astoria".

Classification

The cost and quality of hotels are usually indicative of the range and type of services available. Due to the enormous increase in tourism worldwide during the last decades of the 20th century, standards, especially those of smaller establishments, have improved considerably. For the sake of greater comparability, rating systems have been introduced, with the one to five stars classification being most common and with higher star ratings indicating more luxury. Hotels are independently assessed in traditional systems and these rely heavily on the facilities provided. Some consider this disadvantageous to smaller hotels whose quality of accommodation could fall into one class but the lack of an item such as an elevator would prevent it from reaching a higher categorization. In some countries, there is an official body with standard criteria for classifying hotels, but in many others there is none. There have been attempts at unifying the classification system so that it becomes an internationally recognized and reliable standard but large differences exist in the quality of the accommodation and the food within one category of hotel, sometimes even in the same country. The American Automobile Association (AAA) and their affiliated bodies use diamonds instead of stars to express hotel and restaurant ratings levels.

Historic Hotels

Some hotels have gained their renown through tradition, by hosting significant events or persons, such as Schloss Cecilienhof in Potsdam, Germany, which derives its fame from the Potsdam Conference of the World War II allies Winston Churchill, Harry Truman and Joseph Stalin in 1945. The Taj Mahal Palace & Tower in Mumbai is one of India's most famous and historic hotels because of its association with the Indian independence movement.

Some establishments have given name to a particular meal or beverage, as is the case with the Waldorf Astoria in New York City, United States where the Waldorf Salad was first created or the Hotel Sacher in Vienna, Austria, home of the Sachertorte. Others have achieved fame by association with dishes or cocktails created on their premises, such as the Hotel de Paris where the crêpe Suzette was invented or the Raffles Hotel in Singapore, where the Singapore Sling cocktail was devised.

A number of hotels have entered the public consciousness through popular culture, such as the Ritz Hotel in London, UK, through its association with Irving Berlin's song, 'Puttin' on the Ritz'. The Algonquin Hotel in New York City is famed as the meeting place of the literary group, the Algonquin Round Table, and Hotel Chelsea, also in New York City, has been the subject of a number of songs and the scene of the stabbing of Nancy Spungen (allegedly by her boyfriend Sid Vicious). The luxurious Grand Hotel Europe in Saint Petersburg, Russia achieved fame with its inclusion in the James Bond film GoldenEye.

Unusual Hotels

Many hotels can be considered destinations in themselves, by dint of unusual features of the lodging or its immediate environment:

Treehouse Hotels

Some hotels are built with living trees as structural elements, for example the Costa Rica Tree House in the Gandoca-Manzanillo Wildlife Refuge, Costa Rica; the Treetops Hotel in Aberdare National Park, Kenya; the Ariau Towers near Manaus, Brazil, on the Rio Negro in the Amazon; and Bayram's Tree Houses in Olympos, Turkey.

Cave Hotels

Desert Cave Hotel in Coober Pedy, South Australia and the Cuevas Pedro Antonio de Alarcón (named after the author) in Guadix, Spain, as well as several hotels in Cappadocia, Turkey, are notable for being built into natural cave formations, some with rooms underground.

Capsule Hotels

Capsule hotels are a type of economical hotel that are found in Japan.

Ice and Snow Hotels

The Ice Hotel in Jukkasjärvi, Sweden, and the Hotel de Glace in Duschenay,- Canada, melt every spring and are rebuilt each winter; the Mammut Snow Hotel in Finland is located within the walls of the Kemi snow castle; and the Lainio Snow Hotel is part of a snow village near Ylläs, Finland.

Garden Hotels

Garden hotels, famous for their gardens before they became hotels, include Gravetye Manor, the home of garden designer William Robinson, and Cliveden, designed by Charles Barry with a rose garden by Geoffrey Jellicoe.

Underwater Hotels

Some hotels have accommodation underwater, such as Utter Inn in Lake Mälaren, Sweden. Hydropolis, under construction in Dubai, will have suites on the bottom of the Persian Gulf, and Jules Undersea Lodge in Key Largo, Florida requires scuba diving to access its rooms.

Other Unusual Hotels

- The Library Hotel in New York City is unique in that each of its ten floors are assigned one category from the Dewey Decimal System.
- The Burj al-Arab hotel in Dubai, United Arab Emirates, built on an artificial island, is structured in the shape of a boat's sail.
- The former ocean liner RMS *Queen Mary* in Long Beach, California uses its first-class staterooms as a hotel.
- The Jailhotel Löwengraben in Lucerne, Switzerland is a converted prison now used as a hotel.
- The Luxor, a hotel and casino on The Las Vegas Strip in Paradise, Nevada, United States due to its pyramidal structure.
- The Liberty Hotel in Boston used to be the Charles Street Jail.

MOTELS

A motel (motor-ist's hotel) is a hotel which is for a short stay, usually for a night, whilst you are on a long journey. Has direct access from your room to your vehicle so you can go on.

World Record Setting Hotels

Largest

In 2006, Guinness World Records listed the First World Hotel in Genting Highlands, Malaysia as the world's largest hotel with a total of 6,118 rooms.

Oldest

According to the Guinness Book of World Records, the oldest hotel still in operation is the Hoshi Ryokan, in the Awazu Onsen area of Komatsu, Japan which opened in 717.

Tallest

Burj Al Arab is the tallest building used exclusively as a hotel. However, the Rose Tower, also in Dubai, which has already topped Burj Al Arab's height at 333 m (1,090 ft), will take away this title upon its opening.

Living in Hotels

A number of public figures have notably chosen to take up semi-permanent or permanent residence in hotels.

- Actor Richard Harris lived at the Savoy Hotel while in London. Hotel archivist Susan Scott recounts an anecdote that when he was being taken out of the building on a stretcher shortly before his death he raised his hand and told the diners "it was the food".

Hotel Manager

A **hotel manager** or **hotelier** is a person who handles the everyday function and management of a hotel. Larger hotels often have management teams, instead of individual managers, where each member of the group begins to specialize on a certain area of interest.

Occupational Tasks

Some of the responsibilities of a hotel manager include:

- organizing and directing the hotel's services
  - o concierge
  - o reception
  - o reservations
  - o catering
  - o housekeeping
- controlling budget and formulating financial plans
- promoting the business
  - o marketing
  - o advertising
- Achieving profits and expenses
- meeting with customers, contractors and suppliers
- hiring, training, reviewing and overseeing staff members
- attending to problems or customer complaints and comments
- addressing maintenance and upkeep

- seeing to accommodations
  - o furniture
- meeting safety, health and licensing regulations
  - o security

MOTEL

Entering dictionaries after World War II, the word **motel**, a portmanteau of *motor* and *hotel* or *motorists' hotel,* referred initially to a type of hotel consisting of a single building of connected rooms whose doors faced a parking lot and, in some circumstances, a common area; or a series of small cabins with common parking. As the United States highway system began to develop in the 1920s, long distance road journeys became more common and the need for inexpensive, easily accessible overnight accommodation sited close to the main routes, led to the growth of the motel concept.

The motel concept originated with the Motel Inn of San Luis Obispo, constructed in 1925 by Arthur Heineman. In conceiving of a name for his hotel Heineman abbreviated *motor hotel* to *mo-tel.*

Unlike their predecessors, auto camps and tourist courts, motels quickly adopted a homogenized appearance. They are typically constructed in an 'I'- or 'L'- or 'U'-shaped layout that includes guest rooms, an attached manager's office, a small reception and, in some cases, a small diner. Post-war motels sought more visual distinction, often featuring eye-catching neon signs which employed themes from popular culture, ranging from Western imagery of cowboys and Indians to contemporary images of spaceships and atomic era iconography.

In their early years, motels were "mom-and-pop" facilities on the outskirts of a town. They attracted the first "road warriors" as they crossed the United States in their new automobiles.

Motels differ from hotels in their common location along highways, as opposed to the urban cores favored by hotels, and their orientation to the outside (in contrast to hotels whose doors typically face an interior hallway). Motels almost by definition include a parking lot, while older hotels were not built with automobile parking in mind. With the 1952 introduction of Kemmons Wilson's Holiday Inn, the mom-and-pop motels of that era went into decline. Eventually, the emergence of the interstate highway system, along with other factors, led to a blurring of the motel and the hotel, though family-owned motels with as few as five rooms may still be found, especially along older highways.

Long-term

Motels with low rates sometimes serve as housing for people who are not able to afford an apartment or have recently lost their home and need somewhere to stay until further arrangements are made. Motels catering to long-term stays often have kitchenettes.

Short-time

In most countries of Latin America and some countries of East Asia, motels are also known as short-time hotels, and offer a short-time or "transit" stay with hourly rates primarily intended for people having sexual liaisons and not requiring a full night's accommodation. In Mexico love hotel equivalents are known as "Motel de paso" (Passing Motel) (even if they are actually meant mostly for pedestrian access). In Colombia, Venezuela and Brazil, motels are used by people for sexual intercourse only. In Argentina these establishments are called *albergue transitorio* ("temporary lodging"), though known as *telo* in vesre-slang. In Panama love hotels are known as Push Bottoms. In Paraguay, similarly to Brazil and Colombia, motels may charge only by the hour and are also popularly known as *reservados*. In Singapore, cheap hotels often offer a slightly more euphemistic "transit" stay for short-time visitors. In Manila, a campaign against the hotels, believed by religious conservatives to contribute to social decay in the predominantly Roman Catholic country, ended with the city banning hotels from offering stays of very short duration. As of December 2006 there are still many short time hotels in operation. In Belgium and France, these establishments are known as *hôtels de passe*. In Chile, they are known as *moteles parejeros* (coupling motels), and many of them offer hourly rates. In the United States and Canada, some ordinary motels in low income areas—often called *no-tell motels* or *hot sheet motels*—play a similar role to love hotels.

Films

The Bates Motel is an important part of *Psycho*, a 1959 novel by Robert Bloch and the 1960 Alfred Hitchcock film of the same name. Film sequels *Psycho II* and *Psycho III* feature the motel as does the 1987 television movie *Bates Motel*.

Legal Issues

Motels have also served as a haven for fugitives of the law. In the past, the anonymity and the ability to move around easily between motels in different regions by dropping in and checking out with a simple registration process allowed fugitives to remain head of the law. However, several advances have reduced the capacity of motels to serve this purpose. Crcard transactions, which in the past were more easily approved and took days to report, are now approved or declined on the spot, and are instantly recorded in a database, thereby allowing law enforcement access to this information. This system was implemented in 1993 after the abduction and murder of Donna Martz, whose crcard was used by her killers following her death to purchase food, gasoline, and to pay for overnight motel stays . The story of Martz's disappearance, leading to the development of this system, was described on The FBI Files. Laws in many places now require registering guests to present a government-issued photo ID, especially when paying with cash. Local law enforcement agencies frequently check motels when they suspect a wanted individual may be staying in their jurisdiction.

RESORT

A **resort** is a place used for relaxation or recreation, attracting visitors for holidays or vacations. Resorts are places, towns or sometimes commercial establishment operated by a single company. Such a self-contained resort attempts to provide for most of a vacationer's wants while remaining on the premises, such as food, drink, lodging, sports, entertainment, and shopping. The term "resort" sometimes is misused to identify a hotel that does not provide the other amenities required of a full resort. However, a hotel is frequently a central feature of a resort, such as the Grand Hotel at Mackinac Island, Michigan. A resort is not merely a commercial establishment operated by a single company, although in the late twentieth century this sort of facility became more common.

Towns that contain resorts—or where tourism or vacationing is a major part of the local activity—are often called resort towns. Towns such as Sochi in Russia, Sharm el Sheikh in Egypt, Barizo of Spain, Cortina d'Ampezzo of Italy, Druskininkai of Lithuania, Nice or French Riviera of France or Newport, Rhode Island or St. Moritz, Switzerland, or larger regions, like the Adirondack Mountains or the Italian Riviera are well known resorts. The Walt Disney World Resort is a prominent example of a modern, self-contained commercial resort. Resorts exist throughout the world, increasingly attracting visitors from around the globe. Thailand, for instance, has become a popular destination. Resorts are especially prevalent in Central America and the Caribbean. Closely related to resorts are convention and large meeting sites. Generally these occur in cities where special meeting halls, together with ample accommodations as well as varied dining and entertainment are provided.

Types of Resort

Resort at a Destination

A commercial establishment at a resort destination such as a recreational area, a scenic or historic site, a theme park, a gaming facility or other tourist attraction competes with other businesses at that destination.. Examples would be hotels in and around Walt Disney World, resorts in St. Martin in the Caribbean, and establishments at Aspen, Colorado in the USA.

Destination Resort

A destination resort is a resort that contains, in and of itself, the necessary guest attraction capabilities—that is to say that a destination resort does not need to be near a destination (town, historic site, theme park, or other) to attract its public. Consequently, another characteristic of a destination resort is that it offers food, drink, lodging, sports, entertainment, and shopping within the facility so that guests have no need to leave the facility throughout their stay. Commonly these facilities are of higher quality than would be expected if one were to stay at a hotel or eat in a town's restaurants. Some examples are Atlantis in the Bahamas, Costa do Sauípe in the Northeastern Brazil, Laguna Phuket in Thailand and Sun City near Johannesburg in South Africa.

All-inclusive Resort

An all-inclusive resort is a resort that, besides providing all of the common amenities of a resort, charges a fixed price that includes most or all items. At a minimum, most inclusive resorts include lodging, unlimited food, drink, sports activities, and entertainment for the fixed price. In recent years, the number of resorts offering "all-inclusive" amenities has decreased dramatically; in 1961, over half offered such plans and in 2007, less than ten percent do so.

Historical Resorts

A famous resort of the ancient world was Baiae, Italy, popular over 2,000 years ago. Capri, an island near Naples, Italy, has attracted visitors since Roman times.

Another famous historical resort was Monte Ne near Rogers, Arkansas, which was active in the early 20th century. At its peak more than 10,000 people a year visited its hotels. It closed in the 1930s, and was ultimately submerged under Beaver Lake in the 1960s.

6

Tourism Planning

INTRODUCTION

Tourism is one of many activities in a community or region that requires planning and coordination. This bulletin provides a simple structure and basic guidelines for comprehensive tourism planning at a community or regional level. Planning is the process of identifying objectives and defining and evaluating methods of achieving them. By comprehensive planning we mean planning which considers all of the tourism resources, organizations, markets, and programs within a region. Comprehensive planning also considers economic, environmental, social, and institutional aspects of tourism development.

TWO SIDES OF TOURISM PLANNING

Tourism planning has evolved from two related but distinct sets of planning philosophies and methods. On the one hand, tourism is one of many activities in an area that must be considered as part of physical, environmental, social, and economic planning. Therefore, it is common to find tourism addressed, at least partially, in a regional land use, transportation, recreation, economic development, or comprehensive plan. The degree to which tourism is addressed in such plans depends upon the relative importance of tourism to the community or region and how sensitive the planning authority is to tourism activities.

Tourism may also be viewed as a business in which a community or region chooses to engage. Individual tourism businesses conduct a variety of planning activities including feasibility, marketing, product development, promotion, forecasting, and strategic planning. If tourism is a significant component of an area's economy or development plans, regional or community-wide marketing plans are needed to coordinate the development and marketing activities of different tourism interests in the community.

A comprehensive approach integrates a strategic marketing plan with more traditional public planning activities. This ensures a balance between serving the needs and wants of the tourists versus the needs and wants of local residents. A formal tourism plan provides a vehicle for the various interests within a community to coordinate their activities and work toward common goals. It also is a means of coordinating tourism with other community activities.

STEPS IN THE PLANNING PROCESS

Like any planning, tourism planning is goal-oriented, striving to achieve certain objectives by matching available resources and programs with the needs and wants of people. Comprehensive planning requires a systematic approach, usually involving a series of steps. The process is best viewed as an iterative and on-going one, with each step subject to modification and refinement at any stage of the planning process.

There are six steps in the planning process:

1. Define goals and objectives.
2. Identify the tourism system.
   (a) Resources
   (b) Organizations
   (c) Markets
3. Generate alternatives.
4. Evaluate alternatives.
5. Select and implement.
6. Monitor and evaluate.

STEP ONE: Defining Goals and objectives. Obtaining clear statements of goals and objectives is difficult, but important.

Ideally, tourism development goals should flow from more general community goals and objectives. It is important to understand how a tourism plan serves these broader purposes. Is the community seeking a broader tax base, increased employment opportunities, expanded recreation facilities, better educational programs, a higher quality of life? How can tourism contribute to these objectives?

If tourism is identified as a means of serving broader community goals, it makes sense to develop plans with more specific tourism development objectives. These are generally defined through a continuing process in which various groups and organizations in a community work together toward common goals. A local planning authority, chamber of commerce, visitors bureau, or similar group should assume a leadership role to develop an initial plan and obtain broad involvement of tourism interests in the community. Public support for the planning process and plan is also important.

Having a good understanding of tourism and the tourism system in your community is the first step toward defining goals and objectives for tourism development. The types of goals that are appropriate and the precision with which you are able to define them will depend upon how long your community has been involved in tourism and tourism planning.

In the early stages of tourism development, goals may involve establishing organizational structures and collecting information to better identify the tourism system in the community. Later, more precise objectives can be formulated and more specific development and marketing strategies evaluated.

STEP TWO: Identifying Your Tourism System When planning for any type of activity, it is important to first define its scope and characteristics. Be clear about exactly what your plan encompasses. A good initial question is, "What do you mean by tourism?" Tourism is defined in many ways. Generally, tourism involves people traveling outside of their community for pleasure. Definitions differ on the specifics of how far people must travel, whether or not they must stay overnight, for how long, and what exactly is included under traveling for "pleasure".

Do you want your tourism plan to include day visitors, conventioneers, business travelers, people visiting friends and relatives, people passing through, or seasonal residents? Which community resources and organizations serve tourists or could serve tourists? Generally, tourists share community resources with local residents and businesses. Many organizations serve both tourists and locals. This complicates tourism planning and argues for a clear idea of what your tourism plan entails. You can begin to clarify the tourism system by breaking it down into three subsystems:

(1) tourism resources,

(2) tourism organizations, and

(3) tourism markets.

An initial task in developing a tourism plan is to identify, inventory, and classify the objects within each of these subsystems.

TOURISM RESOURCES are any (1) natural, (2) cultural, (3) human, or (4) capital resources that either are used or can be used to attract or serve tourists. A tourism resource inventory identifies and classifies the resources available that provide opportunities for tourism development. Conduct an objective and realistic assessment of the quality and quantity of resources you have to work with. Table I provides a suggested classification to help obtain a broad and organized picture of your tourism resources.

TOURISM ORGANIZATIONS combine resources in various proportions to provide products and services for the tourist. Table 2 is a partial list and classification of organizations that manage or coordinate tourism-related activities. It is important to recognize the diverse array of public and private organizations involved with tourism.

The most difficult part of tourism planning is to get these groups to work toward common goals. You should develop a list of these organizations within your own community and obtain their input and cooperation in your tourism planning efforts. Setting up appropriate communication systems and institutional arrangements is a key part of community tourism planning.

TABLE 1. TOURISM RESOURCES

Natural Resources

- Climate-seasons
- Water resources-lakes, streams, waterfalls
- Flora-forests, flowers, shrubs, wild edibles
- Fauna-fish & wildlife
- Geological resources-topography, soils, sand dunes, beaches, caves, rocks & minerals, fossils
- Scenery-combinations of all of the above

Cultural Resources

- Historic buildings, sites
- Monuments, shrines
- Cuisine
- Ethnic cultures
- Industry, government, religion, etc.
- Anthropological resources
- Local celebrities

Human Resources

- Hospitality skills
- Management skills
- Seasonal labor force
- Performing artists-music, drama, art, storytellers, etc.
- Craftsman and artisans
- Other labor skills from chefs to lawyers to researchers
- Local populations

Capital

- Availability of capital, financing
- Infrastructure-transportation roads, airports, railroads, harbors & marinas, trails & walkways
- Infrastructure: utilities water, power, waste treatment, communications

TABLE 2. TOURISM MANAGEMENT ORGANIZATIONS AND SERVICES

Off-Site: Coordination, planning, technical assistance, research, regulation:

- Federal & state departments of commerce, transportation, & natural resources
- Federal, state, regional, & local tourism associations
- Educational organizations & consultants, e.g., Travel & Tourism Research Association; U.S. Travel Data Center; Travel Reference Center, Univ. of Colorado, Boulder; Travel, Tourism, & Recreation Resource Center, Michigan State University.
- Travel information & reservation services

On-Site: development, promotion and management, of tourism resources:

- Federal agencies, NB. departments of commerce, transportation, & land management agencies
- State agencies, NB. departments of commerce, transportation, & land/facility management agencies
- Local government organizations, e.g., visitor information, chamber of commerce, convention & visitor's bureaus, parks
- Businesses:
    - Accommodations: Hotels, motels, Lodges, resorts, bed & breakfast cabins & cottages, Condominiums, second homes, Campgrounds
    - Food & Beverage: Restaurants, Grocery, Bars, nightclubs, Fast food, Catering services
    - Transportation: Air, rail, bus; Local transportation: taxi, limo, Auto, bicycle, boat rental; Local tour services
    - Information: Travel agencies, Information and reservation services, Automobile clubs
    - Recreation Facilities & Services: Winter sports: ski, skating, snowmobile areas; Golf courses, miniature

golf; Swimming pools, water slides, beaches; tennis, handball, racquetball courts, bowling alleys; Athletic clubs, health spas; Marinas, boat rentals and charters; hunting & fishing guides; Horseback enterprises; Sporting goods sales & rentals

— Entertainment: Nightclubs, amusement parks, spectator sport facilities; Gambling facilities: casinos, horse racing, bingo; video arcades; art galleries and studios, craft shops, studios, demonstrations; performing arts: theater, dance, music, film; historic & prehistoric sites; museums: art, history, science, technology; arboreta, zoos, nature centers,

— Special festivals and events

— Support services: Auto repair, gasoline service stations; boat & recreation vehicle dealers and service; retail shops: sporting goods, specialties, souvenirs, clothing; health services: hospitals, clinics, pharmacies; laundry and dry cleaning; beauty & barber shops; babysitting services; pet care; communications: newspaper, telephone; banking and financial services

TOURISM MARKETS: Tourists makeup the third, and perhaps most important subsystem. Successful tourism programs require a strong market orientation. The needs and wants of the tourists you choose to attract and serve must be the focus of much of your marketing and development activity. Therefore, it is important to clearly understand which tourism market segments you wish to attract and serve. Tourists fall into a very diverse set of categories with quite distinct needs and wants. You should identify the different types of tourists, or market segments that you presently serve or would like to serve. This may involve one or more tourism market surveys.

A visitor survey identifies the size and nature of the existing market and asks the following questions:

- What are the primary market segments you presently attract?
- Where do they come from?

- What local businesses and facilities do they use?
- What attracted them to the community?
- How did they find out about your community?
- How satisfied are they with your offerings?

A market survey (usually a telephone survey) also can be conducted among households in regions from which you wish to attract tourists. This type of study helps identify potential markets, and means of attracting tourists to your area.

TOURISM MARKET SEGMENTS

In a general tourism plan, some clear target tourism market segments should be identified (See Table 3). You might begin by defining the market area from which you will draw most of your visitors. The size of your market area depends upon the uniqueness and quality of your "product", transportation systems, tastes and preferences of surrounding populations, and your competition. Identifying the market area will help target information and promotion and define transportation routes and modes, competition, and characteristics of your market.

Next, divide your travel market into the following trip length categories:

- day trips from a 50 mile radius,
- day trips from 50 to 200 miles away,
- pass-through travelers,
- overnight trips of 1 or 2 nights (most likely weekends), and
- extended overnight vacation trips.

After you have an idea of your market area and kinds of trips you will be serving, begin defining more specific market segments like vehicle campers, downhill skiers, sightseers, family vacationers, single weekenders, and the like. These segments can be more clearly tied to particular resources, businesses, and facilities in your community.

What kinds of products and services are likely to attract each of these groups? Tourist needs as well as their impact on the local community are quite different for day tourists versus overnight tourists. Areas catering primarily to weekend traffic will experience large fluctuations in use. In deciding the relative importance of these different segments, communities need to assess both their ability to provide required services (do you have enough rooms?), as well as the demand for different types of trips relative to the supply and your competition.

THE ENVIRONMENT: A tourism plan is significantly affected by many factors in the broader environment. Indeed, one of the complexities of tourism planning is the number of variables that are outside of the control of an individual tourism business or community. These include such things as tourism offerings and prices at competing destinations, federal and state policy and legislation, currency exchange rates, the state of the economy, and weather. These factors are discussed more fully in Extension bulletin E-1959 as part of the market environment analysis.

Local populations also must be considered in tourism planning. As they compete with tourists for resources, they can be significantly affected by tourism activity, and they are an important source of support in getting tourism plans implemented. A survey of local residents can be conducted to assess community attitudes toward tourism development, identify impacts of tourism on the community, and obtain local input into tourism plans. Public hearings, workshops, and advisory boards are other ways to obtain public involvement in tourism planning. Local support and cooperation is important to the success of tourism programs and should not be overlooked.

TABLE 3. TOURISM MARKET SEGMENTS

I. Geographic market areas

II. Trip categories

Day Trips:

- short-within 50 miles
- long-up to 200 miles

Pass through traffic:

- day visitors

- overnight stays

Overnight Trips:

- weekend
- vacation

III. Activity or trip purpose

Outdoor Recreation:

- Water-based Activity:
  - Boating: sail, power, cruise, row, canoe, water ski
  - Swimming: pool, beach, sunbathing, scuba
  - Fishing: charter, sport, from pier, boat, shore, ice
- Land-based Activity:
  - Camping: backpacking, primitive, developed
  - Hiking: climbing, beachcombing, spelunking
  - Hunting
  - Skiing: downhill, cross country
  - Snowmobiling
  - Bicycling
  - Horseback riding
  - Picnicking
- Air-based Activity:
  - Airplane rides, hang gliding, ballooning, parachuting
- General:
  - Nature study
  - Photography or landscape painting
  - Viewing natural scenery

Sightseeing & Entertainment:

- Visiting particular sites or areas:
  - historic or pre-historic
  - cultural
  - amusements
  - scenic

- Attending particular events, shows, or demonstrations:
  - ethnic festivals
  - sporting events
  - performances
  - agricultural fair or festival
  - boat show
  - shopping

Other Primary Purpose for Trip:

- Visiting Friends & Relatives
- Convention & Business/Pleasure

STEP THREE: Generating Alternatives. Generating alternative development and marketing options to meet your goals requires some creative thinking and brainstorming. The errors made at this stage are usually thinking too narrowly or screening out alternatives prematurely. It is wise to solicit a wide range of options from a diverse group of people. If tourism expertise is lacking in your community, seek help and advice outside the community.

Tourism planning involves a wide range of interrelated development and marketing decisions. The following development questions will get you started:

- How much importance should be assigned to tourism within a community or region?
- Which general community goals is tourism development designed to serve?
- Which organization(s) will provide the leadership and coordination necessary for community tourism planning? What are the relative roles of public and private sectors?

Tourism marketing decision questions include (Extension bulletin E-1959):

- Segments: Which market segments should be pursued; geographic markets, trip types, activity or demographic subgroups?
- Product: What kinds of tourism products and services should be provided? Who should provide what?

- Place: Where should tourism facilities be located?
- Promotion: What kinds of promotion should be used, by whom, in which media, how much, when? What community tourism theme or image should be established? (See Extension bulletins E-1939, E-1957, E-1940, E-1938, E-2005)
- Price: What prices should be charged for which products and services. Who should capture the revenue? (See Extension bulletin E-1999)

STEP FOUR: Evaluating Alternatives. Tourism development and marketing options are evaluated by assessing the degree to which each option will be able to meet the stated goals and objectives.

There are usually two parts to a systematic evaluation of tourism development and marketing alternatives: (1) Feasibility analysis, and (2) Impact assessment. These two tasks are interrelated, but think of them as trying to answer two basic questions: (1) Can it be done?, and (2) What are the consequences? A decision to take a specific action must be based both on feasibility and desirability.

FEASIBILITY ANALYSIS: First, screen alternatives and eliminate those that are not feasible due to economic, environmental, political, legal, or other factors. Evaluate the remaining set of alternatives in more detail, paying particular attention to the market potential and financial plan.

Make a realistic assessment of your community's ability to attract and serve a market segment or segments. This requires a clear understanding of the tourism market in your area and how this market is changing. Also carefully identify your competition and evaluate your advantages and disadvantages compared to the competition.

Plan toward the future because it takes time to implement decisions and for your actions to take effect. Therefore, look at the likely market and competition for several years to come. Review forecasts for the travel market in your area, if available. Careful tracking of tourism trends in your own community can help identify changes in the market that you will have to adapt to. (See Extension bulletins E-1959 and E-1992 for more details on feasibility and marketing.)

IMPACT ASSESSMENT: When evaluating alternative development and marketing strategies it is important to understand the impacts, both positive and negative, of proposed actions. Table 4 presents a classification of economic, environmental, and social impacts associated with tourism development. The types of impacts and their importance vary across different communities and proposed actions. Generally, the size, extent, and nature of tourism impacts depend upon:

- volume of tourist activity relative to local activity
- length and nature of tourist contacts with the community
- degree of concentration/dispersal of tourist activity in the area
- similarities or differences between local populations and tourists
- stability/sensitivity of local economy, environment, and social structure
- how well tourism is planned, controlled, and managed.

Look at both the benefits and costs of any proposed actions (See Extension bulletin E-1937). While tourism development can increase income, revenues, and employment, it also involves costs. Evaluate benefits and costs of tourism development from the perspectives of local government, businesses, and residents.

TABLE 4. IMPACTS OF TOURISM

Economic Impacts:

- Sales, revenue, and income
- Employment
- Fiscal impact-taxes, infrastructure costs
- Prices
- Economic base & structure

Environmental Impacts:

- Lands
- Waters

- Air
- Infrastructure
- Flora & fauna

Social Impacts:

- Population structure & distribution
- Values & attitudes
- Education
- Occupations
- Safety & security
- Congestion & crowding
- Community spirit & cohesion
- Quality of life

IMPACTS ON LOCAL GOVERNMENT

Local government provides most of the infrastructure and many of the services essential to tourism development, including highways, public parks, law enforcement, water and sewer, garbage collection and disposal. Evaluate tourism decisions with a clear understanding of the capacity of the local infrastructure and services relative to anticipated needs, and take into account both the needs of local populations and tourists.

A fiscal impact analysis evaluates the impact of tourism on the community's tax base and local government costs. It entails predicting the additional infrastructure and service requirements of tourism development, estimating their costs, deciding who will pay for/provide them, and how. Will tourism generate increased local government revenue through fees and charges, local sales or use taxes, increased property values or property tax rates, or larger local shares of federal and state tax revenues?

Impacts on Business and Industry Businesses that are directly serving tourists benefit from sales to tourists. Through secondary impacts, tourism activity also benefits a wide range of businesses in a community. For example, a local textile industry may sell to a linen supply firm that serves hotels and motels catering primarily to tourists. A local forest products industry sells to a lumberyard where local woodcarvers or furniture makers buy their supplies. They in turn sell to tourists through various retail outlets. All of these businesses benefit from tourism.

If most products and services for tourists are bought outside of the local area, much of the tourist spending "leaks" out of the local economy. The more a community is "self-sufficient" in serving tourists, the larger the local impact.

Impacts on Residents

Local residents may experience a broad range of both positive and negative impacts from tourism development. Tourism development may provide increased employment and income for the community. Although tourism jobs are primarily in the service sectors and are often seasonal, part time, and low-paying, these characteristics, are neither universal nor always undesirable. Residents may value opportunities for part time and seasonal work. In particular, employment opportunities and work experiences for students or retirees may be desired.

Residents may also benefit from local services that otherwise would not be available. Tourism development may mean a wider variety of retailers and restaurants, or a better community library. It may also mean more traffic, higher prices, and increases in property values and local taxes. The general quality of the environment and life in the community may go up or down due to tourism development. This depends on the nature of tourism development, the preferences and desires of local residents, and how well tourism is planned and managed.

STEPS FIVE AND SIX:Implementation, and Monitoring and Evaluation. We will not attempt a complete discussion of decisionmaking, plan implementation, and monitoring, but these are critical steps in the success of a tourism plan. A set of specific actions should be prescribed with clearly defined responsibilities and timetables. Monitor progress in implementing the plan and evaluate the success of the plan in meeting its goals and objectives on a regular basis. Plans generally need to be adjusted over time due to changing goals, changing market conditions, and unanticipated impacts. It is a good idea to build monitoring and evaluation systems into your planning efforts.

CONCLUDING REMARKS

Successful tourism planning and development means serving both tourists and local residents. The bulletins in this series stress the importance of a market orientation for attracting and serving tourists. This market orientation must be balanced with a clear view of how tourism serves the broader community interest and an understanding of the positive and negative impacts of tourism development.

Remember, tourism should serve the community first and the tourist second. Tourism development must be compatible with other activities in the area and be supported by the local population. Therefore, the tourism plan should be closely coordinated with other local and regional planning efforts, if not an integral part of them.

7

The Space Tourism Industry in 2030

Over the past few years the general perception of space tourism has changed from being considered "science fiction" to becoming recognised as an important new target for the space industry. This change has been stimulated in part by the Space Tourism Study Program of the Japanese Rocket Society (JRS), which led to the development of a scenario that has received general consensus: if some $12 billion of funding became available in the near future, commercial passenger space travel services to and from Earth orbit could begin in 2010. At a growth rate of some 100,000 passengers/year/year the business could reach 700,000 passengers/ year by 2017, at a price of about $25,000 /passenger.

The importance of this result is that $12 billion is less than half of one year's funding of government space agencies today, and it is therefore readily affordable. The paper extrapolates the JRS scenario to the year 2030, based on market research results. By that time space tourism activities could have grown to a scale of $100 billion/year, creating several million jobs. It thereby demonstrates the very great economic value of such a development - approximately $1 trillion greater than the value of continued taxpayer funding of space agencies' activities without developing space tourism. The paper also discusses the potentially critical importance of this new industry in maintaining economic growth in the world economy against the deflationary pressures caused by excess capacity in older industries, and inadequate investment in new ones.

INTRODUCTION

Several events over the past 2 years have greatly raised the credibility and attention given to the subject of space tourism. These include:

1. Publication of reports by NASA (1), the American Institute of Astronautics and Aeronautics (AIAA) (2), Daimler-Chrysler Aerospace GmbH (3) and others acknowledging that space tourism is the most promising commercial market in space.
2. Speeches by senior figures including the President of the Space Transportation Association (STA) Thomas Rogers, Congressman Dana Rohrabacher, NASA Administrator Daniel Goldin and others referring favourably to the realism and great economic potential of space tourism.
3. Founding of the Space Travel and Tourism Division of the STA in Washington DC, of the Space Tourism Society in Los Angeles, of Space Adventures Inc, Spacetopia Inc, Zegrahm Space Voyages Inc, and of other organisations dedicated to realising space tourism.
4. Holding of dedicated meetings such as the STA Conference, the 2nd International Symposium on Space Tourism, the UK-Japan Space Tourism Workshops, IAF Congress sessions on space tourism, and others.
5. Opening of the Internet Web Site www.spacefuture.com dedicated to disseminating information on space tourism and space power. Introducing the various aspects of space tourism, and containing more than 100 published papers, news and commentary, the site received more than 1/4 million visits in its first 2 years.
6. Founding of the new companies Bigelow Aerospace and Virgin Galactic Airways by wealthy entrepreneurs Robert Bigelow and Richard Branson to realise space tourism.
7. Ever-growing media coverage of space tourism.
8. Significant progress by companies developing reusable space vehicles, such as Kistler Aerospace, Rotary Rocket, Bristol Spaceplanes, and contenders for the "X Prize".

The formal Space Tourism Study Program under way within the Japanese Rocket Society since 1993 is widely accepted as a reasonable baseline for discussion of the potential for establishing a commercial space tourism industry. The scenario developed as part of that study estimated that the development and certification of the " Kankoh-maru" VTOL passenger launch vehicle, designed to carry 50 passengers to low Earth orbit (LEO), and involving 1200 test-flights using 4 vehicles (following aviation practice), would require 10 years and a budget of some $12 billion. It is notable that this is less than half of the annual budget of government space agencies today, and so is clearly a very supportable level of investment.

Assuming the start of orbital passenger space flights in 2010, the JRS scenario foresees production of 8 Kankoh-maru vehicles/year, each capable of 300 flights/year for 10 years. This implies a growth in passenger numbers of approximately 100,000 passengers/year/year, leading to some 700,000 passengers/year in 2017 (4).

The JRS's continuing Study Program has identified several areas that require further study. First, the development and manufacturing cost estimates of Kankoh-maru have been criticised as too high, being roughly twice the estimate made by Lockheed-Martin for the much larger "Venture Star" reusable launch vehicle. (NB Kankoh-maru is both structurally simpler and much smaller than the proposed Venture Star, but it is more ambitious in its flight rate of 300 flights/year.) However, cost-estimating models for rocket launch vehicles are not readily applicable to vehicles planned to perform airline-style operations since there is no data-base of relevant experience. The accumulated experience in the aviation world of designing and operating rocket-powered aircraft is probably more relevant, but this has not yet been assembled in a useful form. Second, no detailed analysis has yet been carried out of the development and production costs of orbital accommodation facilities, which are considered important to generate sufficient demand for passenger flights to orbit.

Nevertheless, based on market research data, economic growth projections, and historical growth rates achieved by other industries, reasonable forecasts can be made for further growth of the space tourism industry from 2017 forward.

2030 VISION

Based on the above discussion, we can lay out a vision of space tourism activities 30 years in the future, based on the provision of a growing range of commercial space travel services to the general public. Extending the JRS scenario linearly to 2020, passenger numbers would reach 1 million/year after 10 years of operation. Thereafter it seems reasonable to project continued growth both in the number of customers and in the range of services offered, as this would follow the pattern seen in the travel and tourism industry on Earth. This growth would be fueled by rising incomes, growing middle class populations, and commercial competition between service providers to attract customers from around the world. On this basis, passenger numbers traveling to low Earth orbit (LEO) of 5-10 million/ year 30 years from now would imply average growth rates of 18% - 26%/year through the decade 2020-2030, which are certainly feasible.

On this scenario, traffic of 5 million passengers/year in 2030 would imply that the cumulative number of passengers at that time would reach some 40 million people - or perhaps 3% of the middle class population of the time. However, in market research, most people say that they would like to travel to space, and in addition a large proportion, particularly of younger people, say that they wish to do so several times.

Furthermore, based on the precedent of decades of commercial aviation experience, we can predict that service prices will fall steadily as passenger numbers increase. And due to this fall in prices as well as to the development of progressively more entertaining facilities in orbit, it seems probable that demand will continue to grow strongly. Consequently a traffic rate of 5 million passengers/ year by 2030 will be very far from satisfying the known demand: serving a mere 3% of the middle class population will not satisfy the market. Hence traffic levels several times higher than this, perhaps 20 million/year, must be considered a possibility. Such traffic rates may seem unrealistically high to some members of the space industry; however they seem rather low to members of the aviation industry, who already carry more than 20 million passengers every week, and are expecting air traffic to quadruple by 2030.

ORBITAL ACCOMMODATION INDUSTRY

Such growth will also have interesting implications for the hotel industry. It is worth noting, first, that the technology required for initial orbital accommodation is much simpler not only than that needed for passenger launch vehicles, but also than that in orbiting research stations: there is no need for highly accurate attitude control, high-speed computers and communications, nor custom-designed research equipment. Nevertheless, by 2030 orbital hotels will have moved beyond the first generation comprising clusters of standard pre-fabricated modules, and will include large structures like resort hotels, entertainment complexes and sports centres assembled in orbit (5).

From market research, the great majority of customers can be expected to stay in orbit for 2-3 days or longer, from which it is simple to calculate that 5-10 million passengers/year will entail some 30,000 - 80,000 guests staying simultaneously in orbital accommodation. Assuming an average occupancy rate of 80%, this will require capacity for some 35,000 to 100,000 guests in orbit. This will therefore become a field for substantial business investment, involving the wide range of activities involved in commercial real estate development on Earth in addition to aerospace engineering (6).

Another implication is that, assuming a staff:guest ratio of between 1:3 and 1:2, the number of hotel staff working in orbit 30 years from now will be between 10,000 and 50,000. Since staff will work shifts of perhaps 1- 2 months in orbit, the total number of people engaged in this work will be at least twice this figure, some 20 - 100,000.

Staff who work in space for the travel and tourism industry as hotel staff and space tour conductors (or " Specon", a contraction of "Space conductor", as they are coming to be known in Japan) can therefore be expected to outnumber government astronauts by hundreds-to-one by 2030. As career-goals for young people to aim towards, this is therefore a much more realistic target than trying to be selected as one of the tiny number of government astronauts (whose selection inevitably takes place in the proverbial "smoke-filled rooms").

Based on this simple analysis, we can project that 30 years from now there will be more than 100 hotels in orbit, since even at the lower end of the projections made above an average capacity of 350 guests/hotel seems rather high. These hotels will probably operate in a small number of defined orbits, in which they will maintain their position within agreed parameters, due to the safety and operational benefits that they will gain (7, 8). Agreement over positions in low Earth orbits is similar in principle to that for geo-stationary orbit, though it will be more complex in practice, and will require a number of legal innovations (7, 8). The majority of the hotels will therefore probably be within one of perhaps two different high- inclination orbits which will allow for economical access from high latitudes (9, 10), as well as providing guests views of much of the Earth. There may also be as many as 20 specialised sports centres, comprising a stadium and accommodation for users and spectators. These sports centres are likely to be in a low equatorial orbit, which is the cheapest orbit to reach, since their customers will generally be more interested in zero gravity sports than in viewing a wide range of different places on Earth. By 2030, sports stadia as large as 100m in length could be in operation, and international sports competitions in both "zero G" and artificial gravity created by rotating the sports stadium seem likely to be developed.

There may be as many as 10 hotels in a polar orbit to give guests detailed views of the entire Earth, and there may also be a few hotels in one or more highly elliptical orbits with apogees of several thousand km in order to provide guests views of the distant Earth. Access to these will be significantly more expensive than to other hotels, but over some 15 years a significant level of market segmentation can be expected to take place. With 100 or more scheduled flights/day to the hotels listed above, and probably many more private flights, aerospace traffic control will be long-established. A system based on the Space and Air Traffic Management System (SATMS) proposed in early 1999 by the US Federal Aviation Authority (FAA) seems likely to have been adopted internationally and developed to include "local" space traffic management systems in the vicinity of each hotel, and for each defined orbit (11).

ADDITIONAL ASPECTS

Due to the commercial incentives that will arise as the scenario described above develops, there is likely to be at least one propellant "service station" in each of the main hotel orbits, supplying water, oxygen and hydrogen initially. The supply of water (for conversion using solar-powered electrolysis into oxygen and hydrogen) and/or oxygen from the lunar surface and from Earth-approaching cometary bodies both to these LEO propellant stations, and to orbital hotels and sports centres will also probably be a regular commercial activity by 2030 (12).

Indeed, 30 years from now, the leading-edge of space tourism will have moved on, with businesses offering round-trips to stay in hotels both in lunar orbit and on the lunar surface, serviced with scheduled daily flights. Bigelow Aerospace is aiming to offer the first such services within about 15 years (13), and so by 2030 lunar tourism could probably support two hotels in lunar orbit, and more on the lunar surface. Likely sites include both lunar poles where water may be readily accessible, and others at sites with particularly good views. Hilton International has specifically quoted the discovery of water on the lunar surface as the reason for starting to plan the first Lunar Hilton (14)

In case the idea of lunar tourism seems futuristic, it should be remembered that the technology needed to travel to the Moon is already more than 30 years old. Once the key step is taken to develop low-cost passenger services to and from low Earth orbit, there is no reason why travel to and from the Moon should not follow quickly. Indeed, lunar hotels are likely to be more attractive to wealthy tourists due to their exclusivity.

Figure 1: Space Tourism in 2030 (15)

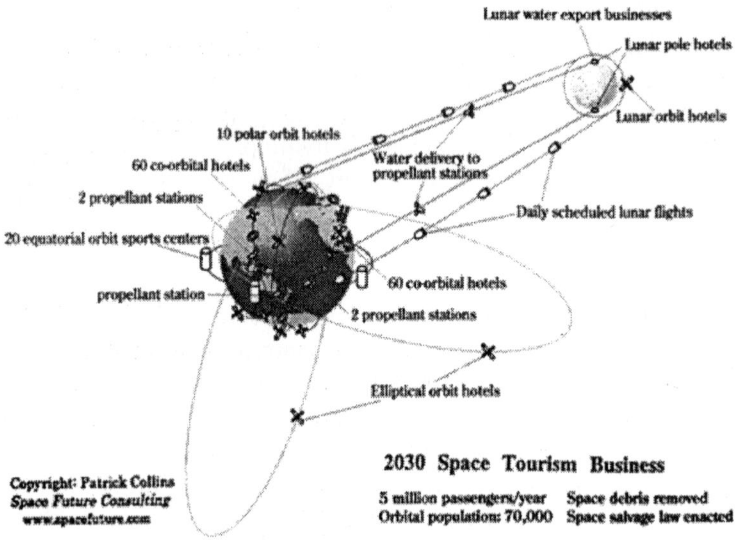

SPACE TOURISM TURNOVER

The tourist activities described above will represent a turnover of the order of some $100 billion/year by 2030, assuming 5 million guests paying $20,000 each. Although this is far larger than space activities today, it will still be only a few percent of civil aviation at that time, which is projected to exceed $2 trillion/year. Over and above the selling of travel services to customers, the provision of accommodation services in addition to space transportation will create new markets in space for a wide range of products and services, creating many new commercial opportunities in these fields.

Based on the cost estimates in the JRS scenario, the development of these activities will have absorbed some $200 billion of cumulative investment by 2030, most of it occurring through the 2020s. Almost all of this investment will come from commercial sources, for which $200 billion is not a large amount - an overall average of $7 billion/year, reaching perhaps $20 billion in 2030. (For comparison, annual expenditure by government space agencies today is $25 billion/year.)

Consequently the total amount invested commercially in passenger space travel services, and in other commercial space activities that develop from them over the next 30 years, could reach several times the amount needed for this scenario without strain. Indeed, it is only the amount that taxpayers would be obliged to pay for government space agencies if funded at today's level over the same time period - though without any comparable economic return. This point is discussed further in the following section. In a more ambitious scenario, the commercial investment of perhaps half a trillion dollars would create several hundred billion dollars/year turnover of new commercial space activities, providing the basis for a well-founded, world-wide economic boom, and opening access to the limitless resources of space. Such an outcome would finally dispel all pessimistic concerns about the Earth's limited resources, the inevitability of poverty for much of the world's population, the end of economic growth, and so on.

This is particularly true in view of the fact that a major beneficiary of the low launch costs that the growth of large-scale space tourism activities will bring about could be the global electricity industry, because the supply of electric power from space to Earth will become commercially feasible at approximately the same launch cost/kg as tourism (16). If an early pilot plant such as the Japanese "SPS 2000" project (17) is implemented in a timely manner and successfully demonstrates the potential economic feasibility of delivering environmentally benign microwave power from space to Earth, this activity could become a second major commercial space activity by 2030, earning tens of $billions/year, and supporting investment on a broadly similar scale to tourism. Thus, by reducing the cost of access to space sharply, space tourism could also be extremely beneficial to the global environment by making the supply of clean power from space economically feasible.

MACRO-ECONOMIC ASPECTS

It is particularly interesting to note that the activities described above will create several million permanent jobs in the aerospace, hospitality and related industries, a large proportion of them in leading industrial countries (although the technical know- how on which they depend will be available in a wider range of countries in 2030 than they are today). This is in striking contrast to the effect of government space spending: the current level of $25 billion/year maintains employment at some 1/2 million - in jobs which will disappear when this taxpayer support ends.

It is instructive to compare these two outcomes in more detail. The continuation of government funding at $25 billion/ year would use $750 billion over 30 years, of which perhaps 25% might return to governments as taxes. The tourism scenario would use about half this amount of investment (of which perhaps 25% would flow to governments as taxes), but most of it would come from private investors to whom it would be returned with a commercial rate of profit. It would in addition generate commercial revenues of $100 billion/year or more (of which perhaps 25% would flow to governments as taxes), and support several million jobs. Cumulative revenues by 2030 would be approaching $1 trillion.

The net difference to the economy between these two scenarios would thus reach of the order of $1 trillion by 2030 - a very substantial contribution to the world economy of that time. Estimates of the present value of this scenario depend on the discount rate used, which might vary from 18.6%, being a recent estimate of the cost of capital for a space tourism venture (18), to as low as 3%, as an estimate of the long-term economic growth rate. The former figure is appropriate for the initial investments at each significantly new phase of development; however, the correct value to use as an average over the next 30 years lies somewhere between these two figures. In this case the present value of $1 trillion in 2030 will lie between some $300 billion and some $4 billion; a 10% discount rate would give some $50 billion. Clearly, whatever discount rate is used, it is economically very desirable to invest in the creation of this new industry.

The decision to implement this scenario will not only be economically valuable in itself, but it is also desirable for its contribution to the development of the world economy which is currently threatened by deflation due to excess capacity in many older industries, and inadequate investment in new ones. The growth of commercial space travel services as illustrated in Figure 1 could therefore play an important role in stimulating and maintaining further economic growth throughout the world.

The economic value of this scenario, in terms of the addition to global turnover and profits, increase in tax revenues, etc, is some $1 trillion. Since there are no alternative proposals for achieving space commercialisation on anywhere near this scale, the decision not to develop a space tourism industry in the near future would therefore impose an unnecessary cost on taxpayers of approximately $1 trillion over the next 30 years. Such a financial burdem is not only heavy in itself; the waste of this opportunity would also prolong the deflationary forces in the world economy. Delaying it unnecessarily for even a few years would impose a cost of tens of $ billions.

This result raises the question "Since the economic effects of such a development are so desirable, what should governments do to ensure its realisation?" Above all, governments should take whatever steps are effective in getting private investment to flow into this field as soon as possible. The lack of effort in this direction by taxpayer-funded space agencies to date reflects their continuing concern for their traditional activities rather than for the wider interests of the general public.

Throughout the world, many major industries have been undergoing severe restructuring in the post-cold-war period - based on adapting their activities to provide services that sufficiently large numbers of the general public wish to pay for. It is time for the space industry also to undergo a similar re-orientation towards providing the public with services that they are prepared to pay for, rather than continuing to spend large amounts of taxpayers' money on unprofitable activities chosen by political processes. The first step is for space agencies to acknowledge, publicly, frequently and authoritatively, the primary importance of the objective of making space travel services available to the general public, as well as its feasibility, its likely profitability, and its economic desirability, as NASA and the AIAA have already admitted in print (1, 2). Such acknowledgment alone could greatly encourage investors to start to take an interest in this field. Thereafter there is a long list of helpful activities that governments can perform, some of which are discussed in (1, 15 & 19).

CONCLUSIONS

In the absence of serious disruption to world economic growth, by 2030 the space tourism industry could be carrying some 5 - 10 million passengers/year to low Earth orbit, with some 50,000 - 100,000 guests staying simultaneously in a range of accommodation facilities in orbit - hostels, hotels, resort hotels, sports centers. Tourism services to hotels orbiting the Moon and on the lunar surface can also be expected to be under way, based on technical capabilities that are already more than 30 years old today.

Although this scenario may seem more ambitious than the plans of government space agencies, it would require substantially less investment than the $25 billion/year that governments currently spend on civilian space activities. More importantly, the great majority of the investment involved would come from commercial sources, not from taxpayers, and would be returned with substantial profit to investors, thereby adding to the wealth of society.

The major reduction in launch costs which the development of large-scale space travel services would cause would also create other commercial opportunities in space, including possibly making the supply of environmentally clean electricity from space competitive with other sources.

This paper has shown that the vigorous development of space tourism over the next 3 decades has an economic value, in terms of addition to global income and wealth, increase in tax revenues, etc, of some $1 trillion. The longer the delay in changing the priority of space activities to aim at realising this highly desirable outcome, the greater the cost to taxpayers.

8

The Economic Impact of Visitors to the Community

Impact studies that examine the economic effects within a community of development projects such as a new hotel are usually confined to a fiscal analysis of local government costs and revenues. But increasing emphasis on the total environment-social, biological, and business-calls for an appraisal of broader impacts within the community for a wholistic perspective. Economic impact studies need to provide information about the effects on jobs, income, or housing, as well as how a project will affect the community's overall environment. The effects a project has on various groups within a community (i.e. its distribution effects) are often more important than its economic efficiency.

An economic impact assessment can become a useful tool for a community to use in working out what is most economically effective considering the goals for family income, distribution of benefits and costs, fiscal impacts, benefits over time, etc. The approach to setting up such a study will depend on the situation, the community, and the analyst's judgment. The study is not the final word on whether a particular choice should be made; it simply presents alternatives and their effects. The purpose of an economic study is to put some practical problems in proper perspective for a public decision-making process. Frequently, decisions must be made with less information than any community would desire.

Communities must also combat a number of misconceptions about economic impact studies, including an unrealistic expectation that the analysis can be completely accurate and comprehensive. Every attempt to increase the accuracy of a study, also increases its cost and time required. A balance must be struck between what a community wants to spend and the desired level of accuracy. Errors in assessing economic impacts will affect a decision only if they are so large that the apparent desirability of alternatives is reversed. If the best alternative appears substantially superior to the next best alternative, then it may take only rough computations to confirm that superiority. If the first and second best alternatives are not widely separated, it will take greater accuracy to identify the best choice, but a wrong decision will result in a relatively small loss. It may be relatively easy to estimate total benefits and costs, but much more difficult to estimate the differences in distribution of income and costs within the community. If distribution impacts are important there will be more work to do.

Another misconception is that economic impact analysis is irrelevant because decisions are made on a political basis. Growing constraints on public spending and tax collection make it difficult to decide what programs to fund and what projects to approve. Hard choices have to be made when funding is available for only one of several worthwhile projects which annually compete for scarce revenues. The problem is to decide which project will benefit the community most, given the goals. Despite the fact the economic impact assessment has not been used a great deal, more and more communities find it a valuable tool for understanding the consequences of political decisions.

Step 1: Define the scope of the study and alternatives to be considered in the analysis.

Local government decisions fall into three general categories: plans, policies, and projects. The effects associated with each category vary somewhat and require different levels of detail in an analysis. It may take some time to understand what local officials and leaders want from an analysis, but care in defining the scope of the study will save time later and make the results more useful to those who must interpret them. In general, plans often provide for broad assumptions and community goal statements while policies and projects become increasingly specific.

Whether a plan, policy, or project is under consideration, the basic method of an economic impact study is to compare alternatives to discover the differences in their economic effects. In some cases, it may seem easier to analyze only the original proposal and not to consider any alternatives, but this will limit the usefulness of the study because it forgoes consideration of variations that might make the proposal better suited to the community. In extreme cases, a decision not to consider alternatives could lead to rejection of a proposal that, with small changes, could have benefited the community.

The number of alternatives that should be considered depends on the number of realistic options available and on other constraints, such as time, information, funding, and political realities. Whatever alternatives are chosen, there must be sufficient information to permit analysis of the economic impacts at a level that will aid realistic decision making. It is useful for leadership to limit alternatives to be included in the analysis to a realistic number.

Step 2: Define exactly what decisions need to be made, what information is being requested, and what questions the study should answer.

Far too often the consultant or analyst determines what information a community needs and what assumptions are to be made about the community's goals and resources. An analyst must understand precisely what decisions local officials need to make and what information is being requested to conduct a useful economic impact study. Even if staff members have been given the responsibility for choosing alternatives and shaping the study, they may still want to consult those who will use the study to be sure it covers the essential points and contains the most useful information possible. For example, if the staff has been asked to analyze the economic impact of several general plan alternatives, there may be certain areas of particular concern to local government, such as the fiscal effects of different levels of growth or the effects on employment. These decisions are the responsibility of the community, perhaps facilitated by the analyst. The community should start by listing the types of questions that the study is to answer. Not all questions can be anticipated; the study itself may highlight other areas that need consideration. With an initial list of areas to be included, however, the analyst can move to the next step.

Step 3: Determine how detailed the analysis should be.

The scope of the study will depend on several factors:

- What type of proposal is under consideration; a plan, policy, or project.
- Whether the study is part of a continuing process of economic analysis or is a one-time request for analysis of a particular proposal.
- Time and budget constraints.
- Expertise of the available staff within the community.
- The audience for the study; the city council, board of supervisors, or a department chief.
- The geographic area covered and the length of time considered.

The level of detail a study requires will depend primarily on the type of proposal being considered. Comprehensive plans for the entire community obviously will involve extensive analysis of the present economic conditions and the expected effects of the plan's alternatives, while a plan for a particular service in one area of the community could be analyzed with far less work. Policies and projects will involve different levels of detail, depending on their scope or size in relation to the rest of the community. A second important consideration in determining a study's level of detail is whether it is a one-time analysis or part of a continuing program. The initial economic impact studies will entail more work in gathering the necessary data and information, but if the analysis is continued, each report that follows will be easier to prepare. Beginning the work at the broadest plan level will provide a framework within which to analyze other decisions.

The scope of the study may be partly determined by the individuals or groups who have requested the analysis. The city council or planning commission might want only a short summary of the general impacts of a proposal, while a department chief might need a detailed study of all the important impacts. Other constraints on the level of detail in a study, such as time and budget limitations, will be beyond the control of the staff. A staff's unfamiliarity with methods of economic analysis may also add to these constraints. Local governments may wish to use analysts and others from outside the community to do much of the initial work and training.

Two additional limitations on a study are the area it encompasses and its duration. The area included in an economic impact assessment should be clearly defined, and the reasons for its delineation explained, because the boundaries of political jurisdictions do not necessarily correspond to the boundaries for housing, land, employment, economic impacts, or even fiscal impacts on local government. Some impacts will be zero within certain areas. For example, new hotel construction may have no effect on tourism growth in the region, even though it influences the local area. Or additional hotel rooms in one area may mean less demand for accommodations in the rest of the region. Particularly in a metropolitan region, communities cannot always pinpoint the effects a proposal will have on their own tourist-related employment or land-use. To do so often requires an awareness of regional interactions and of factors outside the local community or government's control.

The availability of data will play an important role in defining the study area. The geographic area is generally that political unit (the city, county, or standard metropolitan statistical area) for which published statistics exist. As a practical matter, the final choice of the geographic area may have to be left open until the details on the various alternatives are clear. This may mean working for a period of time with overlapping geographic areas.

The length of time considered in an impact assessment can also significantly affect the results. The assessment should take into account the period that the economic impacts will be important; the first five years, perhaps, could be covered in detail and a broader look given to the life of the impacts. The longer the period of analysis, the less certain projections become. Plans usually specify the period for which they apply; the assessment should provide analysis for the same period. Since policies may involve temporary decisions or establishment of guidelines for a community, the analyst needs to provide an estimate of how long the effects of a proposed policy are likely to last. Projects have an initial effect during the construction phase, a continuing effect through their middle age, and often a different effect during their declining years. Thus, the economic impacts should be considered not only during the building period, but for the entire life of the project, as long as reasonable estimates can be made, which may require certain assumptions about things such as future real estate values, property tax rates, inflation rates, and consumer demand.

Step 4: List in the study all fundamental assumptions and limitations.

A study's assumptions may cover a wide range of variables, such as changes in the national economy; the rate of growth in population, employment, or income; or the continuation of or change in trends. Whatever alternatives are chosen, the comparison of impacts will be valid only if the same methods have been used consistently throughout the assessment. For example, if inflation effects are considered in one alternative, they should be considered in all alternatives. The study should clearly state which methods are being used and if, for any reason, one alternative is treated differently, the difference should be explained. It may be necessary to add to the initial list of assumptions during the analysis. There may be opportunities to indicate which assumptions most influence the long-term benefits and costs of the project. This is helpful in evaluating the risks associated with the project.

Limitations in the analysis should be identified. For example, if the time available to prepare the study is limited, and some economic areas cannot be covered as thoroughly as desired, the analyst will want to explain this limitation and how it affects the study. Likewise, any limitations in the method of analysis should be thoroughly discussed to give decision makers an idea of risks inherent in the outcome.

Step 5: List all economic impacts that are considered.

For a very large project or a major plan, all economic impact areas will probably be affected, while for specialized plans, policies, or projects, certain areas may not be affected. For example, a community's general plan probably will affect everything from population size to the delivery of public services, while a ten-unit housing development will not have significant effects on income levels or government services except for a small community.

Step 6: Determine what data are needed, what are available, and how they will shape the study.

In order to evaluate the economic impacts of a change in land use for a large tourism project, it is useful to detail past growth trends and to prepare a current community profile. The analysis of economic impacts may warrant collection of past and current data to help address the following:

- Visitor expenditures and their impact on local revenues.
- Estimate of community visitor days so we know if existing work force and facilities can handle the expected demand. (i.e., measurement of employment, housing, existing land use, etc.)
- Data to determine the dollar cost and benefit of local tourism development will help the community assess who will gain and who will not benefit from the development. (i.e., local property and sales taxes, costs associated with traffic congestion, pollution damage, etc.)

Projections of future growth and change also will be needed. These could be based on historical trends or on a number of assumptions about the probability of certain changes occurring. Projections of population and business activity will be particularly important in evaluating development proposals.

Finding adequate data can be a major obstacle. A vast amount of data has been collected and published by governments and private organizations, but all too often these data do not provide the exact information needed. All data must be evaluated on the basis of how they were collected, what assumptions were made, what items were excluded, why they were collected, and by whom. The decision to collect new data will depend on the cost and time involved, compared to the quality and adaptability of existing data.

The data available and the need to prepare new data can shape the type of analysis. If good data are not available and time does not permit preparation of new information, these limits should be clearly identified. For example, the analyst might explain that certain projections of employment and income are very rough estimates, but they will have to be relied upon for estimating the effects of the proposal on public services and land area requirements.

Step 7: Analyze the effect of each alternative on the individual economic areas being considered and analyze indirect effects (or cross-impacts) among economic areas.

A plan, policy, or project which imposes a change in one economic sector of the community may trigger a change in many of the other sectors as well. When these ties are understood, the indirect or secondary impacts of a proposal can also be identified. Figure 1 describes a proposal that a local government might consider and the kinds of direct and indirect consequences-economic, demographic, and environmental-which might result from tourism development.

Step 8: Present results so alternatives can be compared, identifying the aggregate and distributional impacts of each alternative.

The aggregate economic impacts include the total effects in one sector, such as the aggregate employment impacts or the aggregate impact on housing. Distributional impacts are those that affect some individuals, groups, institutions, businesses, and communities more than others. For instance, land use restrictions imposed on high density housing may drive up the cost of cheaper housing, thereby directly affecting lower income families.

ESTIMATING COMMUNITY VISITOR DAYS

It is important to know the cost of a visit to your community relative to the cost of a visit to another community. That cost includes expenditures for food, lodging, travel, and entertainment. Many of these amounts, however, are outside of a community's control (such as the cost of travel to your area).

Communities may be able to cooperate to influence the effects of transportation costs on tourists. The Durango/Silverton railroad, for example, is a multi-community effort that enhances regional tourism. Other expenses are those not usually considered in terms of dollars and cents. The most important cost of driving may not be the gasoline or depreciation of the car, but the hours spent.

The price of a visit must be balanced with the benefits offered to visitors. Are there natural attractions-beaches, rivers, canyons, scenic viewsor events that are interesting to a visitor?

However we must face the reality that factors other than price influence tourism potential. A primary factor is personal income of the tourist you intent to target with your product. Are personal incomes increasing (are the media mentioning a prospering or expanding economy) or remaining constant? Is there a recession? What is the state of the economy-both national and international?

If incomes are rising, people will have more to spend on tourism. This may mean that more people will visit your area and that they will pay more for a trip, or stay longer. It may also mean that tourists decide to go to more expensive areas in the United States, or to foreign countries, but keep in mind that international travel may be affected by factors other than income, such as the currency exchange rate and political stability. The effect of any changes in income level are difficult to assess, however, they should be considered because income level relates closely to the types of tourists attracted. Of particular interest is how income levels are changing for the tourists that are most likely to visit your community.

In evaluating the tourism potential it is important to consider the number of competing communities that would affect your town. If you are surrounded by other community's with strong tourism industries you will need to focus on the "distinctive" qualities that your town has to offer. These qualities might be natural (parks, beaches, climate) or man-made (museums, historical attractions, special events, sports attractions). Depending on your competitive environment, you may find advantages in multi-community collaborative attractions; again, the Silverton/Durango Railroad is an example. Complementary tourism resources are also important. Many cities have cooperatively (and sometimes not so cooperatively) developed tourism based on the historical nature of a region, for example, many areas in the western U.S. emphasize Oregon Trail attractions.

An example of competing communities will illustrate the importance of this issue. Along the California coast, Santa Barbara, Pismo Beach, Santa Cruz, and the communities between them attract visitors on the basis of their warm, pleasant climates and the interesting historical aspects of their cities. All have substantial tourism industries, yet the distance between these cities can easily be covered in a day's drive. These cities view each other as competitors; each, therefore, tries to differentiate itself from the other. Each city is aware of the attractiveness of the others. This is clearly evident in their promotional literature and in the new areas of interest that the cities develop. All are successful in attracting visitors, despite their proximity.

ESTIMATING TOURIST POTENTIAL FOR EXISTING ATTRACTIONS

The most appropriate starting point for estimating economic potential of existing attractions is the level of visitation for previous years. Using Figure 1, list the average annual visits and the peak day visits for each year (for the last ten years, if available). Use daily, weekly, or monthly visit figures as appropriate for your community. If you are not collecting these figures now, you should start to establish a basis for assessing your situation and potential.

For each year after the first year listed, calculate the percentage growth from the previous year using the formula:

$$\frac{\text{Visits for Year - Visits Previous Year}}{\text{Visits Previous Year}} \times 100\% = \%\ \text{Change in Visitors}$$

You can also calculate for peak visits by month or day.

If the previous year's visitation was higher than that for the current year, the percentage growth will be negative. Both average and peak number of visits should be calculated.

After calculating the growth in average and peak visitation, write down any special events planned for the year, such as the opening of a new attraction or festival. Also, write down any outside events that might have affected visits that year, such as a recession or a world's fair. Calculate an average growth rate for the period. You should attempt to modify the growth rates to remove the effects of special events or attractions and outside events. Major peaks or valleys need to be explained to help understand the long term trends and to know if different rates of change might be expected in the future. Using the estimated growth rate, calculate potential visit figures for each year ahead in your planning horizon. For each year use the following formula:

Estimated Visits for the Year

= Previous Year's Estimated Visits × % Annual Growth Rate

Start with visits for the current year and calculate year by year into the future. Adjust these levels to consider any special events or attractions or any outside events you expect in future years.

Figure. Estimates of visitors to Western City, U.S.A.

Year	Average number of visitors	Growth from previous year	Peak number of visitors	Special events and/or attractions	Outside/other events that affected visits
1991	*200/wk*	*NA*	*350 July 4*	*None*	*new highway open*
1992	*600/wk*	*200%*	*1500 July 4*	*western days*	*chamber efforts*

Estimating tourist potential for new tourist attractions

It is obviously very difficult to come to a firm estimate of visits for new attractions because there are no current levels to use as a starting point. Generally, the best procedure is to seek out other tourist areas with similar types of attractions, similar target markets, and similar competition and use current visit levels there to estimate the levels likely for your community and attraction.

There will not be an existing area that perfectly matches the proposed one but current visitation figures for other areas can be adjusted to reflect differences in:

- Size of potential target markets.
- Nearness and convenience of target markets.
- Availability of competitive areas to the target markets.
- "Drawing power" of the area's attractions.
- Costs to the target markets of visiting the areas.

ASSESSING SUPPORT SERVICES TO MEET ESTIMATED VISITATION LEVEL

An inventory of support services will provide essential information about anticipated needs, and may be useful in advertising and marketing. For example, do the motels have facilities that appeal to families (do they have swimming pools and playgrounds), or to convention goers (do they have convention facilities and nighttime entertainment)? Does the restaurant inventory include those capable of catering gourmet meals or are they predominantly fast food establishments? Do the food services include a variety?

The general process of evaluating community needs and the costs to satisfy them involves several steps. The following pattern may be useful.

Determine the present level of facilities and associated capacity.

Identify the kinds of tourism and visitors contemplated. En route visitors will require fewer services than destination (overnight or longer) travelers.

Estimate the quantity of tourists (and duration of season). This may be a projection of your past experience adjusted for expected economic conditions, or an estimate based on the experience of similar attractions elsewhere.

Estimate the increase in facilities and services needed for the estimated quantity of visitors at the expected level of service. In most cases, simple surveys using guidelines provided here are sufficient. Consider methods of financing these additions and develop a budget and schedule for these provisions.

Below is a sample form (Figure 2) for determining facilities necessary to meet anticipated demand. The breadth and depth of inventories depend, among other things, upon the size of the community and the scope of the development plan. Surveys may be expensive or inexpensive depending on the scope, the size of the area to be surveyed, and the amount of cooperation from the support services.

Remember that inventories are not one-time affairs. Continual inventories (annual, seasonal, monthly-whatever you consider most appropriate for your needs) are essential measures of the success or failure of tourism. Special needs of visitors should be considered in assessing need for additional attractions and facilities. These needs include disability and accessibility requirements, language barriers, and cultural differences.

IMPACT OF VISITOR EXPENDITURES ON LOCAL REVENUES

The money tourists spend in a community is the benefit which people probably recognize most readily. Other benefits might include improved recreation facilities, expanded cultural and social opportunities, and pride in one's community, but additional dollars provide the usual appeal for tourism development. These dollars benefit sectors throughout the community, including those not directly connected to tourism, such as the construction industry.

Communities contemplating development to encourage tourism can estimate the amount of money visitors will spend in their area. These estimates are useful in several ways.

- To indicate the value of tourism to a larger region.
- To show the impact on specific local economic sectors, for instance main street business, households, local governments.

- To plan new tourism attractions or facilities.
- To determine the impacts of tourism on the economy in terms of receipts, employment, payroll, and tax revenues.

Steps to construct a custom income multiplier

1. Collect data on the volume and pattern of tourist spending. This information will come from survey data or regional use figures.
2. Estimate the percentage of sales income which remains in the area. Interviews with knowledgeable business people in each sector will provide this estimate.
3. Determine the percentage of tourist expenditures that directly increase local revenue. This is a "weighted" average of all sectors where the weights are the percent of the tourist expenditure in each sector.
4. Estimate the percentage of income that local people spend in your community.
5. Estimate the percentage of goods and services sold locally that are produced locally.
6. Multiply the percent estimated in Step 4 by the percent estimated in Step 5.
7. Subtract the percent calculated in Step 6 from 100 percent and divide the result into 100 percent.
8. Calculate the income multiplier by multiplying the result obtained in Step 7 by the percent calculated in Step 3.
9. Determine the increase in local income by multiplying total tourist expenditure by the income multiplier.

Measuring visitor expenditures

There are four methods that communities may use to collect estimates of total dollars spend by visitors to their area.

Diaries

A diary format that continuously records spending is the most accurate method for obtaining expenditure information. Diaries require minimum recall on the part of respondents, which is advantageous if highly detailed information is sought.

There are two major shortcomings, however. First, recording expenses may change the tourist's spending habits and therefore bias total tourism spending estimates. Second, participation tends to be low because few vacationers welcome an additional chore. Innovative incentives might offset this problem.

Tourists with certain types of personalities may be more likely than others to keep diaries. Personality differences might also be reflected in spending behavior.

Exit interviews

Another method of gathering expenditure information is to interview people as they leave an area. People can be asked to estimate their total expenditures for the entire visit to an area, or for only their last day there. Since fewer people will refuse to complete an exit interview, you can expect to find a more representative group of respondents with this method than with diaries. People will tend to forget many expenditures, however. They will remember better the expenses from the last day than from earlier days.

A variation on the exit interview is to interview people randomly in an attempt to reach them on each day of their visit. This reduces the bias found when interviews are concentrated on the last day of a visit, but it does not eliminate the problem of recall.

Mail surveys at home

Questionnaires may be sent to visitors at their home addresses, using a random sample derived from various registration data. This type of questionnaire typically gets a higher response rate than the diary method, but a lower response rate than exit interviews. The time lapse in mail surveys increases the tendency to underestimate actual expenses.

Surveying tourist-related business

Businesses directly affected by visitor expenditures include hotels, shops, and restaurants. Information gathered from proprietors or managers of these establishments is subject to their ability to differentiate between tourist-related sales and sales to residents.

Measurement of impact on local revenues

There are two methods to measure the impact of tourist expenditures on local revenue:

- Adapt coefficients from existing national or regional studies.
- Develop specific impact relationships for the community being studied.

There may be analysts who can assist a community with this task. There may be consultants or perhaps a council of governments, a regional development organization, a college, or Extension faculty who would welcome the opportunity to cooperate in a project of this sort. The cost of analysis may influence how the community chooses to address this need.

Use of regional or county revenue multipliers

(Note: Revenue is used here to differentiate from family income. The usual convention among economists is to speak of income multipliers, but we are talking of changes in "income" throughout the local economy, not just to families.) Regional or county revenue multipliers provide a rough estimate of the increase in local revenue as a result of tourist related expenditures. A multiplier is a factor used to estimate the impact on local revenue from tourism sales.

Evidence indicates that in the northwestern United States local income from tourism falls within a range of 30 to 50 percent of tourist expenditures. (This should not be confused with "revenue multipliers" which are much larger.) In most areas, a $100 tourist expenditure can be expected to increase local revenue by $30 to $50. If a multiplier is not available, a ballpark estimate can be made by considering the following factors:

- The estimate will probably fall within the range of 0.3 to 0.5.
- The multiplier will tend to be at the upper end of the range if the region is urban (more self sufficient) rather than rural, and if tourists buy products which require considerable local labor in production (e.g., hotel-motel expenditures, purchase of local arts and crafts).

There may be an economic analysis office in the State government or in the business department of a university that knows of multipliers for this or a similar region. The U.S. Forest Service or Extension Service through the IMPLAN program may be able to provide the multiplier estimates for the area.

Construction of a custom multiplier

If the program is past the preliminary stage and the community already does considerable tourist buisness, it may make sense to develop a custom multiplier. Information required is:

- The pattern and volume of tourist expenditure in the region.
- The percentage of goods and services produced locally.
- The percentage of local revenue that is spent locally.

If a custom multiplier is the option of choice, the community will usually need to acquire outside assistance to complete the work.

Examples of visitor expenditure patterns.

The pattern and volume of tourist expenditures will be the first type of data collected in evaluating tourist impact. Of every $100 spent by tourists in Arizona in 1984, for example, about $26 was spent for food and beverages, another $26 for lodging, a little more than $23 for transportation, $7 for entertainment, and $15 for retail purchases. The money which accrues to local residents depends on the amount of tourist expenditures .

The more money each tourist spends in the area, and the more tourists who visit, the greater the increase in local incomes. The amount of local income created will depend on the pattern of expenditure by the tourists and on the amount of goods and services that can be provided by the local community.

For example, if the expenditure is for fuel, the money quickly leaves the community to pay for the fuel, unless there is a local wholesaler, when it stays in the community longer.

Percentage of goods and services produced locally.

Also important is the extent to which different sectors within the local area purchase goods and services from each other. If the local restaurant is able to purchase food from wholesalers in the region, more of the tourist expenditure will accrue as local revenue. For sectors important to tourist trade, it is useful to estimate the percent of each purchase that is produced locally. Interviews with knowledgeable business people in each sector can provide this information.

Again, some economic analysis office in the state should be able to estimate the effect throughout the economy of money spent locally. For example, when the percentage of goods and services produced locally and the distribution of tourist expenditures were computed in one area, 32 percent of tourist expenditures went to restaurants and food stores. Of that amount, almost 59 percent went to local businesses and residents as additional revenue. As might be expected, lodging is the sector with the highest percentage of goods and services supplied locally, and thus the highest potential for generating local revenue.

Percentage of money spent locally

Once the percentage of goods and services produced locally has been estimated and the pattern of tourist expenditure established, the amount of money coming into the local area can be calculated. If $28.70 is spent for lodging, and if 38 percent of this sum must go to buy goods and services outside the area, then 62 percent of the money, or less than $18, stays in the local community.

This is not the end of the matter, however. Recipients of this revenue will spend a portion for goods and services, some produced locally and some imported. The motel proprietor buys groceries at the local market and gasoline at the filling station, generating additional local revenue. These second round recipients will have less of the total money to spend than the first round recipients-those who received revenue from the initial tourist purchase-and third round recipients will have even less than second round participants.

The result of this "chain of spending" is a multiplier process whereby money spent locally is multiplied to give the total impact of the new money spent in the community.

The amount of revenue generated locally in the second, third, and subsequent rounds of spending is determined by the same considerations that determined the direct impact-the proportion of money spent on local goods and services, in this case by local residents, and the percentage of these goods and services produced locally. Figure 1 takes a $200 tourist expenditure into the second round of spending. Taxes are treated as a payment for services performed by outsiders. $200 in local purchases created $100 revenue for local residents in the first round. They, in turn, spent $55, or 55%, at local shops and businesses. The other $45 went into savings, or taxes, or into other communities as a portion of the revenue was spent outside the community. The $55 in local revenue adds to community business. The addition to local economic activity, however, will be less than the amount of the sales. If 40 percent of the goods and services purchased with that $55 are produced locally, then another $22 will be added to local revenues, which will lead to further increases in local sales and incomes.

In the literature on tourism, it is not uncommon to find statements to the effect that initial expenditures by tourists are multiplied many times over as a result of subsequent rounds of spending. Such statements may be misleading. We are concerned not with the volume of sales attributable to the tourist expenditure, but with the portion of that expenditure which ends up as local income. Smaller and smaller portions of the original expenditure continue to ripple through the local economy. The multiplier accounts for the actual economic size of these smaller and smaller ripples for a more accurate estimate of the actual economic impact.

9

Measuring Tourism Impacts at the Community Level

INTRODUCTION

Many rural communities in the U.S. have experienced significant change in the last two decades. Some have prospered from the urban-to-rural migration patterns of the 1970's and expanded employment opportunities; others have declined because of the farm problems of the 1980's and the lack of employment opportunities for residents. In either case, the changes have made the governance of rural America more complex. An influx of people from urban areas with different values and expectations creates new demands for local government services. However, the revenue base of rural communities may not be sufficient to fulfill the expectations of new residents. In those communities with constant or declining populations, community leaders are seeking new economic opportunities to stabilize or reverse the economic problems they face.

In the Northeast, one of the viable economic opportunities available to rural communities continues to be tourism and related outdoor recreational activities. Tourism currently contributes to the economic base of many rural communities in the region, and other communities are interested in attracting tourism development to increase job opportunities. The impacts of tourism development are usually local in nature, and planning decisions regarding such developments are made by local officials. However, community leaders often lack the knowledge to effectively evaluate the positive and negative impacts that tourism may have on the local area. Because of this lack of information, rural community leaders are seeking assistance from extension and research personnel at the land-grant universities.

In 1986, a six-year Northeast regional research project entitled "Tourism Impacts and Development Alternatives from the Local Rural Government Perspective"(commonly referred to as NE-163) was initiated to address some of the issues facing local government officials regarding tourism development. Researchers from the land-grant universities in the following states have participated in the project: Maine, Vermont, Massachusetts, Rhode Island, Connecticut, New York, New Jersey, Delaware, and Michigan. Representatives from New Jersey and Connecticut retired early in the life of the project and were not replaced.

One of the objectives of the project is to develop, test, and refine procedures that would enable local officials to evaluate the relative benefits and costs of future tourism development alternatives. The purpose of this publication is to present the results of several studies conducted by members of the NE-163 research committee that contributed to this objective.

The first two papers address the question of identifying the importance of tourism in the states, counties, or communities in the Northeast. The study by Tom Brown at Cornell University uses shift-share analysis and location quotients for the lodging sector to assess changes in the tourism industry in the region. The results show that the tourism sector, as approximated by lodging receipts, grew at a rate greater than the overall retail sector in the Northeast.

However, the rate of growth varied substantially among states and counties, thereby causing significant changes in the geographical distribution of tourism activity within the region. The results are useful in that they identify the counties where tourism activity is concentrated in the region. This allows local communities to determine where they stand in terms of current tourism activities, relative to other counties in the Northeast.

The paper by Mal Bevins of the University of Vermont and Rod Zwick of Lyndon State College in Vermont uses cluster analysis to classify Vermont communities. Two of the seven community clusters identified are related to tourism. The results of the cluster analysis are then used to determine whether a simpler procedure based on secondary data could be used to classify communities. A spreadsheet approach based on key community characteristics is developed that approximately reproduces the results of the cluster analysis. Finally, the community clusters are analyzed in terms of the property tax burden on local residents. The results indicate that residents of the two tourist-related community clusters have lower property tax burdens than residents in the non-tourist-related community clusters, thus suggesting that the tourism development in those communities reduces the property tax burden on local landowners.

The third paper by Tim Tyrrell of the University of Rhode Island presents the Tourism Development Simulation Model (TDSM). Originally, this model was envisioned to provide a way for community planners to make "ball park" estimates of the impacts associated with different types of tourism development. In the early phases of construction, however, it became clear that impacts vary substantially with the characteristics of the community and its responses to development, as well as with the characteristics of the development itself and the types of tourists it attracts. A complex set of interactions make it difficult to specify "average impacts" for different types of tourism development in different types of communities.

Consequently, the model was transformed into a simulation game in which the player is forced to consider the consequences of development and the complex interactions within the community that, together, determine the ultimate impact of the development. The value of the game is that the player begins to recognize a much broader range of potential impacts than just jobs or income. For example, the model forces the user to consider the need to balance local government budgets and the potential environmental and social impacts associated with the tourism activity. The model is based on results of several tourism research projects; hence the model offers a realistic view of the issues that a community must address in assessing the ultimate impacts associated with tourism development.

One of the more difficult and expensive aspects of tourism studies designed to measure the economic impact of tourism is the need to determine the spending profile of tourists who are attracted to a community by a new development. This spending profile depends on several factors including whether visitors are local or non-local residents, day users or overnight visitors, and the type of lodging used by overnight visitors.

Complex visitor surveys often have to be conducted to construct the visitor spending profiles. The fourth paper by Dan Stynes and Dennis Propst at Michigan State University addresses this issue by constructing visitor spending profiles for different types of visitors or segments of tourists, such as day visitors, overnight visitors who camp, and overnight visitors who use motels for lodging. By constructing separate spending profiles for the different segments of homogeneous visitors, the spending profiles are more stable across space. Hence, local planners can determine the types and numbers of visitors that a tourism development will attract and then use the spending profiles constructed from data collected at other locations to determine the level of tourist spending associated with the new development. This approach significantly reduces the time and cost of estimating the total tourist spending associated with a new development.

Stynes and Propst also discuss how input-output models, in conjunction with the total expenditures of tourists, can be used to measure the indirect and induced effect associated with the tourists' expenditures in the local area. The last paper by Mario Teisl and Steve Reiling at the University of Maine examines the impact that tourism has on local governments' cost of providing local government services. Like residents, tourists consume local government services during the time they stay in the community. These services include police and fire protection, water and sewer services, and solid waste disposal. Again, the amount and types of services demanded vary with the type of tourist. For example, day visitors demand a different mix and quantity of services than do overnight visitors or seasonal residents. Their paper presents the results of a study that estimated how tourism affects the costs of providing nine different local government services using data for 379 towns in Maine. They conclude that tourism does have an impact of the costs of delivering several types of the public services, but the additional costs incurred to provide services to tourists is quite small relative to the total costs of providing local services.

All of these papers contribute to the stated objective to develop, test, and refine procedures that enable local officials to evaluate the potential benefits and costs of tourism development. Although additional work is needed to further assist local officials, the contributions presented in this report should simplify the task of evaluating the potential impacts that communities may incur from tourism development.

ASSESSING CHANGES IN TOURISM IN THE NORTHEAST

Tourism is acknowledged to be among the leading industries in each state in the Northeast. Yet tourism is so diverse that it is often difficult to measure. Only at the site level, such as at a park, resort, or for a specific fishery, can researchers use survey methods to estimate the economic impacts of tourism in a straightforward and relatively uncomplicated way. As examples of such research see Gitelson and Grafe (1990) and Connelly et al. (1986). These methods also have been applied to special events such as community festivals (Mitchell and Wall 1989).

For larger geographic entities, it becomes much more difficult to accurately measure the economic impacts of tourism. The basic measurement problem stems from the fact that most tourist expenditures occur at retail establishments such as restaurants, sporting goods stores, marinas, golf courses, and amusement areas whose clientele also include local residents. The owners of such businesses usually have only a vague estimate of the proportion of annual receipts that is derived from tourists versus local residents. Indeed, this proportion often changes from weekday to weekend and from season to season.

In cases where secondary data are available on a monthly basis, such as state employment statistics broken down by counties and municipalities, one can derive reasonable estimates of the proportion of employment and business receipts that are from tourists versus local residents (e.g., Connelly and Brown 1988; Brown and Connelly 1986). Such estimates are derived intuitively from graphics and assume a base level of trade from local residents. Sales or employment above this base level are then attributed to tourism. This type of analysis is useful at the state or sub-state level, but the cooperation of the state commerce or economic development agency is needed before the monthly employment and sales data can be obtained.

Estimates and comparisons of tourism over time for a broader region require not only the use of secondary data, but of regional analysis methods to develop indices of change. In an earlier analysis Brown (1980) used shift-share analysis of lodging receipts to estimate changes in the share of Northeastern tourism that each state in the Northeast received from 1972 to 1977. He then used location quotients to examine the relative dependence of both Northeastern states and counties on tourism in 1977 and changes from 1972. This study presents an update of the Brown (1980) study and compares data from 1977 to 1987.

METHODS

The comparative analysis of tourism uses lodging receipts as the index of tourism. The rationale for this is first that of all the Standard Industrial Codes (SIC) of economic sectors pertaining to tourism, only the lodging sector has an insignificant amount of trade from local residents. Second, most tourism studies find lodging receipts to be a significant portion of total trip expenditures, and it is unusual to find localities where tourism originating from day-use visits is an important economic force.

The degree to which states gained or lost in their "share" of tourism is analyzed by the use of shift-share analysis. This traditional method has been described in detail by Dunn (1960) and Ashby (1964). It was applied to tourism in the Northeast by Brown (1980) and also by Cole (1980). Brown (1982) also used shift-share analysis to examine changes in tourism among major regions of the U.S.

Various measures using location quotients are used to examine the relative dependence of county and state economies on tourism. Described in detail by Izard (1976), location quotients (LQs) can be developed for employment, sales, income, or other economic measures. LQs compare the proportion of a smaller area's economy (i.e., states and counties, in this study) devoted to a particular sector (i.e., lodging) with the analogous portion for a larger geographic area (i.e., the Northeast) of which the smaller area is a part. Thus, if a given county in the Northeast had a lodging sales LQ of 1.0 with respect to the Northeast, the proportion of the county's retail sales derived from lodging would be the same as for the Northeast as a whole. An analogous LQ of 2.0 would signify that the proportion of the county's receipts derived from lodging was twice that of the Northeast. Brown (1981) found that heavily tourist-oriented counties in New York had 1977 LQs that exceeded 11.0.

The database used for this study is the Census of Selected Services, a publication of the Bureau of the Census, U.S. Department of Commerce. Data from this quinquennial publication for 1972, 1977, and 1987 (the most recent year available) were used. Major problems occurred with the 1982 Census of Selected Services in the categorizing of individual firms into standard industrial codes (SIC). As a result, 1982 data are not comparable to other years and were not used.

Lodging is classified under SIC codes as a service, but nevertheless is a part of the broader retail economy. To operationally define the "broader retail economy" of which lodging is a component, we selected the total of retail trade plus the service industries as reported by Bureau of the Census. The Bureau of the Census definition of services changed somewhat from 1977 to 1987, although this change did not effect the lodging industry. For comparability in showing broader economic changes from 1977 to 1987, we retained the 1977 definition of services. We then converted 1977 data to 1987 constant dollars. One major factor occurred in the Northeast between 1977 and 1987 that had a profound effect on some businesses classified as lodging establishments: 'the advent of casino gambling in Atlantic City (Atlantic County), New Jersey. As classified, lodging receipts in New Jersey increased four-fold from $1.0 billion in 1977 to $4.0 billion in 1987 (1987 constant dollars). While much of this real spending increase is attributable to tourism, most of the receipts are not lodging receipts per se, and are not comparable with lodging data elsewhere in the Northeast. As a result, an approximation was made to eliminate the portion of receipts attributable to casino gambling. This was done by assigning the 68 lodging establishments in Atlantic County with more than 25 rooms total lodging receipts of the average hotel/motel in the rest of New Jersey. Doing so reduced the estimate of 1987 lodging receipts for the state from $4.0 billion to $1.15 billion.

All dollar values expressed in the Results section are in constant 1987 dollars to facilitate comparison of real growth. All data are derived from the Census of Selected Services or Census of Retail Trade.

RESULTS

Receipts in the retail trade and services sector of the economy grew 22.1% over the decade from 1977 to 1987, from $428.6 billion in 1977 to $523.5 billion in 1987. During the same period, lodging receipts increased by over twice that rate (48.5%), from $7.1 billion to $10.5 billion (Table 1). Lodging receipts grew in absolute terms in every state in the Northeast (Table 1, column 3).

Figure 1 shows categories of net percentage change in lodging receipts adjusted for inflation, at the county level, comparing 1987 and 1977 data. Some of the counties with the largest net percentage growth in lodging receipts were urban and suburban counties. These include counties containing the cities of Boston and Springfield, NU; Stamford and Bridgeport, CT; Rochester and Nassau County (western Long Island), NY; and some Philadelphia-area counties. A number of rural counties also posted gains of at least 50% in lodging receipts between 1977 and 1987. Many of these counties, though rural in character, are within a short drive of major metropolitan areas. Notable exceptions occur in northern and central Vermont, in northeastern and central Pennsylvania, and in southern West Virginia.

Many other counties in the Northeast experienced gains in lodging receipts that fell within the second category in Figure 1 of 11% to 49%. Such counties were found in each state and were generally well spread throughout the region.

Counties for which data are available that declined notably in lodging receipts between 1977 and 1987 were generally those that either are not well developed with tourism attractions, and/or are at a locational disadvantage with respect to distance from population centers. Examples of such declines include much of noncoastal Maine, parts of the Adirondacks and far northern New York, and the Southern Tier of New York and the Northern Tier of Pennsylvania.

Shift-Share Analysis

Traditional shift-share analysis breaks the total economic change over a given period into three components: regional growth, industrial mix, and state shares. These are shown in columns 2-4 of Table 2; the sum of these columns equals the total change (column 1). The first component, regional growth, indicates the amount of growth that would have occurred had lodging grown at only the rate of the retail service economy in the Northeast. A comparison of columns 1 and 2 shows that West Virginia was the only state for which lodging grew less rapidly (only slightly so) than the retail-service economy in the Northeast. The second component of total change, the industrial mix (Table 2, column 3), reflects the performance of the lodging sector in comparison to the retail-service economy. It is calculated by multiplying the 1977 lodging receipts for each state by the difference between the percentage growth in the lodging sector in the Northeast (48.5%) and the percentage growth in lodging receipts in the Northeast (22. 1%). Because lodging growth outperformed the overall retail-service sectors in the Northeast by 26.4%, the industrial mix for each state is positive and equal to 26.4% of its 1977 lodging receipts.

The third component, the state shares, measures the degree to which each state increased or decreased its share of regional lodging receipts. It is calculated by multiplying each state's 1977 lodging receipts by the difference in percentage change of the state's increase and the region's increase in lodging receipts from 1977 to 1987. From Table 2, column 4, we see that some major changes occurred in the state shares of lodging receipts over this period. Massachusetts increased its share by nearly $350 million, while Pennsylvania's share decreased by a similar amount, $334 million. Other states with sizable increases (over $50 million) in their share include Connecticut, Maryland, New Jersey, and the District of Columbia. States with comparable decreases in their share of lodging receipts include New York and West Virginia; Maine fell just short of a $50 million loss in its share.

The net relative change, column 5 of Table 2, is the amount of change over and above the regional growth (Column 1 minus Column 2). (It is also the sum of changes related to the industrial mix and state shares, columns 2 and 3). As pointed out above, West Virginia is the only state with less lodging growth than in the overall retail-service economy, and therefore a negative net relative change.

Columns 6 through 8 provide some of the parameters at the top of Table 2 in percentage format. Column 6 shows that lodging receipts in Massachusetts and Connecticut roughly doubled from 1977 to 1987, and that all states increased their lodging receipts by at least 20%. Column 7 percentages the total industrial shift among the states. Of all the growth in lodging receipts over and above the retail-service economy growth rate of 22.1%, 34.1% occurred in New York, and over half occurred in the two economically large states of New York and Pennsylvania. Finally, Column 8 percentages the positive and negative shifts in the state shares. Half of the positive shifts in the state shares occurred in Massachusetts, while Pennsylvania and New York combined for over 75% of the losses in state shares.

Location Quotient Analysis

A comparison of 1987 and 1977 location quotients (LQs) for lodging receipts for the Northeastern states is shown in Table 3. In 1987, the retail-service economy of Vermont was over three times as dependent on lodging as the Northeast as a whole. West Virginia and Maine had LQs of 2.55 and 2.00, respectively. Connecticut, Rhode Island, Maryland, and New Jersey were relatively less dependent on tourism, with LQs of approximately 0.8.

The 1987/1977 lodging sales LQ provides an index of the change in the relative dependence of the economy on tourism over this ten-year period. It should be pointed out that for large entities such as states, we would not expect retail or service LQs to deviate substantially over a ten-year period except for cases of emerging industries or unusual situations. West Virginia had the highest 1987/1977 lodging LQ (1.20).

Approximately 25 counties in the northeast had lodging sales LQs of greater than 5.0. For the most part, these include the most popular tourism destination areas in the Northeast. Among them are areas of coastal Maine that include Acadia National Park; parts of the White Mountains of New Hampshire; parts of the Green Mountains and some of the renowned ski areas of northern Vermont; Cape Cod, Nantucket, and Martha's Vineyard; the Adirondacks, some parts of the Catskills, and the Thousand Islands regions of New York; the Maryland Eastern Shore, including Ocean City and the Assateague Island National Seashore; the Pocono Mountains of Pennsylvania; and portions of the Blue Ridge Mountains in West Virginia.

Approximately 45 additional counties fell within the second category of having LQs of between 2.00 and 5.00. Some of these counties represent excellent tourist destination areas that are located where the economy is more diversified than counties in the first category. Examples include all of southern and central Vermont; Niagara Falls, Chautauqua Lake, and the Lake Champlain Valley in New York; the Berkshires in Massachusetts; the Amish country in Pennsylvania; Newport and coastal Rhode Island; the Delaware shore; and Atlantic City, New Jersey.

Counties with low to average LQs fall into two general categories. The first is large urban areas. These areas have very diversified economies, and although they may receive very large numbers of tourists (e.g., New York City, Boston, Philadelphia), their retail and service economies as a whole are not highly dependent on tourism. This is also true of many suburban counties that are proximate to large urban centers. The second category would include counties that are heavily agricultural or forested, often located great distances from urban centers or in areas that are not connected by interstate highways, and where major tourism attractions have not been developed. Particular examples include several counties in western New York and southern West Virginia.

SUMMARY

The combination of shift-share analysis and location quotients (LQs) provide an excellent means of assessing the importance of tourism in the various states and counties in the Northeast, and whether the dependence of these areas on tourism is increasing or decreasing. These methods are most useful for making preliminary assessments and comparisons. More in-depth analyses would be necessary to develop an understanding of the factors that are related to increased or decreased tourism dependence.

It should be pointed out that having a high lodging LQ, which implies a strong dependence of an area on tourism, is of itself not necessarily a positive statistic. A high lodging LQ also implies that some other areas of the economy have low LQs and are thus underdeveloped. LQs are valuable in demonstrating the relative dependence of an area on tourism, and in combination with actual data on receipts from lodging and other important tourism sectors (e.g., eating and drinking places, miscellaneous amusement and recreation firms, sporting goods firms) can provide information on whether tourism is growing or declining.

Shift-share analysis can be applied to any level of geographic entity, but is probably most useful at the state or large regional level. With several hundred counties in the

Northeast, each would have only a tiny share of the region's tourism receipts; hence a shift-share analysis would be relatively meaningless. An examination of net percentage change over time (i.e., Figure 1) would be more meaningful. At the state level, where there are a limited number of units, it is much more reasonable to think of shares and whether each state has kept its "share" of Northeast tourism dollars, or whether that share has increased or decreased over time.

These methods of regional analysis are useful to practitioners as well as to researchers. Because the methods are rather intuitive, they can be used successfully with planners and local tourism advisory committees to help them evaluate the stance of their county or area with respect to tourism.

10

Classification of Recreation and Tourism Communities

INTRODUCTION

Policy makers, planners, and the public commonly characterize communities in broad categories when initiating investment, planning, and regulatory decisions. Often categorization schemes (e.g., rural vs. urban) are based on planners' or policy makers' subjective perceptions of communities (Kinds of Communities Working Group 1986). In some states, policy formulators have dichotomized communities as"growing or decaying," "agricultural or industrial," and "old or new" as a consequence of the community's traditional economic base.

Because the traditional economic base is declining, many rural communities have embraced tourism and recreation development as strategies to improve their economic well-being (Liu and Var 1987; Allen et al. 1988). These changes in rural development strategies and economic base of communities suggest that previous categorization schemes may not be viable. New classifications, therefore, should be explored that differentiate rural communities based on tourism and recreation-related attributes, and attributes related to economic growth. Such attributes (variables) may be useful in describing and comparing communities and for determining rural policy initiatives.

Classification schemes (typologies) should be empirically derived if they are to be useful for analyzing and comparing communities, distributing resources (e.g., state and federal revenues), and establishing public policy (e.g., location of a state park). Empirically derived classifications (typologies) provide a means by which we can better predict performance and behavior in the "real world" (Bealer 1987). Some rural community typologies have been developed from socioeconomic data obtained from secondary sources, such as census and state generated data (Humphrey et al. 1987; KOC 1986). Many, however, continue to be based on subjective judgements. Few classification schemes of rural communities have focused on physical attractiveness, growth, or degree of tourism development, except as variables related to resident attitudes or reactions to tourism expansion (Ahmed 1986; Liu and Var 1987; Pizam 1980; Allen et. al. 1988).

Once classification schemes have been constructed, their usefulness in describing "real world" aspects of rural areas should be tested. Too often classifications are developed that are not linked to public policy. Such classifications do not help the practitioner comprehend and work with the socio-political aspects of communities (Feldman 1987). The test of usefulness of the classification scheme then is the linkage between the scheme and "real world" events.

The purpose of this study was to develop an empirical classification (typology) of rural communities based on attributes related to tourism, growth, and recreation amenities, and to determine if the developed typology can distinguish between communities on a variable of socio-political concern, (i.e., property taxes). Two questions guided the research:

1. Can a typology of communities be constructed from secondary data source attributes related to recreation, tourism development, and growth?
2. Does the constructed typology distinguish between community tax burdens (i.e., index of median property tax related to an index of median income)?

The changing economic base of rural areas requires a rethinking of our classification of rural communities. Our communities have become too complex to use a single type descriptor for analytical purposes. One tool, cluster analysis, lets us simultaneously analyze several variables to generate a more useful, mutually exclusive community label or "typology. Such classifications may then help organize our thinking about communities by systematizing and reducing data into discrete categories. The development of meaningful public policy to wisely address community needs requires the use of such techniques.

CLUSTER ANALYSIS APPROACH

Our approach in developing a constructed typology (classification scheme) involved using only secondary data sources. Data for this study were obtained from the Center for Rural Studies at the University of Vermont, data collected by the authors in previous studies, secondary source data from the Agency of Development and Community Affairs, and from other Vermont state agencies. The attributes selected consisted of factors that would differentiate among communities in terms of growth, tourism development, and recreation amenities, while satisfying criteria for inclusion in a clustering solution. Humphrey et al. (1987:52) suggest that variables used as input to clustering solutions should

- be limited in number,
- be relatively uncorrelated with each other (i.e., unique),
- have comparable means and standard deviations.

Ten attributes were selected to differentiate among communities. The selection of attributes was based on (1) the attribute's relation to community growth, recreation attractiveness, and development of tourism; (2) uniqueness; and (3) availability of secondary data source materials for all 246 Vermont communities.

Ten independent variables describing Vermont community conditions in 1985 and 1986 were assessed:

1. Population change between 1980 and 1986.
2. Total value of all property per capita.
3. Total value of all property per acre.
4. Value of all commercial property.
5. Value of all agricultural property.

6. Value of all properties used as second homes.
7. Population density.
8. Water acreage (lake or major river).
9. Degree to which residents find work within the hometown.
10. Commercial lodging capacity.

These attributes were chosen as surrogates for (1) local growth communities, (2) area "class" (two attributes), (3) commercial services, (4) open space land use, (5) area desirability, (6) area congestion, (7) water recreation potential, (8) overall business activity, and (9) traveler attraction potential. In the aggregate they reflect the city and town attributes that are in the forefront of policy formulation facing Vermont today.

Because city and town data are highly skewed on many of the attributes considered in this study, the data had to be standardized to meet the criteria of comparable means and standard deviations. For example towns differed considerably on the value of their commercial property, thus a process had to be found to transform data to lessen the natural variation and highly skewed differences that exist. Likewise, towns vary on one attribute more than another (e.g., residential population density vs. percentage of population working outside the town), thus population density would be more highly weighted in cluster analysis. Using a process outlined by the Kinds of Communities (KOC) Working Group (1986) for examining clusters of Massachusetts cities and towns, the attributes for towns in this study were converted to rank orders and the ranks were subjected to cluster analysis. This transformation simultaneously solves the problems of "outlier" data and natural variability while allowing for simplicity of understanding (KOC 1986). Attributes were ranked so that the highest value had a rank of "1"; towns or cities having a higher median rank on an attribute, therefore, have more of that attribute.

Community attributes were then submitted to cluster analysis. Cluster analysis is a descriptive data reduction procedure that combines what appear to be relatively unrelated cases (e.g., towns and cities) into homogeneous subsets or categories (i.e., towns and/or cities having commonality). Used in a wide variety of disciplines, cluster analysis is essentially a mapping procedure(KOC 1986).The output from the mapping allows one to identify and label the cluster, and understand how cases group together. Various types of cluster analytic procedures are available, but generally they can be divided between hierarchical and nonhierarchical techniques. A nonhierarchical procedure was selected for this study because of the relatively large number of cases. The nonhierarchical technique uses multivariate profiles to sort the cases into k-clusters based on "seed" points (Goldsmith 1987). The initial seed points are automatically defined by the cluster program, and each case is assigned to an initial seed. A centroid for the clusters is computed and used as a seed point for the next iteration on which the cases are sorted (Goldsmith 1987). Programs such as SAS's FASTCLUS program allow the user to specify the number of clusters they wish to explore. While the selection of the number of clusters in many cases is arbitrary in nature, the researcher can compare different numbers of clusters from successive cluster runs to determine which number of clusters most clearly and simply describes the similarities between towns. Similarity in nonhierarchical cluster analysis is defined as the similarity of a town or city to the cluster center; the average Euclidean distance within a cluster, then, is an indication of how well the cluster accounts for the towns arrayed in the cluster (KOC 1986). The smaller the average distance, the tighter the cluster and the more alike are the towns within that cluster, and the easier it becomes to interpret the cluster solution.

Clusters that emerge from the cluster analytic procedure can be thought of as constructed types possessing some common characteristics. This commonality (or homogeneity) can then be used for comparison or for distinguishing between types on other variables in the "real" world. For example if community types are similar with respect to growth attributes they may be equally homogeneous in characteristics such as tax revenue per capita. Two dependent variables subsequently were analyzed within the seven cluster frame: (1) tax burden (i.e., relationship between income earned and property taxes paid), and (2) amount of local property owned by community residents. Clearly, cluster analysis worked well, as a research tool, in objectively classifying communities. It worked equally as well in applying such a classification scheme to differentiate the impact of development.

DATA MANAGEMENT APPROACH

We are living in a state of rapid change. Communities may shift from one type to another type as development occurs. Therefore, a model, easier and faster to use than the cluster analysis model, is needed to monitor change at a relatively low cost. The cluster analysis model described above is an effective tool to monitor change, but to reevaluate ten variables on an annual basis is extremely time consuming and expensive.

It was apparent from our cluster analysis model that property values (disaggregated) was the most important variable explaining community classification. The second most important variable was population density. Armed with this knowledge, we set forth to develop a simple system that could be used to classify communities over time. Our goal was to develop a system that could be handled with a desktop personal computer, thereby opening use of this analytical tool to a much larger group.

After investigating many spreadsheet programs, we decided to use Computer Associates' SuperCalc. We found the data management program (within the SuperCalc spreadsheet) to be very effective and relatively easy to use. Nearly all of our basic data were already in a spreadsheet format and could be used directly or imported into SuperCalc.

SuperCalc's data management function was used to perform a boolean search of the full data set, to extract a list of communities that met a given set of criteria values. The criteria were different for each community type, so that a community would fall into one class only (mutually exclusive classification).

However, it became apparent that more accurate type names should be used. All communities that were primarily residential should carry the name residential—thus the old name "commercial high density" was re-named "residential commercial center." The old "rural bedroom community" was re-named "residential rural." The old "waterfront bedroom" community became "residential limited commercial."

It was decided that all communities that were primarily recreational should carry that name in its title. Thus, "major resort" communities were re-named "recreational commercial centers." The old "recreational" communities were re-named "recreational non-commercial." Lastly, "rural woodland" communities were renamed "lowest population density" communities (several that fell into this class had very little forested acreage).

Residential property tax burden was calculated for 1989 using the clusters identified through the boolean search procedure. The principal advantage that the boolean technique has over cluster analysis is the ability to analyze community change over a period of years. Property values in Vermont towns in 1970 were compared with property values in 1989, for each community type.

This analysis shows that residential property values in recreational commercial centers increased from 12 percent of the state residential total value in 1970 to 23 percent of the state total in 1989. The reverse situation was found in residential commercial centers where the portion of the total state residential value dropped from 43 percent to 33 percent in this 19-year period. This was an important finding, as it clearly showed movement of permanent residences from the higher density cities to the lower density rural recreation centers.

A similar gain and loss situation was found in analyzing changes in commercial property values. While the urban centers had 58 percent of the state total commercial value in 1970, they had only 51 percent in 1989. In 1970, the rural recreation centers had 20 percent of the state total commercial value. In 1989, this increased to 39 percent.

The impact of such shifts on local government is clear—there was a loss of tax base in urban residential areas and gain in tax base in rural commercial recreation areas. Another favorable impact on the rural commercial recreation communities was the increased diversity in the tax base, important in times of economic uncertainty. The non-commercial rural recreation centers failed to share in the good fortune of the commercial recreation centers. There was very little growth in these communities between 1970 and 1989. Their share of second homes values dropped from 35 to 21 percent of the state total.

IMPLICATIONS

The two approaches tested in this research resulted in the creation of a scientifically useful method of classifying communities for further analysis. The two types of recreation/ tourism communities that the models identified are very different and call for very different policies to guide growth and development.

This research does not provide the answers to complex questions relating to growth and development, but it does provide a reasonable frame for balanced dialogue on such issues. Such dialogue is necessary if we are to develop sound long-range policies governing community growth in Vermont and the nation.

11

Tourism Development Simulation Model

INTRODUCTION

Tourism industry development has its greatest impacts at the community level. These impacts reach far beyond jobs, wages, and revenues. Social and environmental consequences such as crime, congestion, and water pollution also can have serious impacts on the quality of life of residents as well as on the quality of vacations for tourists. Community leaders and planners have indicated a need for information about these impacts.

Since 1980, researchers at a number of universities in the Northeast and elsewhere have worked toward developing a framework and a database with which any locality could make "ball-park" estimates of the impacts of typical types of tourism development. A major research finding has been that it is not easy to define typical communities, typical developments, or average impacts.

Another finding has been that the complex interactions between residents, tourists, industry, and government make it difficult to justify a simple framework for analysis. On the other hand it is difficult to present the correct framework (assuming one exists) in a simple manner. In order to test our preliminary research hypotheses, a tourism-planning computer game has been developed which pits the player against the development pressures of a hypothetical small New England community.

In addition to meeting our objective of illustrating our long-term research goals in a palatable format the game has been used successfully in the classroom and, in fact, has taken on a project status of its own.

Project Background: A Game?

The Tourism Development Simulation Model (TDSM) is a computer program developed in conjunction with a series of projects on the impacts of tourism development. The emphasis in the earliest project was on the development of a methodology that could be used by individual municipalities and state agencies to estimate and project impacts caused by alternative tourism product mixes at the local level. A follow-up project focused on the fiscal impact portion of the model.

In the early stages of design and development of this model, it became readily apparent that the scope of the work was very broad-too broad to produce the quick and comprehensive results users wanted. It was, in fact, difficult to describe the goals of the project or its potential value to targeted users. It was decided, therefore, that a simplified version of the model could provide the basis of a computer game, and that this game concerning tourism development in a hypothetical community could provide an alternative means of describing the usefulness of the major project objectives.

The production and distribution of the game has been so successful that it has taken on a project status of its own. Priced at cost, it was initially distributed as an amusing "think piece" for researchers and planners, and as an palatable introduction to related research projects.

The game is loosely based on the impact assessment framework developed in a study of the impacts of tourism on thirteen coastal communities in the Northeast (Tyrrell et al. 1985). A typical small New England community was characterized using some empirical results and some "best guess" approximations to relationships between major variables. The relationships were then refined to reflect the "reality" exhibited in recent community case studies (NE-137 Block 1985).

In addition to providing the intended introduction to long-term project goals, the processes of designing and constructing the game and using it as a community behavior simulator have taught us much about the implications of "reality" and "reasonableness" on mathematical representations of community behavior. These lessons have had a considerable impact on our primary goal of developing a tourism development simulation model.

Designed to illustrate the principles of community budgeting and planning in the context of tourism industry development, the game has been used as an educational tool for students of tourism planning at the graduate and undergraduate level, and non-degree participants in leadership development programs in both the U.S. and Canada. For all audience types, the educational vehicle provided by the computer game is accepted enthusiastically. As with others (Loukissas 1983), we have found this approach to have definite advantages over traditional seminar presentations.

This paper describes the details of the game's design and describes the importance of the "reasonableness" criterion used in the development of the underlying model. It also attempts to persuade the reader that a computer game, based on a "best-guess" model, can provide a useful research and educational tool.

The Tourism Industry Focus

The tourism industry has many dimensions of concern to community researchers. It is recognized to include a wide range of business types whose activities impact a broad cross-section of the host community (Murphy 1985). Tourists are of many types as are the residents of the affected community. In conducting community-based tourism research it is therefore important to identify and measure impact generators and recipients by their types so that policies can address specific problems and needs. In the model underlying this game, however, all tourist-related businesses are represented by an industry average, and all non-tourist-related businesses are represented by another average. In a similar way, residents are grouped and tourists are grouped. In contrast to the research approach, the emphasis here is on the general dynamics of the tourism industry as it relates to other societal components in a typical community setting. A flow chart of the major components is provided in Figure 1.

The community is viewed as a circle whose outer ring is the natural resource base. Within that is the social system which provides the context for all community activities. Finally, in the center are the four major components of the model: the tourism industry, "other" industry, local government, and the residents. Outside the community are four factors that influence and are influenced by community activities: exports, non-resident capital, non-resident laborers, and tourists. The arrows that connect the components and outside factors illustrate the major linkages assumed by the model that underlies the game.

Specific adjustments in behavior of tourism businesses, "other" businesses, residents, and tourists are determined by equations relating causal factors to specific actions. This follows the basic econometric approach of modeling market systems (Pindyck and Rubinfeld 1976). By sacrificing the behavioral differences of different types of producers and consumers, the simulation-game goes beyond equations that are typically estimated in research projects and speculates about a very complex set of important interactions within the community. Of particular interest were the social and environmental impacts of development that can change the "quality of life" for residents, the "bottom line' for businesses, and the "quality of the vacation" for tourists. Such impacts are well documented in the literature (Mathieson and Wall 1982). Finally, the game recognizes the political nature of the decision-making process, the budget-balancing skills required by individual community officers, and the unpredictable disturbances to the planning process caused by unforeseen events.

A Community Setting

In order to simulate tourism development in the most realistic way possible, the model centers on the decisions made by an administrative officer of a typical small town in New

England in the late 1970's. At the beginning of a game there are 20,000 residents in 10,000 households, and the population is growing at 1% per year. Half the population is considered to be in the labor force. 7500 of these are employed by the tourism industry, 2250 are employed in the "other" industry of the local economy, and the unemployment rate is initially 2.5%. Wage rates are $ 10,000 per year in the tourism industry and $20,000 per year in the other industry. Although average firms in both tourism and "other" industries begin the simulation breaking even, profits earned in the subsequent years are distributed to the residents of the community as additional income. Consequently disposable household income averages $11,255 per year in year 1.

The natural resource base of the community is assumed to be a major recreation area, thus the draw for tourists and a major factor in the quality of life in the community. This resource might be a park or beach that is valued by the community and attractive enough to draw tourists to town, but fragile in the sense that increased use, in the absence of preventative investment, will result in a reduction in its aesthetic qualities. A number of works report on such impacts on recreational resources (Young 1973).

In the initial year of the simulation 200,000 tourists visit the community, staying an average of 7 days each, and visiting the natural resource recreation site on every day of their stay. Residents each make 10 visits per year to the recreation site. Residents and tourists pay the same price per visit to the recreational site, which is managed by the industry, however the tourists pay a visitor's fee to the town.

The town administrator has the authority to invest these and other town revenues in the protection/enhancement of the natural resource base.

Year-to-year variation in weather is one example of the unpredictable nature of the community environment. The model assumes that changes in the average seasonal temperature from its norm of 75 degrees F will influence use of the recreational resource by residents as well as tourists. Each year of the simulation, average seasonal temperature is assigned a random value from 70 to 80 degrees. When temperatures drop below 75 degrees, visits to the site decrease, and when temperatures exceed 75, they increase.

As residential and tourist populations increase they are assumed to impact the social and environmental characteristics of the community as well as its economy. These are manifested in crime and congestion rates and water quality measures known to the community, reported as social and environmental indexes and as headlines in the local press. Thus, the quality of life in the community is assumed to be reflected in indexes for three basic community qualities: economic, social, and environmental. The environmental index is assumed to reflect the quality of the recreational resource (Wennergren and Fullerton 1972). The geometric mean of the three indexes, weighted by the population of the community, is used as an overall measure of community well-being. Such quality of life indexes have been pursued for a number of years, with varying degrees of success. (Booz, Allen, Inc. 1973). This well-being measure might also be thought of an indicator of the economist's social welfare function (Henderson and Quandt 1958).

In addition to the raw indexes, the game player is presented news headlines that correspond to the severity of the index above or below their initial, equilibrium position. For example, when the social index drops 30% below its initial value the player is informed "Crime and Congestion at Record Levels. Police Frustrated." And when the environmental index rises 30% above its initial value the player is informed "National Task Force Adopts Local Environmental Plan as Model."

The Game Player

The game player assumes the role of an unusually potent town administrator who must guide development using tourism promotion and three other types of expenditure programs: "other" industrial development programs, social programs, and environmental projects. These expenditure categories are assumed to include all major expenditure items in a town's budget except for administration, which is ignored by the model. In order to balance the town's budget the player must adjust tax rates for residential and business property and decide upon daily tourist fees. The player's objective is to achieve balanced economic, social, and environmental development as measured by their respective indexes. At the end of each year of office the player is presented with quantitative and qualitative assessments of performance, and given the opportunity to change any of the seven fiscal controls. The game ends after 10 years of service or when the player quits or is fired, which ever comes first.

THE TOURISM DEVELOPMENT MODEL

Model Structure

Some 40 equations containing more than fifty parameters characterize the components of community activity and development in the small hypothetical town. Most of these (19 equations) characterize the tourism industry and "other" industry behavior. These include basic supply and demand relationships for the tourism product and the "other" product produced in the town, as well as derived demands for labor and supplies and business relocation. The multi-market model framework is common to macro modeling efforts (Pindyck and Rubinfeld 1976).

Supply and demand equations are logarithmic and contain a lagged dependent variable. This formulation characterizes behavior as "partially" adjusting toward some distant equilibrium value. The amount of the adjustment declines each year following the initial change in the independent variable. The rate of adjustment is determined by the size of the lag coefficient. Such models are frequent in econometric research studies since their coefficients are directly interpretable, and the implied dynamics is intuitively appealing.

The logarithmic specification implies that the coefficient of each explanatory variable is a short-run elasticity (the percentage change in the dependent variable in the first year resulting from a 1% change in the independent variable). Long-run elasticities (the ultimate percentage change in the dependent variable after a 1% change in the independent variable) are computed as the ratio of the short-run elasticity to (1 - lag coefficient). The complete set of behavioral equations and their coefficients are listed in Appendix A.

Random Events

As described above, weather is an important cause of random variations in visits to the recreation site and has important implications for the tourism industry. Part of the change in export sales by the "other" industry in the community is also generated as a random event. The model assumes the percentage deviation of current from previous export sales is randomly selected in the range from -5% to +5%.

Early in the administration of the town it is unlikely that any unforeseen event will alter the outcome of control decisions. By the fifth year of the administration, however, there is a 60% probability that some such unforeseen event has occurred. These events are announced as "Important News Flash(es)."

Five types of random events are built into the model:

F: FIRE DESTROYS ___ % OF THE INDUSTRIAL DISTRICT,

G: GAS SHORTAGE THREATENS TO REDUCE TOURIST VISITS BY ___%, 0: OIL TANKER SPILLS - REDUCES WATER QUALITY INDEX BY ___%,

U: UNEXPECTED MEDIA ATTENTION PROMISES TO INCREASE TOURIST VISITS BY ___% and

B: BAD DEBTS LEFT BY PREVIOUS PLANNER UNCOVERED AMOUNTING TO $_______

The percentages and the dollar amount indicated by the News Flashes are also determined randomly. The percentages range from 25 to 100%, and the dollar amount of the deficit can range from 0 to $250,000.

The choice of the five events was meant to correspond to five of the major uncertainties facing tourism community administrators: unexpected catastrophes in tourism and the "other" industry, a direct threat to tourism attractiveness because of pollution, unforeseen (and unplanned) rapid growth in tourism, and a personal threat to the job security of the administrator.

The player is given the opportunity to respond to these events before the impact is levied on the social, environmental, and economic indexes. The successful planner will take corrective actions given this opportunity. The probability of a subsequent event is low for the immediate future after an event, but increases as the years pass. This may be an unrealistic representation of the planner who spends considerable time responding to crises. The game events may be repeated or not and the severity of the events, as measured by the percentage or dollar amount, will vary from occurrence to occurrence and game to game. It is very unlikely that any two games will be similar.

COMMUNITY IMPACTS

Population Change

The 20,000 or so residents of the game community work either in the tourism industry or the "other" industry. There is a natural growth in the population of 1% per year as well as migration into and out of the community depending on the difference between the percentage of unemployed workers and an assumed "frictional" employment level of 3%. If the unemployment rate is above the frictional level there will be population migration out of the community; if the unemployment rate is less than 3% there will be some migration of population into the community.

Income Generation and Wealth

Residential income is the sum of wages paid to workers and profits earned by owners in the tourism and "other" industries. It is assumed that the major portion of current income is expended on necessities purchased from the "other" industry and luxuries including recreation- days purchased from the natural resource managers, the tourism industry. The wealth of residents is characterized by the value of residential property (broadly defined). Residential property values are influenced by the number of residents; with more residents, demand for property rises and property values increase. Property taxes are the only taxes paid by residents, and they are controlled by the rate set by the game player.

Town Finances

The town derives revenues from five sources: daily tourist fees, residential property taxes, tourism industry property taxes, "other" industry property taxes, and interest income on any accumulated budget surplus from previous years (at a 10% annual rate). The town allocates its budget to five categories of expenditures: tourism promotion, "other" economic programs, social programs, environmental programs, and an automatic interest expense deducted for any accumulated deficit from previous years (also at a 10% annual rate).

The Quality of Life

Economic, Social and Environmental Impacts

In addition to the income generated for residents by the tourism and "other" industries in the communities, there are a host of other economic, social, and environmental characteristics that constitute the quality of community life. All these characteristics are assumed be represented by a set of four indexes. The economic index rises with the average wage rate and falls with unemployment. The social and environmental indexes rise with expenditures on social and environmental programs and fall with increases in the numbers of tourist-days and residential recreational visits.

A social-environmental index, which is also used as a measure of tourism attractiveness in the demand equation for tourist visits, is provided by the geometric mean of the social and environmental indexes. A quality of community life is provided by the geometric mean of the social-environmental index and the economic index. This index is assumed to be the objective function for the community and determines the annual game score.

GAME PLAY AND USE OF CONTROLS

Active Play

The first active screen of the game requests that the player provides three initials for identification. These are later used to record the player's final score for comparison with other scores. The player is asked at once whether the seven economic controls should be changed from their initial settings. Figure 2 shows the actual screen presented by the game.

As soon as the player is "READY FOR THE NEXT YEAR TO BEGIN," a community overview screen is shown such as the one in Figure 3. This screen provides current and past values for tourism industry revenue, "other" industry revenue, real disposable household income, the unemployment rate, and the accumulated town surplus or deficit. This screen also presents up to five news headlines determined by the indexes described above and the player's current and cumulative score.

The following sequence of screens afford the player the opportunity to view five detailed informational screens including:

"LOCAL GOVERNMENT FINANCIAL STATEMENTS," "SOCIAL ENVIRONMENTAL STATISTICS," "TOURISM BUSINESS STATISTICS," and "OTHER INDUSTRY STATISTICS."

When the player is finally satisfied that enough information has been viewed and that the appropriate adjustments to the seven controls have been made, the next year begins, and the model calculates changes to the community and its industries. Overview results for the next year are presented summarizing these calculations.

When a player chooses to change one or more of the economic controls, a screen is presented that indicates the current level of each of the controls and how controls can be changed (Figure 4.) When all controls have been changed to the desired values, the player begins the next year of the administration.

Player Performance

The first informational screen of each year provides the annual score for the player based on the overall well- being index. However, the player (administrator) also must attempt to balance the budget in order to keep from being fired. If the deficit (or surplus) exceeds more than a few percent of the total budget the planner is defamed in the press. If the deficit (or surplus) is greater than about 10% the player will be fired despite the overall well- being of the community. Thus, the relative size of the town's budget deficit or surplus

THE GAME: You have been hired as the town planner for a community with an important tourism industry, it generates 55% of local income. The town budget is currently $11.9 million. Town revenues last year were generated from a $1 daily tourist tax ($1.4 Million last year), and property taxes from residents ($8 M), tourism businesses ($2 M),and other businesses ($0.5 M). The last administration allocated $5.5 M to social programs, $1.5 M to tourism promotion, $4.5 M to environmental programs, and $0.4 M to other economic development programs. Your task is to adjust tax rates and expenditures to achieve:

YOUR GOAL: GET THE HIGHEST POSSIBLE SCORE IN 10 YEARS

By maximizing social welfare in the town and keeping yourjob as long as possible. Social welfare is defined as a product of three indexes: economic, social and environmental. Each is affected by the residents and tourists.

Strike a key when ready...

PLEASE ENTER 3 INITIALS TO IDENTIFY YOURSELF ? TJT

THANK YOU, TJT

ECONOMIC CONTROLS LEFT IN PLACE BY THE PREVIOUS ADMINISTRATION:

C(1) = $ 1.00 = FEE CHARGED EACH TOURIST

C(2) = $ 20.00 = EFFECTIVE RESIDENTIAL PROPERTY TAX RATE (PER $1000)

C(3) = $20.00 = EFFECTIVE COMM./IND. PROPERTY TAX RATE (FOR $1000)

C(4) = $1,500,000.00 = BUDGET FOR TOURIST PROMOTION

C(5) = $400,000.00 = BUDGET FOR OTHER ECONOMIC PROGRAMS

C(6) = $5,500,000.00 = BUDGET FOR SOCIAL PROGRAMS

C(7) = $4,500,000.00 = BUDGET FOR ENVIRONMENTAL PROGRAMS

DO YOU WANT TO LEAVE CONTROLS UNCHANGED (Y OR N) ? Y

YEAR OF OFFICE = 1

TOURISM IND.REVNU. $82,181,280 This yr.; $79,999,880 Last yr.; 2.73 percent change

OTHER IND.REVENUE $65,444,108 This yr.; $66,115,800 Last yr.; -1.02 percent change

REAL DISP HHD INC. $11,419 This yr.; $11,255 Last yr.; 1.45 percent change

UNEMPLOYMENT RATE 3.3 This yr.; 2.5 Last yr.; 32.83 percent change

ACCUMULATED TOWN SURPLUS (DEFICIT-) $39,089 This yr.; $3- Last yr.

TOWN BUDGET:BALANCING ACT APPLAUDED BY TOWN'S PEOPLE.

PLANNER NEWS:MAYOR APPLAUDS PLANNING STAFF - PROJECTS GOOD TIMES AHEAD

SCORE FOR TJT, THIS YEAR: 102, THIS GAME: 102

DO YOU WISH TO SEE LOCAL GOVERNMENT FINANCIAL STATEMENTS (Y OR N) ? Y

Figure 4. Changing Controls

DO YOU WANT TO LEAVE CONTROLS UNCHANGED (Y OR N) ?

MOVE CURSOR TO CONTROL TO BE CHANGED (USING UP AND DOWN ARROWS)

C(l) = $1.00 = FEE CHARGED EACH TOURIST

C(2) = $20.00 = EFFECTIVE RESIDENTIAL PROPERTY TAX RATE (PER $1000)

C(3) = $20.00 = EFFECTIVE COMM./IND. PROPERTY TAX RATE (PER $1000)

C(4) = $1,500,000.00 = BUDGET FOR TOURIST PROMOTION

C(5) = $400,000.00 = BUDGET FOR OTHER ECONOMIC PROGRAMS

C(6) = $5,500,000.00 = BUDGET-FOR SOCIAL PROGRAMS

C(7) = $4,500,000.00 = BUDGET FOR ENVIRONMENTAL PROGRAMS

TYPE F1 TO EXIT

TYPE F2 TO CHANGE VALUE F2

ENTER NEW VALUE FOR CONTROL, THEN PRESS RETURN. C(1) = 1.50

F1 plus the overall well-being index are used to evaluate the player's job performance. It is in fact the budget-balancing problem that forces most game players into early retirement.

The End of The Game and Scores

The game ends when the planner quits, is fired, or survives 10 years in office. The score consists of the average of the community well-being index weighted by the residential population and summed over the number of years in office normalized so that 100 points per year reflects maintaining the initial levels of all indexes. The distribution of scores generated from 100 plays where the only criterion was to balance the budget is given in figure 5. The scores underlying the illustration ranged from 402 to 1072 with only thirteen scores above the norm of 100 points per year for the entire ten-year period.

The distribution of scores obtained when following a specific decision rule has been a major aide in assessing the performance of the model. For example, the scores in Figure 5 were determined by the rule that each year the tourist fee would be changed by exactly the ratio of the current deficit (or surplus) to the current number of tourist days. We have adopted this budget-balancing, status-quo type decision rule as our base line distribution of scores. In this distribution, the major cause of variation was games in which the player was fired prior to the ten-year maximum. The secondary cause of variation was the influence of random events on community well-being. As the bimodal distribution of the figure suggests, a typical game involved two events. When the first event was serious, the budget-balancing, status-quo player could not compensate and was fired between the fourth and seventh year as reflected in the cluster of scores between 400 and 700. The second event occasionally resulted in a firing, but because of its timing late in the game most players reached the tenth year.

Every game ends with the opportunity to view a listing of the ranked scores from the previous 100 games played. These results identify the players by initials, and the individual games played by the score earned, the number of years the office was held, and the nature of the "NEWS FLASH" events that occurred while in office. These are indicated by the initial letter of the news flash (F, G, 0, U, or B) and provide a basis to evaluate the specific events that have most dramatically affected the well-being of the game community. This list of scores has been useful to teachers for evaluating uses of the game and relative success of individual students in dealing with hypothetical community problems.

APPLICATIONS

In Education

Beyond individual play as described above, the game has proved to be of value in classroom exercises to simulate town politics and decision making. In this application each member of the class is assigned a role and a role card which indicates a specific attitude about development issues. Game years are marked off every 30 minutes. At the beginning of each new year individuals meet in groups to develop policy and strategies for dealing with other groups. As the year progresses groups interact. At the end of the year the mayor and the rest of the administration is advised by various public and private groups about actions to be taken on behalf of the community. These actions are input as changes to the seven controls on the local economy and the game provides a report of the influence of the changes and news on any special occurrences.

It is of particular interest to note that a major problem with the model was uncovered by students who figured out how to "beat the game." Property taxes, in the model, are treated as reductions in income prior to its allocation to leisure and non-leisure goods. As such, the model predicts no social outrage following rapid property tax increases that are put back into social and environmental programs. Accordingly, students have found that extremely high scores can be earned by raising property taxes and spreading the proceeds across social programs. This result has lead to revisions in the game as well as the identification of new topics for tourism research.

In Research

As suggested by the distribution of scores shown in Figure 5, the game acts as a stochastic simulation model when a specific decision rule is adopted. A research version of the game offers the player the opportunity to change behavioral parameters and automatically restart with specific decision rules. This enables the study of the influence of individual parameters and identification of behavioral relationships that lead to extreme scores. This is the basis for an ongoing study of the model, its parameters, and future refinements of the model.

SUMMARY AND CONCLUSIONS

It has been the purpose of this paper to present the details of a project that started toward a research objective, later became an educational project, and is currently on-going as a combined research and educational program. Based in research findings from a variety of studies, a "straw-man" computer game was constructed to help in the presentation of a difficult concept in a new research effort: the dynamic and stochastic nature of tourism community behavior. This game was "borrowed" for use in the classroom and subsequently revised for educational purposes. We are convinced that game play is a very exciting way of teaching tourism planning. We have also found that students and others playing the game can provide us with an unexpectedly rich source of research assistance'. In our quest for a "reasonable" characterization of tourism community behavior. We have therefore altered our research procedures to explicitly account for the research-education interaction. It has been to our great delight that, on more than one occasion, students have identified inadequacies in the model by their ability to "beat the game."

The future for this type of project is bright. The model has been used by over 50 researchers and 500 students, and feedback from its use has suggested a wide range of revisions. These include adding more sectors of the economy toward the goal of a Leontief model of transactions, adding more types of tourists and residents, and adding more specific impacts thus far only generalized as social and environmental impacts. It has also been suggested that more of the complexities of community government be included such as the role of zoning on development. Many of these suggestions could result in major improvements to the model; however, the game's simplicity would need to be sacrificed. In the process of deciding upon such improvements, it will be our overriding concern to maintain a balance between the model's usefulness as an educational tool and as a research vehicle.

12

The Impact of Tourism on Local Government Public Service Expenditures

INTRODUCTION

Background

Tourism is an important component of the Maine economy. Tourists spent about $1.6 billion in Maine during 1987 (Center for Survey and Marketing Research 1988). These expenditures supported over 58,000 full-time equivalent jobs that paid about $470 million in wages. In addition, a total of $85 million was collected by the state in the form of sales and gasoline taxes paid by tourists, and income taxes paid by people working in the tourism industry. These numbers reflect only the direct or primary impacts of tourism on the Maine economy. The impacts are even larger when the indirect and induced effects of tourist expenditures are included in the impact measures. Nevertheless, the direct impacts alone provide a strong justification for those who refer to Maine as "vacationland."

Studies measuring the economic benefits of recreation and tourism have become quite common in the last 20 years (for example, see Chapters 9 and 10 in Napier 1981 and Bergstrom et al. 1990). However, a complete economic evaluation of tourism requires measurement of the economic costs of tourism as well as the economic benefits. Tourism-related costs can take several forms, including traffic congestion, crowding at recreation and tourist facilities, environmental degradation, higher housing costs, and a general increase in the cost of living. Tourism can change the character of tourist communities and reduce the quality of life for residents. Tourism also can increase the cost of providing public services within communities. Like residents, tourists "consume" public services, such as water and sewer services, solid waste disposal services, and road services provided by local governments. The types and quantities of services consumed by tourists depend in part on the amount of time they spend in the community and the types of activities in which they participate. For example, seasonal home owners consume a larger quantity and more diversified mix of public services than tourists who spend only a few hours at a tourist attraction within a community.

Several studies have investigated the relationship between tourism and local government expenditures. Barrows and Nilsestuen (1974) studied the fiscal impacts of reservoir development in the Kickapoo Valley in Wisconsin and observed increases in local government expenditures for new roads and road maintenance, police and fire protection, and water, sewer and waste disposal facilities. Young (1973) also reports that tourism development increases the demand for local public services and stresses existing delivery systems. Schultz and Stronge (1980) note that tourism increased public service costs in Florida to alleviate traffic congestion, higher crime rates, and overcrowding of hospitals and other health-care facilities. All of these studies suggest that tourism growth and developmentaffect some of the public services provided by local governments.

The American Society of Planning Officials (1976) examined the effects of recreational second home development on local government expenditures. Some of the fiscal impacts identified include: -increases in solid waste disposal costs because second home owners generate more waste per household, and because solid waste collection costs are higher for second homes due to their remote location and seasonal variation in service;

— increases in road maintenance costs because of the need to improve roads and to snowplow roads that previously were not plowed;

— increases in police, fire protection, and health-care costs to provide services to seasonal residents; retirement communities and skiing developments often require expanded local health-care services;

— local education expenditures are usually unchanged by second home development, unless second homes are converted to year-'round use, or the recreational development causes secondary population growth in the year-round population.

Dwyer and Espeseth (1977) studied four rural counties bordering a newly constructed reservoir in Illinois. Eight years after the reservoir was completed, they found a large increase in the number of visitors to the site, but no significant second home development. Local governments experienced increases in road construction and maintenance costs and law enforcement costs.

Finally, Cole and Kuserk (1984) analyzed the fiscal impacts of four groups: permanent residents, seasonal residents, overnight tourists, and day tourists on five municipalities along the Delaware shore. Local government revenues and expenditures attributable to each group were measured. The results indicate that seasonal residents contribute more to local government revenues than the cost of providing them with services. This result reflects the fact that seasonal residents only demand services during part of the year, but pay the same property tax rate as year-round residents. On the other hand, overnight tourists and day tourists consume more in local government services than they contribute to the towns in revenues. One of the recommendations of the study is to initiate or expand user fees for parking and beach use so that towns can collect a greater share of the costs incurred to provide services to overnight and day tourists.

Purpose of Report

The overall purpose of this report is to present the results ofa study designed to determine how tourism affects the level of public service expenditures made by Maine communities. Because tourists consume public services while visiting a town, the basic hypothesis of this study is that per capita expenditures incurred by towns to provide public services will be higher in those towns that accommodate high levels of tourist activity. This study attempts to test this hypothesis using data on public service expenditures and tourism activity for 379 towns in Maine. The specific study objective is to develop an expenditure determinants model to determine how community characteristics, including tourism, affect per capita expenditures incurred to provide public services.

This study only addresses one type of cost that tourism may impose on the community: the costs of providing public services. The study does not attempt to assess directly the other types of social, economic, or environmental costs that can accompany tourism development. However, communities may respond to these costs by providing more or better quality public services. These types of responses would be reflected in higher public service delivery costs, and therefore, may be partially accounted for in the expenditure determinants equations estimated in this study.

In addition, no attempt is made in this study to determine how tourism activities contribute to the revenue base of local communities. Because Maine towns are highly dependent on property taxes as a revenue source, tourist-related facilities (second homes, hotels, motels and restaurants, and retail establishments that cater to tourists), can contribute positively to the tax revenue base of a town. This study, however, only examines tourism's impact on public service expenditures.

Organization of the Report

Section II contains a discussion of the methodology used in this study. Data collection and estimation procedures are discussed in Section III, and the results are presented in Section IV. Finally, the implications of the results are discussed in Section V.

METHODOLOGY

Estimation of cost functions is a common practice in economics. Cost functions show the relationship between the cost and the quantity of the good or service provided while holding constant the other factors that influence costs:

Total Costs = f(Quantity) Quality, Price of Inputs, Other Supply Factors)

Total costs are directly related to the quantity of the good provided. That is, total costs increase (decrease) as the level of output increases (decreases), other things being equal. Hence, the total cost curve has a positive slope over all ranges of output. However, average total costs may decrease (increase) as the level of output increases, due the presence of economies (diseconomies) of size.

The quality of the good or service, the prices of inputs, and all other factors that influence costs are constant along a given total cost curve. If one or more of these factors change, the entire cost curve will shift up or down. For example, the total cost function would shift upward as the quality of the good or service increases, and as the prices of inputs used to produce the good or service increases. Other factors also influence total costs. In the case of local government services, population density and the physical size of the community are examples of factors that can affect the costs of providing some public services. Changes in these supply-condition variables also cause the entire total cost curve to shift up or down.

Total cost functions for public services could be estimated to determine the influence of tourism on public service delivery costs. However, there are two problems with this approach. First, the construction of cost equations for publicly provided services is problematic because public service output levels are difficult to measure. For example, it is difficult to quantify the "output" of fire protection services provided by the town. Without acceptable measures of the quantity of public services provided, the appropriate cost functions can not be estimated.

Another problem with the cost function approach is that it only represents one side of the market. Factors related to the demand side of the market also influence the level of public services provided by a community. For example, communities with high per capita incomes often provide more and/or higher quality services than communities with low per capita incomes.

Furthermore, tourists may increase the demand for some public services. As a result, the community may have to increase the quantity of service provided which, in turn, will increase the total cost of providing the service. Therefore, demand conditions have to be included in an analysis of the factors that influence the cost of providing local government services.

Ideally, one could estimate demand and cost functions simultaneously to determinethe level of services provided by the community. However, this approach also requires adequate measure of the quantity of services provided. Because these measures are not readily available, most researchers have adopted the expenditure determinants method to identify factors that influence local government expenditures for public services (Hirsch 1970).

Expenditure determinants models were introduced in the 1940s and have been refined over the years. Currently, expenditure determinants models are estimated using multiple regression analysis. However, these models lack a strong theoretical base because they incorporate both supply and demand variables in the same equation. Nevertheless, Hirsch (1970) has noted that these models advance our understanding of the factors that cause expenditure levels to vary among communities.

In its general form, the cost determinants model assumes that per capita expenditures on public services depend on several factors that affect the cost of providing a public service (Hirsch 1970):

EXPENDITURES PER CAPITA = F(QUANTITY, QUALITY, INPUT PRICES, OTHER SUPPLY CONDITIONS, DEMAND CONDITIONS).

Note that the expenditure determinants equation includes the independent variables used in the cost function approach, including quantity and quality measures of the service provided, the prices of inputs used to produce the services, and other supply factors or conditions that affect public service expenditures. Because of the lack of adequate measures of the quantity and quality of output provided, proxy variables are used to represent quantity and quality measures. For example, the population of the town is often used to approximate the quantity of the service provided, and the crime rate, fire insurance rating, and student-teacher ratios are examples of the variables used to reflect the quality of some of the public services provided.

Supply conditions, such as population density, the degree of urbanization in the area, and the level of non-local government aid also influence public service expenditures. For example, sewer collection costs are usually lower in towns where the population is concentrated in a small geographic area. Similarly, state aid for road maintenance has a substantial impact on road maintenance expenditures because the town is reimbursed for all or part of the maintenance expenses.

Unlike the cost function approach, the expenditure determinants equation also includes variables that reflect demand conditions. These are included because they play an important role in community decisions regarding the quantity or level of public service to provide. Demand conditions include per capita income levels, real property values per capita, and the types of industries in the community. For example, a manufacturing plant that generates large quantities of waste water can increase the level of expenditures for waste water treatment facilities in the town. Similarly, the presence of tourism can increase the demand for some types of public services. Commuting patterns also influence the demand for public services, as do the demographic characteristics of the population. For example, retirement communities often spend more per capita for health-related public services than other communities. Similarly, communities comprised of a large number of families with children often spend more per pupil for education services.

Tourism's potential impact on public service expenditures can enter the expenditure determinants model in a number of ways. For example, tourism can be viewed as a demand condition that influences public service costs. However, some forms of tourism development can have an impact through supply condition variables. Second home developments are often located some distance from the central core of the community, thereby increasing solid waste collection, road maintenance, and other public service costs. Furthermore, second home owners often have different demographic characteristics than year-round residents and may, therefore, demand a different type or level of services (American Society of Planning Officials 1976).

Finally, it is important to recognize that several different types of "tourists" exist, including seasonal home residents, vacationers that spend one or more nights in a community, and day visitors that spend only a few hours at their destination. Clearly, different types of tourists demand different types or quantities of public services. As noted above, seasonal residents who live in the community part of the year utilize a wider range of services than visitors who only spend an afternoon at the beach. Consequently, three types of tourists are included in the study: seasonal residents, vacationers*, and day tourists. The three types of tourists are included separately in an attempt to measure the impact of each type of tourist on local public service costs.

Unfortunately, data are unavailable on the number of tourists who visit a community in Maine. Consequently, proxy measures have to be used to represent the level of tourist activity in Maine communities. The number of seasonal residents is represented by the number of seasonal homes in the community. The number of vacationing tourists in a given community is represented by the commercial lodging capacity (hotel, motel rooms and campsites at commercial campgrounds) in the town. Finally, the seating capacity of seasonal restaurants in the community is used to represent the number of day visitors. Although the number of seasonal homes and the commercial lodging capacity are considered to be good proxies for seasonal residents and vacationing tourists, respectively, the use of seating capacity at seasonal eating establishments is not considered to be a good measure of day-trip visitors. However, no other measure was available.

Separate expenditure equations are specified for each of the major public services provided by Maine towns, including police, fire, welfare, health, recreation, sanitation, public works, general administration and education. The expenditure equations for each public service and the hypothesized sign on each independent variable are presented below.

POLICE

POLICE EXPENDITURES PER CAPITA = f(POPULATION, POPULATION SQUARED, MILES TO NEAREST SMA, CRIME RATE, CRIME CLEARANCE RATE, PER CAPITA INCOME, PER CAPITA REAL PROPERTY VALUES, POPULATION PER SQUARE MILE, IN COMMUTERS PER CAPITA, TOWN IS ON ISLAND, PRESENCE OF TOWN POLICE DEPARTMENT, SEASONAL HOMES PER CAPITA, PER CAPITA LODGING CAPACITY, AND PER CAPITA SEASONAL RESTAURANT SEATING)

Population and population squared are included in this and other equations to partially capture the level or quantity of service provided. The population squared variable reflects the total expenditure function's classical properties and tests the hypothesis that per capita expenditures are subject to economies or diseconomies with respect to population size. Miles to nearest Standard Metropolitan Area (S.M.A.) is an urbanization measure to test the hypothesis that per capita police expenditures increase with increasing urbanization (Borcherding and Deacon 1972). The crime rate is used to reflect the demand for police services, and the crime rate is used to reflect the quality of police services (Walzer 1972). Both of these variables should be positively related to per capita police expenditures. However, the crime rate can also reflect the quality or quantity of police services (i.e., a high crime rate may indicate a low quantity or quality of police services); therefore, the crime rate may be negatively related to per capita police expenditures. Per capita income reflects the ability to pay for services and should be positively related to per capita police expenditures (Weicher 1970).

Per capita real property values reflect the available tax base of the community and the value of assets requiring police protection; it is hypothesized to be positively related to per capita police expenditures. Population per square mile reflects population density and should be positively related to per capita police expenditures (Weicher 1970), although Sacks and Harris (1964) found density to be insignificant in explaining per capita police expenditures. In-commuters reflect the commercial and industrial activity in the town and should be positively related to per capita police expenditures (Muller 1975). "Town is on island" is a qualitative variable to reflect the hypothesis that island towns (with no physical connection to the mainland) have a different public service cost structure. These towns may be more self-sufficient in the provision of certain services because they can not rely on other towns when additional services are needed.

Presence of a town police department is a qualitative variable to indicate whether the town has its own police department. Some towns rely on police services provided by the county or the state. Presence of a police department should be positively related to per capita police expenditures. The three tourism-related variables are hypothesized to be positively related with per capita police expenditures (Barrows and Nilsestuen 1974; Dwyer and Espeseth 1977).

FIRE

FIRE EXPENDITURES PER CAPITA = f(POPULATION, POPULATION SQUARED, ARSON PER CAPITA, FIRE PROTECTION RATING, REAL PROPERTY VALUES PER CAPITA, PER CAPITA INCOME, POPULATION PER SQUARE MILE, PERCENT REAL PROPERTY WHICH IS INDUSTRIAL, TOWN IS ON ISLAND, SEASONAL HOMES PER CAPITA, PER CAPITA LODGING CAPACITY, AND PER CAPITA SEASONAL RESTAURANT SEATING)

Arson fires per capita is included to reflect the demand for fire services and is hypothesized to be positively related to per capita fire expenditures. The fire protection rating is an insurance industry rating of fire protection quality or effectiveness. Ratings range from one to ten, with one being a superior rating; thus, there should be a negative relationship between the fire protection rating and per capita fire expenditures. Real property values per capita proxies the amount of property to be protected and is expected to be positively related to per capita fire expenditures. Per capita income, a demand shifter, should be positivelyrelated to per capita fire expenditures (Borcherding and Deacon 1972). Population per square mile is hypothesized to be positively related to per capita fire expenditures (Fisher 1961) because higher density areas may require special fire fighting equipment (i.e., ladder trucks for multi-story structures) and "a high population density will aggravate the danger from fire" (Weicher 1970:388).

Percentage of real property valuation that is industrial reflects the importance of industrial activities in the community and may identify special demand factors for fire protection services (potential of chemical spills, fires, etc.). Therefore, percent industrial should be positively related to per capita fire expenditures. The island town dummy variable is hypothesized to have a positive relationship with per capita fire expenditures because island towns need to be more self-sufficient in providing fire protection. The tourism variables are hypothesized to be positively related to per capita fire expenditures (Barrows and Nilsestuen 1974).

WELFARE

WELFARE EXPENDITURES PER CAPITA = f(POPULATION, POPULATION SQUARED, UNEMPLOYMENT RATE, PER CAPITA INCOME, WELFARE AID PER CAPITA, TOWN IS ON ISLAND, SEASONAL HOMES PER CAPITA, PER CAPITA LODGING CAPACITY, AND PER CAPITA SEASONAL RESTAURANT SEATING)

The unemployment rate represents a demand factor and is hypothesized to be positively related to per capita welfare expenditures. Per capita income should be positively related to per capita welfare expenditures (Sacks and Harris 1964). Non-local government aid for general assistance lowers the local cost of providing welfare services and, therefore, should be positively related to per capita welfare expenditures. The tourism variables are included in the equation to test the hypothesis that they are insignificant in explaining per capita welfare expenditures.

HEALTH

HEALTH EXPENDITURES PER CAPITA = f(POPULATION, POPULATION SQUARED, PER CAPITA INCOME, FIRE PROTECTION RATING, PERCENT OF POPULATION OVER 65, MILES TO NEAREST SMA, PERCENT OF REAL PROPERTY WHICH IS INDUSTRIAL, TOWN IS ON ISLAND, HOMES PER CAPITA, PER CAPITA LODGING CAPACITY, AND PER CAPITA SEASONAL RESTAURANT SEATING)

Per capita income is expected to be positively related to per capita health expenditures (Borcherding and Deacon 1972). The fire protection rating proxies as a quality measure because it is hypothesized that the quality of the local ambulance/ rescue squad is closely related to the quality of the local fire department.

The percentage of the town's population over 65 is used to reflect demand for health services and should be positively related to per capita health expenditures (Gabler 1971). However, people over the age of 65 are eligible to have their ambulance services paid for by Medicare, whereas non-medicare recipients often do not pay for ambulance services. Therefore, towns may subsidize the ambulance squad to cover the operating costs not paid by Medicare recipients. If this is the case, the percentage of population over 65 may have a negative relationship with per capita health expenditures.

Miles to nearest SMA proxies as an urbanization measure, and it is hypothesized towns located farther away from larger, well-equipped, urban health facilities need to spend more on per capita health expenditures. Percent of real property which is industrial reflects the demand for special health services associated with industrial accidents, and should be positively related with per capita health expenditures.

The island town dummy variable is expected to be positively related to per capita health expenditures because island towns need to be more self-sufficient in providing health services. The tourism variables are hypothesized to be positively related to per capita health expenditures because seasonal residents and special recreation facilities, such as skiing areas, may strain local health services (American Society of Planning Officials 1976).

RECREATION

RECREATION EXPENDITURES PER CAPITA = f(POPULATION, POPULATION SQUARED, PER CAPITA INCOME, REAL PROPERTY VALUES PER CAPITA, INCOMMUTERS PER CAPITA, OUTCOMMUTERS PER CAPITA, MILES TO NEAREST SMA, TOWN IS ON ISLAND, SEASONAL HOMES PER CAPITA, PER CAPITA LODGING CAPACITY, AND PER CAPITA SEASONAL RESTAURANT SEATING).

Per capita income and real property values per capita reflect ability to pay for recreation services and proxy for effective demand; wealthier communities are hypothesized to spend more per capita for recreation (Borcherding and Deacon 1972). Incommuters and outcommuters may demand recreation opportunities in the towns in which they work; thus incommuters should be positively related, and outcommuters should be negatively related, to per capita recreation expenditures (Keeling 1986). Miles to nearest SMA is used to proxy the presence of substitute recreational opportunities. Cities generally have more recreation and entertainment opportunities that can be used by neighboring communities; therefore, towns located farther from cities may have to provide more recreation opportunities.

It is hypothesized that seasonal restaurant seating capacity is positively related to per capita recreation expenditures because day-tourists increase the demand for recreation opportunities and thereby increase town recreation expenditures per capita (i.e., increased beach and park maintenance). On the other hand, seasonal residents are expected to demand fewer recreational opportunities because seasonal homes are often concentrated in locations (lake front, around ski areas, etc.) where owners can provide their own recreation. Commercial lodging capacity is hypothesized to be unrelated to per capita recreation expenditures because vacationers are usually attracted to a destination for reasons unrelated to town-related recreational opportunities.

SANITATION

SANITATION EXPENDITURES PER CAPITA = f(POPULATION, POPULATION SQUARED, PERCENT CHANGE IN POPULATION, PER CAPITA INCOME, POPULATION PER SQUARE MILE, INCOMMUTERS PER CAPITA, PERCENT OF REAL PROPERTY WHICH IS INDUSTRIAL, TOWN IS ON ISLAND, SEASONAL HOMES PER CAPITA, PER CAPITA LODGING CAPACITY, AND PER CAPITA SEASONAL RESTAURANT SEATING)

Sanitation services exhibit high capital costs and short-run capacity constraints. Consequently, one would expect a lag in the response of sanitation expenditures to changes in population; therefore, we hypothesize a negative relationship between sanitation services per capita and the percent change in population. Per capita income, a demand shifter, should be positively related with per capita sanitation expenditures (Borcherding and Deacon 1972). Population per square mile is included to test the hypothesis that less densely populated towns provide fewer sanitation services because of high collection costs. An alternative hypothesis is that towns with low population densities do provide sanitation services and incur higher per capita sanitation expenditures (Weicher 1970). Incommuters per capita should be positively related to per capita sanitation expenditures. Percentage of real property which is industrial is included to test the hypothesis that towns with large industries incur higher per capita sanitation expenditures. However, industries often provide their own sanitation services; therefore, percent industrial may be insignificant in explaining per capita sanitation expenditures. All of the tourism variables are hypothesized to have a positive effect on per capita sanitation expenditures (Barrows and Nilsestuen 1974).

PUBLIC WORKS

PUBLIC WORKS EXPENDITURES PER CAPITA = f(POPULATION, POPULATION SQUARED, PER CAPITA INCOME, REAL PROPERTY VALUES PER CAPITA, ROAD AID PER CAPITA, INCOMMUTERS PER CAPITA,

POPULATION PER SQUARE MILE, TOWN IS ON ISLAND, SEASONAL HOMES PER CAPITA, PER CAPITA LODGING CAPACITY, AND PER CAPITA SEASONAL RESTAURANT SEATING)

Per capita income and per capita real property values should be positively related to per capita public works expenditures (Ohls and Wales 1972). Non-local road aid per capita also should be positively related to public works expenditures per capita. Incommuters per capita reflect the size of the commercial sector of the town and should be positively related to per capita public works expenditures (Muller 1975). Population per square mile is a density factor and should be negatively related to per capita public works expenditures. Per capita seasonal homes, per capita lodging capacity, and per capita seasonal restaurant seating are expected to be positively related to public works expenditures because of increased demand for road maintenance (Dwyer and Espeseth 1977).

ADMINISTRATION

ADMINISTRATION EXPENDITURES PER CAPITA = f(TOTAL EXPENDITURES, TOTAL EXPENDITURES SQUARED, TOTAL NON-LOCAL AID PER CAPITA, PER CAPITA INCOME, REAL PROPERTY VALUES PER CAPITA, OUTCOMMUTERS PER CAPITA, TOWN IS ON ISLAND, SEASONAL HOMES PER CAPITA, PER CAPITA LODGING CAPACITY, AND PER CAPITA SEASONAL RESTAURANT SEATING)

Administrative expenditures per capita are not directly tied to the provision of any particular public service, but are a positive function of the level of all other public service expenditures (not including administrative expenditures). The squaring of total expenditures tests the hypothesis that administration expenditures per capita are subject to economies or diseconomies with respect to the level of town expenditures. Total non-local aid per capita should be positively related to the level of administration expenditures per capita (Keeling 1986). Per capita income and real property values per capita should be positively related to administration expenditures because wealthier communities demand higher levels of spending and therefore, more administrative services. The number of outcommuters per capita is included to test the hypothesis that communities with a high number of outcommuters per capita provide a higher level of public services per capita. Per capita seasonal homes, per capita lodging, and seasonal restaurant seating are expected to be positively related to per capita administration expenditures because of increased demand for administrative services.

EDUCATION

PER PUPIL EDUCATION EXPENDITURES = f(ENROLLMENT, ENROLLMENT SQUARED, PERCENTAGE CHANGE IN ENROLLMENT, TEACHER/PUPIL RATIO, PER CAPITA INCOME, REAL PROPERTY VALUES PER CAPITA, EDUCATION AID PER CAPITA, EMPLOYMENT PER CAPITA, TOWN IS ON ISLAND, SEASONAL HOMES PER CAPITA, PER CAPITA LODGING CAPACITY, AND PER CAPITA SEASONAL RESTAURANT SEATING)

Enrollment and enrollment squared test the hypothesis that per pupil education expenditures are subject to economies or diseconomies with respect to enrollment. However, the Maine State Government attempts to equalize per student education spending between towns. Therefore, the enrollment variables may be insignificant in explaining per pupil education expenditures. Percentage change in enrollment should be negatively related to education expenditures per pupil because teaching positions and education administration do not vary in the short run (Keeling 1986).

The teacher/pupil ratio is a proxy for quality of education and should be positively related to per pupil education expenditures. Per capita income and real property values per capita should be positively related to per capita education expenditures because wealthier communities often spend more per student for educational services. However, if the state subsidy for education works to equalize per pupil spending, then the community's level of wealth and income may be insignificant in explaining per pupil expenditures.

Non-local (state) education aid should be positively related to per capita education expenditures. Employment per capita is hypothesized to be positively related to the level of education expenditures because businesses demand better-educated workers (Keeling 1986). The island town dummy variable is hypothesized to be positively related to per capita education expenditures to reflect the increased cost of tuitioning out students to schools on the mainland. The tourism variables are expected to be insignificant in the education equation.

DATA COLLECTION AND ESTIMATION PROCEDURES

Actual 1985 expenditures for the public services discussed above were collected for 379 towns in Maine from the annual reports published by the towns. Although an attempt was made to obtain the data for all incorporated towns in the state, the data were not available for some communities. However, the 379 towns are representative of all towns in Maine in terms of size distribution (Teisl 1990).

The expenditures obtained from the annual reports are divided by the town's population in 1985 to form the dependent variables in the expenditure determinants model. Police expenditures represent all expenditures made for police protection and animal control, while fire expenditures represent all expenses for fire protection, including fire control, hydrant rental, and dispatch/communication costs. Welfare expenditures include general assistance aid and town contributions to social service groups, such as community action programs, senior citizen programs, and family crisis services.

Health expenditures represent local ambulance/rescue squad costs and local government contributions to alcohol and mental health counseling services; recreation expenditures are for community athletic programs and maintenance oflocal parks and recreational facilities. Sanitation expenses include solid waste collection, transfer stations and recycling expenditures, and sewer collection and treatment expenses. Although we would have preferred to estimate separate equations for solid waste disposal and sewer treatment services, many towns do not report costs separately for these two services. Public works expenditures primarily represent maintenance costs for roads and other transportation facilities, but also include streetlighting and cemetery maintenance for some towns. General administration expenses include code enforcement, regional planning, legal, financial and informational services, and other general administration tasks. Finally, education expenses include both public school and adult education costs.

Data representing the independent variables in the equations were collected from various secondary sources for each of the 379 towns in Maine. Sources include Census data, the Maine Department of Labor, Maine Department of Public Safety, Maine State Planning Office, the Maine Bureau of Insurance, and the Maine Department of Education. Seasonal home data at the community level were obtained from previous research (Reiling and Cook 1985) and from Census data. Lodging and seasonal restaurant seating capacity were collected from records provided by the Maine Department of Human Services. The reader is referred to Teisl (1990) for a more complete discussion of the sources from which the independent variables were obtained.

Once the data were obtained, the equations presented above were estimated using Zellner's Seemingly Unrelated Regression (SUR) technique. This technique is used because the error terms in the nine expenditure equations may be correlated with each other for two reasons. First, expenditure levels for different public services are interdependent because their sum is restricted by the total revenue available to cover public service costs. Hence, a higher expenditure level for one service may force a decrease in spending on other services. Second, there may be spill-over effects between different service areas provided by local government. For example, a decrease in police expenditures may cause an increase in vandalism, which may require increased maintenance expenditures by some other town departments such as public works and recreation.

Correlation among the error terms causes inefficient parameter estimates if the equations are estimated using Ordinary Least Squares techniques. The SUR method gives maximum likelihood estimators that possess the minimum variance within the class of all unbiased estimators (Judge et al. 1988). The reader is referred to Theil (1971) and Judge et al.(1988) for a more complete discussion of SUR.

RESULTS

The results of the research are reported in this section. Each of the estimated equations are presented and discussed in terms of the hypotheses identified earlier. Particular attention is paid to the tourism-related variables and their effect on public service expenditures per capita.

Before presenting the specific results, it should be noted that the data set was examined for heteroskedasticity and multicollinearity. Although the former does not exist, the degree of multicollinearity is quite high among the following two sets of independent variables: population, population squared, and population per square mile; and per capita real property values, seasonal homes per capita, and seasonal seating capacity per capita.

The high correlation between two of the three variables representing tourism is especially troublesome for the purposes of this study and should be kept in mind when interpreting the results presented below. The high correlation may result in the correlated variables being insignificant in the estimated equations that contain two or more of the correlated variables.

The weighted coefficient of determination or R2 for the system of equations estimated using the SUR technique is 0.63. That is, the independent variables in the set of equations account for 63 percent of the variation in the level of public service expenditures among the 379 towns.

The F-statistic for the equation system (101 variables and 3309 degrees of freedom) is equal to 1.36, which is statistically significant at the one percent level. Both of these statistics indicate that the equations explain a significant amount of the variation in public service expenditures among towns. The estimated equations for each of the nine public services are presented below and discussed briefly.

Police

The estimated expenditure determinants equation for police services is presented in Table 1. The insignificant coefficients for population and population squared indicate per capita police expenditures do not vary with respect to population size.

Among the statistically significant variables in the equation, per capita income, which represents a demand shifter, is positively related to capita police expenditures. Per capita real property values, which reflects the available tax base of the community and the value of assets requiring police protection, also is positively related to per capita police expenditures. Population density and incommuters per capita are also positively related to per capita police expenditures, as hypothesized. Presence of a town police department indicates per capita police expenditures are higher for towns that have their own police department. Miles to nearest S.M.A. and the crime rate, included to reflect the demand for police services, are not statistically significant in the equation. The crime clearance rate, which was included to reflect the quality of police services, also is insignificant. However, presence of a police department is significant and may reflect quality variations. In earlier estimates, the crime clearance rate was positive and significant when the police department dummy variable was not included in the police equation. Town on an island is not significant in explaining per capita police expenditures. Per capita seasonal homes and per capita seasonal restaurant seating capacity have negative and significant relationships with per capita police expenditures. However, lodging capacity is significant and positively related to per capita police expenditures. The negative signs on the seasonal home and seasonal restaurant seating capacity variables were not expected. It was hypothesized that all three tourism variables would be significant and would have positive signs in the police expenditure equation.

Fire

The estimated equation for fire services is reported in Table 2. The statistically insignificant coefficients for population and population squared suggest that per capita fire expenditures do not vary across towns with different population levels.

Statistically significant variables in the equation include per capita real property values, the fire insurance rating, percent industrial, and the island town dummy variable. Per capita real property values, included as a demand shifter to signify the amount of property to be protected, is positively related with per capita fire expenditures. Per capita fire expenditures also increase significantly as the quality of fire protection, as measured by the fire insurance rating, increases. Towns with proportionally large amounts of industrial property also incur higher per capita fire expenditures. Finally, island towns, which have to be more self-reliant in fire suppression services, also incur higher costs per capita in providing fire protection.

Arson per capita, per capita income, and population density, included to reflect demand factors for fire protection, are not statistically significant in the equation. However, other demand shifting variables, including real property per capita and percent of property that is industrial, are significant.

The tourism variables are not significant in explaining per capita fire expenditures. The insignificance of per capita seasonal homes and per capita lodging capacity was not expected. It was hypothesized that these variables would be significant and positively related to per capita fire expenditures because of the increase in the number of dwellings and businesses to be protected. The high correlation between some of the tourism variables and per capita real property values may contribute to the insignificance of the tourism variables in the equation. However, detailed discussions with town officials in Bar Harbor suggest that tourism has very little impact on town expenditures for fire services.

Welfare

The SUR results for the welfare equation are reported in Table 3. The positive coefficient for population and the insignificant coefficient for population squared indicate per capita welfare expenditures increase linearly with population and therefore, exhibit diseconomies of size with respect to population. The unemployment rate and welfare aid per capita are significant. The unemployment rate represents a demand factor of per capita welfare expenditures. Per capita welfare expenditures increase by $ 0.98 for every dollar increase in general assistance aid received from the state or federal government. This result suggests that welfare expenditures for general assistance are strongly influenced by the aid received by the towns.

Per capita income, included to reflect demand, is not significant in the welfare equation. Furthermore, there is no statistically significant difference in per capita welfare expenditures for island and mainland towns.

The three tourism variables of per capita seasonal homes, per capita lodging capacity, and per capita seasonal restaurant seating are, as hypothesized, not statistically significant in explaining per capita welfare spending.

Health

The estimated health expenditures equation is reported in Table 4. The coefficients for population and population squared indicate per capita health expenditures are subject to economies of size for towns with populations less than 27,250, and exhibit diseconomies of size for larger towns.

Significant variables in the equation include the fire insurance rating, the percentage of the population over 65 years of age, miles to S.M.A., percent industrial, and the island town dummy variable. The fire insurance rating indicates per capita health expenditures increase with increasing quality.

As the percentage of the town's population over 65 increases, there is a decrease in per capita health expenditures. This seems to confirm that towns subsidize the operating costs of ambulance and rescue services provided to non-medicare recipients. Towns located farther from urban health facilities spend more on per capita health expenditures. This is as hypothesized because towns located further away from well-equipped health facilities need to spend more on equipping their local ambulance/rescue squads and have higher transportation costs. Rural communities also may have higher rescue squad needs. Industrial property as a percentage of total property, included to reflect special demand conditions, increase per capita health expenditures. Islands towns incur higher per capita costs of providing health services because these towns have to be more self-reliant in terms of providing health care than mainland towns. Per capita income, included to reflect demand, is not significant in explaining per capita health expenditures.

Seasonal homes per capita and per capita lodging capacity are not significant in explaining per capita health expenditures. Per capita seasonal restaurant seating is positively related to per capita health expenditures. Analysis of the data suggests that the seasonal seating variable reflects the demand for local health services by skiers who use ski areas located in some Maine towns.

Recreation

The SUR results for the recreation equation are reported in Table 5. The coefficients for population and population squared indicate per capita recreation expenditures are subject to diseconomies of size for towns with a population of less than 37,203 and exhibit economies of size for larger towns.

Real property values per capita, reflecting demand factors, is positively related to per capita recreation expenditures. The signs of the coefficients for incommuters per capita and outcommuters per capita are as hypothesized, although the outcommuters variable is not significant in explaining per capita recreation expenditures. This indicates incommuters' increased awareness of recreation opportunities near their worksite increases the demand, thus increasing per capita recreation expenditures. This increased demand comes from a group that contributes little to town revenues, thus placing the fiscal impacts on local residents. Towns located near urban areas have lower per capita recreation expenditures, as hypothesized. Per capita income, which reflects demand, is not significant in explaining per capita recreation expenditures.

Seasonal homes per capita is significant and negatively related to recreation expenditures per capita.

This seems reasonable because seasonal home-owners often have access to recreational resources at their doorstep. Per capita lodging capacity is insignificant, perhaps indicating that tourists staying in commercial lodging establishments use recreation facilities provided by the private sector or other levels of government. Per capita recreation expenditures increase with increasing per capita seasonal restaurant seating. This may indicate towns with large day-trip tourist populations incur higher maintenance costs for parks and public beaches.

Sanitation

The regression results for the sanitation equation are reported in Table 6. The insignificant coefficient for population and positive coefficient for population squared indicate per capita sanitation expenditures are subject to diseconomies of size for towns of all sizes. Among significant variables, per capita income, included as a demand shifter, positively affects per capita sanitation expenditures. Incommuters per capita, reflecting demand from the commercial sector, indicates per capita sanitation expenditures increase with increasing commercial activity. Percentage change in population, used to test the hypothesis that there is a lag in the response of sanitation expenditures to a change in population, has the correct sign but is not significant. Population density, included to test the hypothesis that less densely populated towns provide fewer sanitation services, is not significant. Percent industrial is not significant in explaining per capita sanitation expenditures, indicating industries may often provide their own sanitation services. Island towns are not significantly different in their per capita sanitation expenditures.

Per capita seasonal homes and per capita lodging capacity both have positive and significant effects on per capita sanitation expenditures. However, per capita seasonal restaurant seating capacity is not significant in the equation.

Public Works

The regression results for the public works equation are reported in Table 7. The insignificant coefficients for population and population squared indicate per capita public works expenditures are invariant with respect to population. Significant variables include per capita income, per capita real property values, road aid per capita, and the island town dummy variable. Per capita public works expenditures increase with increases in per capita income. However, per capita real property values are negatively related to per capita public works expenditures. This result is contrary to our hypothesis, but can be explained by analyzing the methods used by the Maine Department of Transportation to allocate per capita road aid. One of the most important factors considered in the allocation of road aid is real property values per capita to reflect the town's own ability to pay for road maintenance. Towns with higher per capita real property values receive less road aid. Therefore, the negative relationship between per capita real property and per capita public works is not surprising.

Road aid per capita increases per capita public works expenditures by $2.02. Island towns incur higher costs of providing public works which may be caused by high transport costs of materials and higher labor costs. Incommuters per capita and population density, included to reflect special demand conditions, are not significant in explaining per capita public works expenditures. However, other demand variables are significant.

Per capita seasonal homes and per capita seasonal restaurant seating capacity are significant and positively related to public works expenditures, as hypothesized. However, the per capita lodging capacity variable is not significant.

Administration

The regression results for the administration equation are reported in Table 8. The coefficients for total expenditures and total expenditures squared indicate per capita administration expenditures are subject to diseconomies of size for all expenditures levels.

Administration expenditures per capita increase with increased levels of non-local aid per capita. Island towns face higher costs per capita of providing administration than mainland towns.

Per capita income, per capita real property values, and the number of outcommuters per capita are not significant in explaining per capita administration expenditures.

Per capita seasonal homes and per capita seasonal restaurant seating are positively related to per capita administration expenditures, indicating increased expenditures for administrative services per capita as the tourism variables increase. Per capita lodging capacity is positive, but insignificant in explaining per capita administration expenditures.

Education

The regression results for the education equation are reported in Table 9. Enrollment and enrollment squared are not significant confirming the hypothesis that enrollment does not affect per pupil education expenditures because of state programs to equalize per pupil education expenditures among towns.

Percentage change in enrollment indicates teaching positions and education administration are fixed in the short run, thus causing a lag in per pupil education expenditures. Per pupil education expenditures increase with increases in the teacher/pupil ratio, a common measure of education quality. Per capita aid to education also is significant and positively related to per capita education expenditures.

Per capita income and real property values per capita are not significant in explaining per pupil education expenditures, indicating the state subsidy for education works well to equalize per pupil spending across towns with different per capita income and per capita real property values. Employment per capita, included to reflect business demand for skilled workers, is not significant in explaining per pupil education expenditures. The three tourism-related variables are also insignificant, as hypothesized.

SUMMARY AND DISCUSSION

The overall objective of this study is to determine, through the use of expenditure determinants analysis, the impact that tourism has on the costs incurred by Maine towns to provide public services. Although the theoretical framework for expenditure determinants analysis is rather weak, it is used in this initial attempt to measure the tourism's impact on local public service provision costs. Tourism's impact is assessed through the use of three variables in the expenditure determinants regression equations that approximate the level of tourism in the 379 Maine towns included in the study. The number of seasonal homes per capita is used to approximate the number of seasonal residents, and the commercial lodging capacity (hotel and motel rooms and campsites at campgrounds) is used to measure overnight or vacation tourists staying in a town. Finally, the seating capacity at seasonal restaurants is used to represent the number of day-trip tourists that visit a town. Other variables are included in the regression equations to represent the quantity and quality of the public services provided, and to account for other demand and supply conditions that are hypothesized to influence public service costs.

The performance of the tourism variables varies among the nine public service equations estimated. None of the tourism variables are statistically significant in three of the equations: fire, welfare and education expenditures per capita. The insignificance of the tourism variables in the latter two equations are consistent with prior expectations. However, in a more detailed case study of the town of Bar Harbor, one of the leading tourist towns in Maine, it was discovered that tourism can have an impact on education expenditures (Reiling and Deller 1991). Seasonal homes and other tourist-related commercial establishments increase per capita property values for the town. Higher per capita property values reduce the level of state funding for education received by the community, thereby requiring an increase in the local community's contribution to education funding. Hence, although the results of the education equation are consistent with expectations, tourism may have some impact on education costs paid by the town. That is, even though total expenditures per pupil are the same in tourist and non-tourist towns, towns with a large tourism sector may pay a larger share of the total costs of education than do towns that do not have a large tourism sector. This impact needs to be studied further.

The insignificance of the tourism variables in the fire expenditures equation is not consistent with expectations. We had hypothesized that the presence of seasonal home and other tourist-related structures would result in higher per capita fire expenditures. However, fire department personnel in Bar Harbor indicated that tourism did not significantly affect per capita fire expenditures. Although there are many tourist-related structures in the town, other types of businesses and structures would be present if tourism did not exist, and some of these other types of businesses or structures may be more prone to fire than the tourism businesses/structures. Hence, this is another issue that should be examined in more detail.

In the police expenditures equation, seasonal homes per capita and seasonal restaurant seating capacity are significant and negative; however, lodging capacity per capita is significant and positive. Our hypothesis was that all three tourism-related variables would be positive and significant. We have no explanation for actual results. Police personnel in Bar Harbor indicated that tourism increases police expenditures per capita because of the need for overtime and additional seasonal workers during the peak tourist season. However, they could not separate the effects caused by different types of tourists.

Two of the three tourism variables are positive and significant in the sanitation, public works, and administration equations. The other tourism variable is statistically insignificant in these equations. Hence, the tourism variables generally conform to expectations in these equations. Only one of the tourism-related variables (seasonal seating capacity per capita) is significant in the health equation. All of the tourism-related variables are significant and have the hypothesized signs in the recreation expenditures equation.

At least one of the three tourism-related variables is positive and significant in six of the nine equations estimated: police, health, recreation, sanitation, public works, and administration. These results suggest that tourism increases per capita expenditures for these six public services. However, these six public services only account for 30 percent of the average budget of Maine towns. The three public service equations in which none of the tourism variables are significant (fire, welfare, and education) account for the remaining 70 percent of town budgets, with education accounting for 65 percent of town expenditures. Hence, even though the equations suggest that six of nine public services are positively affected by tourism, the magnitude of the impact may not be large relative to the total expenditures of town for providing public services. This conclusion is supported by the case study of Bar Harbor (Reiling and Deller, 1991). Public service expenditures associated with tourism in Bar Harbor constitute only 10.7 percent of the total municipal budget, excluding education.

Additional work is needed to refine the techniques used to estimate the impact of tourism on local public service expenditures. One area that deserves additional attention is the search for a better proxy variable of day-trip tourism. The seasonal restaurant seating capacity used in this study is not considered to be a good representation of day-trip tourism. Its high correlation with the number of seasonal homes suggests that the two variables are measuring the same effect, and that the seasonal restaurants may, to a large degree, serve seasonal residents.

Overall, we believe the expenditure determinants equations provide a useful initial investigation of the impact of tourism on pubic service delivery costs. Although additional refinement is needed, the results are fairly consistent with expectations and provide an initial analysis of the impact of tourism on public service costs.

However, it is also recognized that the theoretical justification for the expenditure determinants approach is weak. A more acceptable approach would be to develop a simultaneous equation system model that examines both expenditures and revenues. This approach not only has a better theoretical base, it also considers both the revenue and expenditure sides of the fiscal activities of local government. Further research should focus on the simultaneous equation approach. 12 Marketing the Uniqueness of Small Towns In recent decades, the rural-urban migration trend has reversed. People are moving back to small communities in increasing numbers. Likewise, nonmetropolitan communities are attracting an increasing percentage of new industrial plant locations. Some small communities have capitalized on this national trend; others have not.

This publication relates the science of marketing to communities. A small town can strengthen its local economy as a result of business people and concerned citizens collectively identifying that community's special uniqueness and then capitalizing on it. Seven simple techniques are provided in this publication to help residents of a small town identify and market what is unique about their community. A case example is included. Marketing is a new but rapidly growing field. As recently as the 1950's, there was no established definition for marketing, though many managers were beginning to see the importance of what advocates of this new field were teaching. Large companies began to restructure their organizational charts to include marketing divisions. Over the past 20 years, the field of marketing has developed rapidly to become one of the most important areas of modern business activity.

More recently, creative managers have begun to apply modern marketing techniques to the nonprofit sector. The American Marketing Association defines marketing as "the performance of business activities that direct the flow of goods and services from producer to consumer," Hospital directors, museum managers, political campaign managers, and college presidents are all beginning to realize that they are in the marketing business. Hospital directors market health care; museum managers market historical education and nostalgia; political campaign managers market their candidates; college presidents market education.

Community leaders must recognize that they, too, are engaged in a marketing enterprise-that of marketing their towns to prospective "customers" who could make use of what the town, its people, and its businesses have to offer.

The Differential Advantage

Potential customers often are faced with a wide range of alternative products, all very similar to each other. It is the marketer's job to create in the customer's mind an idea that a particular product is different in an important way, so that the product will have a competitive edge over others in the marketplace. This uniqueness or competitive edge is what is known in the marketing field as a differential advantage,

In the context of community development, it is the job of the community leaders to persuade potential tourists, residents, and outside businesses that your town is unique—or has a differential advantage—in a way that could be important to them in their decision of where to visit or where to locate. This creation of a differential advantage could turn out to be the deciding factor for a family considering where to spend their next vacation. It could influence a family who is thinking of moving to another community, or it could steer a business to locate in your town over other towns which don't appear to have anything unique to offer. In cases where other towns offer similar features, if your community leaders have created a differential advantage in the potential customer's mind, your town is more likely to win out.

A marketing strategy is designed to create and nurture a differential advantage. "The Four P's" of the marketing mix—product, place, price, and promotion—form the center of marketing strategy.

In marketing a town, the various features of the town itself become the product. The concept of the town as a product encompasses the town's scenery, natural resources, friendly atmosphere, transportation routes, history, architecture, educational facilities, shopping areas, and much more. All of these aspects help to determine the individual character of a given town. Often, some of these features will be unique to that town alone but they can sometimes characterize an area of the country as well. For towns in the southwestern United States, an advantage often cited is the excellent climate. This feature helps to make towns in the Southwest different from those in other parts of the country.

Place refers to the physical channel—for example, a grocery store or a lumber company- through which a product is sold. For some marketers, selection of the outlet through which the product will be sold can have a major impact upon the ultimate success or failure of the product in the marketplace.

When we speak of price as an element of a community's marketing mix, we are referring to costs that the community imposes upon residents, tourists, and resident businesses for the privilege of carrying out activities in the town—cost of living, taxes, transportation costs, value of real estate, etc. Often, small towns have distinct price advantages over other locations. These price advantages can become an integral part of a town's marketable uniqueness.

Finally, differential advantages of product and price must be promoted effectively. Essentially, promotion is communication, Community leaders must communicate the message of their town's uniqueness to prospective customers. Reaching the right audience is often the most difficult task, because promotion costs money and most small towns are constrained by a tight promotional budget, But a low-cost promotion program can be effective if it is well-conceived.

In review, community leaders are engaged in marketing a complex product—their town. Principles of marketing tell us that community marketers should develop and nurture a differential advantage for their product, based on the uniqueness of the product itself and the price of the product. This differential advantage must then be promoted to a target audience within applicable budget constraints. Though the steps in developing and carrying out a marketing plan can be time-consuming, they can pay off in the form of a broadened economic base for your community.

Identifying Your Town's Differential Advantage

Your town's competitive edge is a composite of all the factors that make the town unique. Too often, towns try to be successful by copying marketing strategies that have worked for others, only to find that the program they borrowed doesn't work as well as they thought it would.

Each town is unique, and what works for one town will not necessarily work for another. As a basis for your town's marketing program, community leaders must identify and capitalize upon the town's special uniqueness. That uniqueness may be the presence of a valuable natural resource such as rich farmland or thermo-wells, or the community may have a strategic location in serving a given population, or it may have scenic beauty, or historical significance, or a famous native son, or pleasant climate, or pleasing architecture, or a combination of these and other aesthetic values.

Often, those who live and work in the community lose sight of their community's uniqueness or they take it for granted.

To bring your town's uniqueness into focus, solicit ideas from many different sources- residents, newcomers, visitors, and others, Each group can offer a different perspective, and each different perspective can contribute in building your town's differential advantage.

Too often, community-leaders assume that they already know what is unique and marketable about their town. They don't take the time to test out these assumptions with their town's customers, and when they do, it is done in a very unscientific manner. ("A couple from Michigan stopped in here last month and they said. . . ")

Many of us overlook the fact that the overall uniqueness of a community is usually the result of a combination of elements rather than one or two big things.

In identifying your community's uniqueness, be specific and be realistic. Vague generalities and intangible adjectives are of limited value. Remember, uniqueness lies in the eye of the beholder. What is beautiful to one person may be boring and unexciting to another.

The following techniques are designed to help communities gain important insights in the development of a town's competitive edge. Any of these exercises will help you develop a solid marketing program for your town. Naturally, the more of these projects your town can do, the more it will be. able to sharpen its competitive edge. If you have questions or if you need assistance regarding these techniques, your county Extension office can put you in touch with a community development specialist in your state. (Another WRDC publication, entitled "Coping with Growth: Community Needs Assessment Techniques," might also be of interest to you.)

Brainstorming Session

The most basic method of zeroing in on your town's differential advantage is a brainstorming session involving people who know your community. The session can be held at any convenient time and location. It will be more beneficial if you choose a cross section of the community so that different viewpoints can be brought into the discussion. It is equally important that there be a group facilitator chosen in advance to steer the session when it gets off the track.

The brainstorming session should be designed to find out what the participants feel is unique about your town. Plan to have the session take at least an hour. (These sessions tend to run more smoothly when refreshments are provided.) Appoint someone to record the ideas as they are presented on large sheets of newsprint or a blackboard. Then review these ideas after the session is over to decide which are the most promising. Be sure to thank all participants.

The facilitator's first responsibility is the orientation of the brainstorming group. After everyone has been introduced and refreshments have been served, the facilitator should explain that the group is gathered to brainstorm about the uniqueness of the town. Explain that the group's ideas will be used in the development of a marketing package.

The assignment to the group might be: In your opinion, what makes this community unique? What do you particularly like about this community? Keep the brainstorming going by asking questions such as: What else is special about this community?

Brainstorming rules are fairly simple:

- List every idea mentioned.
- Do not discuss ideas.
- Do not judge ideas.
- Do not worry about repetition.
- Do not worry about spelling as ideas are recorded.

These rules must be strictly followed so that no potentially good ideas will be held back by any of the participants. No put-downs or arguments are allowed! The difficulty of the facilitator's job lies not in acquainting participants with these guidelines, but in enforcing them as the exercise continues.

After a list of unique characteristics has been developed, the facilitator may wish to challenge the group to be more specific: What specifically do you mean by "friendly people"? Please explain what you meant by "good climate."

The end result of your brainstorming session should be a usable list of unique, marketable community characteristics. These characteristics, along with other unique aspects of the town uncovered through some combination of the following six techniques, should be stressed in promotions directed to outsiders. If this uniqueness is properly communicated, the town will create for itself a true competitive edge.

Visitor Questionnaire

It is also important and relatively inexpensive to find out what visitors believe is unique about your town. This insight is a valuable aid in the development of the town's competitive edge,

Most towns have a location where visitors can come to ask questions and get information about the area. Usually, this is a visitors' center or chamber of commerce office. Most people who visit these centers are there to gain information for themselves, but smart community leaders can balance this exchange by asking visitors to fill out a brief questionnaire.

First, the questionnaire should find out the visitor's place of residence. Name and address should be optional since this is personal information, but it is important that respondents give their home town and state. With this information, you can pinpoint those areas currently contributing a heavy concentration of visitors to your town. These areas can then become prime targets for promotional activity.

Secondly, the questionnaire should ask the purpose (business or pleasure) and the destination of the visitor's trip. These questions should yield a brief profile of what brings visitors into the community. If a large proportion of the questionnaires show similar responses of one type or another, you can gain insight valuable as you plan your approach for the promotional campaign. For example, if you found that many visitors were passing through your town on the way from New Mexico to California vacation spots, you would select a promotional medium that would reach prospective vacationers from New Mexico, and you would tailor the promotional message to appeal to that audience.

Another question that should be included: What have you particularly noticed that you like about our town? This question will draw a variety of responses. If a pattern develops such as "good road service" or "historical sites" or "that big cactus on the road into town," then you will be armed with a feature of the community that is, in the opinion of outsiders, unique and marketable.

Add more questions if you feel they are necessary, but remember: the more questions on the form, the more likely it is that prospective respondents will leave blanks or refuse to bother with the questionnaire. Keep it short. One side of an 8 1/2" x 11" sheet of paper is least intimidating-to both the respondent and the person analyzing the completed questionnaires. (A sample questionnaire is provided in the case study section at the end of this publication.)

If you don't want to use a questionnaire, a guest registry is a good source of location information. The easiest way to compile location information is with a map and pins. This will give a visual display of the results. Whatever method you use, something along these lines should be instituted. It is a good, inexpensive source of information that will help you plan an effective promotional campaign.

Photography Contest

Photography is an integral part of any good promotional presentation. But good pictures of interesting sights around town can be hard to come by.

Nearly everyone will have a different idea of what particular sight is interesting and unique to a town. Through a well-publicized photography contest, these individual perspectives can be recorded. Some of the pictures could surprise you!

The purpose of such a contest is two-fold. A photography contest can provide a number of quality photographs for use in the town's promotional literature. But just as importantly, it can be an inexpensive way to boost community pride and get residents thinking about their town in a positive way.

Most often, such a photography contest is sponsored by the chamber of commerce, though other groups could undertake it. It is important that one group coordinate the project to avoid wasteful, confusing, and possibly disastrous duplication of efforts. The coordinating body must have an address where entries can be sent, and it must have at least one volunteer, or employee who is willing to keep track of entries as they come in.

Rules are specified by the contest coordinators. The contest will run more smoothly if a few simple guidelines are followed:

- Inform contestants that all entries will become the sole property of the contest coordinators and might be used in promotional literature or other promotional activities.
- Stipulate in detail how entries must be submitted, and to what address. State whether entries should be color or black/white prints. This will, of course, depend upon whether or not you plan to use color photographs in your brochure. Full-color printing is expensive but often necessary to show off local scenery to its best advantage. (If slide/tape presentations have a place in your marketing scheme, consider a category for color slides as well.) Also outline what size entries must be. A standard size is 8" x 1 0" , and it is helpful and more fair if all prints are the same size. All entries should include a brief description of when and where the photo was taken, in addition to the entrant's name, address, and phone number. Encourage multiple entries.
- Set a beginning date and an ending date for the contest. Give people plenty of time to have film developed and duplicates made, but don't let it drag out for so long that

it loses momentum. Six weeks should be a comfortable time limit.

- Inform contestants how their photographs will be judged. Most contests judge entries on technical quality and on subject matter. In this case, the subject should be: "scenes, faces, and activities that are unique to our town."
- Entries should be judged in at least two, preferably three categories. So that amateurs will not be discouraged, amateur entries should be judged separately from entries sent in by professional photographers. In a small town, there may be only a couple of professional entries (consequently all professionals may win a prize). These contributions are worth special consideration because they are often among the best of the contest. Some communities may also want to include a junior category for those 16 years old and under to encourage participation by younger citizens.
- The rules must state that the decision of the judges will be final. This will avoid unnecessary headaches after the contest is over.

Promotion for the contest should be as wide as possible, at the least possible cost. Here are some suggestions:

- Newspapers. Such a contest is newsworthy to local residents. A well-written, concise press release sent to the newspaper's city editor has the best chance of getting printed as a news story (as opposed to a piece of purchased advertising).
- Radio/TV. Local stations are often willing to announce such items for no charge- either as news or as a public service message. This is a great way to let people know about the contest.
- Posters, Handbill-sized posters can be printed for a nominal charge. Such posters should include contest details and can usually be posted in stores and other conspicuous spots around town.

- Schools. If you include a junior division in the contest, speak with local school officials about having the contest announced in the schools.
- Newspaper advertising. It maybe necessary to run a newspaper ad describing the details of the contest, but this type of advertising is usually expensive.

Judges should be chosen before the contest begins. The basic criteria for selecting judges are impartiality and an understanding of the contest's purpose. Judges and their families may not enter.

Prizes should include, recognition and monetary rewards. The following guidelines may be helpful:

- Recognition. Plaques should be offered for first, second, and third place in each division. These can be small and relatively inexpensive, but they should have the name and date of the contest inscribed on them. (Note: Winners of the professional division probably would prefer plaques to hang in their places of business.)
- Credits. The photographer should be credited for all photos used in promotional material.
- Monetary rewards may be found inexpensively. Check with local photo shops to see if they would be willing to donate gift certificates as prizes. Other merchants may also wish to participate. If no donors can be found, remember that U.S. savings bonds can be purchased for less than face value, and they make good, patriotic prizes.

Using the photos. When the contest is over, the sponsoring organization will hopefully have a good selection of usable photographs of unique aspects of the local community. They can be put to use in a number of ways.

- Use the pictures as illustrations in any promotional brochure or printed flyer that is published for distribution to the town's prospective "customers."
- Make a montage of the more interesting photos and display it at the visitors' center, the chamber of commerce, or some other location where visitors and

residents will be likely to see them. Photographs are the best way for visitors to become acquainted with the town in a very short time.

- Increase community awareness by using some of the best photos in a supplement to the town newspaper. Papers will sometimes run such a supplement free, in the community interest, but you will probably have to find advertisers to-sponsor the insert, Finding sponsors can take some effort, but advertisers are often happy for the good exposure that comes f rom participating in such a project. Arrangements should be made with the newspaper to print at least 500 or 1000 additional copies of the supplement.
- Develop a slide presentation from the photographs. Slide shows (with either live or taped narration) can be presented to service clubs and civic organizations to help rekindle interest in the community. If the program is well-received, you might, consider showing it in neighboring cities or wherever your customers are coming from.
- Use either a black/white or a color photo for a poster, depending on your budget. A professional-quality poster can provide excellent exposure for your community when displayed in offices, tourist locations, and travel agencies.
- Develop a "town tour" brochure with your black/white photographs. Pictures can be supplemented with explanations and a map showing locations of the various points of interest, A small, single-color brochure is not very expensive to produce, and it can be a big help to visitors in your community.

Interview New Businesses

To promote expansion by attracting new businesses, this exercise is a must. When a new enterprise locates in town, the chamber of commerce or the city/town council should have a member visit the newcomers to welcome them to the community. If your group is not doing this already, you are missing an opportunity to pick up some valuable marketing information, as well as a chance to help the newcomers feel at home. In this initial contact, no effort should be made to solicit membership in civic organizations. This will detract from the interview.

This interview should be designed to gather pertinent information on why the business person moved to your town. The interview should determine:

1) How the business person found out about the town; and 2) Why they decided to move to town.

If you find through these interviews that certain promotional channels have been effective in bringing in new businesses, then you may want to expand your efforts through these channels. For example, if a business person found out about the community in a newspaper article published in Phoenix, then the town should try even harder to get similar newspaper publicity run in newspapers in other towns, and even rerun in Phoenix. These interviews can uncover marketing strategies that have already been proven to work for your town.

Little preparation is required for these interviews; the interviewer is only interested in the answers to two questions. The first question should be asked after the interviewer has visited with the newcomer for awhile to break the ice. Before asking any questions, assure the respondent that all information received will be treated confidentially, and that you are merely trying to get a general idea of how to improve the town's marketing strategies. A straightforward "How did you first come to learn about our town?" will do nicely, As the subject stops talking, follow up with some probing questions, like "Had you ever heard about our town anywhere else?" and "Why did you decide to read (listen to, etc.) this particular source?"

When you are satisfied that the first basic question has been answered thoroughly, ask the second question: "What made you decide to move your business here, rather than somewhere else?" This can also be followed up until you are satisfied with the detail of the answer. The entire interview should take only about 15 minutes.

Ideally, the interviews should be tape-recorded and transcribed later. The tape recorder should be introduced casually so that your respondent will not become flustered or apprehensive. Respondents talk much faster than you can probably write. The thoughts you miss while writing may turn out to be important later on, even it they seemed to be trivial during the interview. If the interview cannot be recorded, it is essential to take notes while the subject is talking, Notes will be sketchy at best; details should be fleshed in as soon as possible after the interview, while the information is still fresh in your mind. After a few such interviews, the results should be compared to find similarities. If certain statements show up repeatedly, community leaders will be armed with some valuable information that will help make your town's marketing strategy even more effective.

Focus Groups

Focus groups are basically group discussion sessions run by a trained professional who attempts to "focus" group discussion on a specific topic. For small-town marketers, focus groups can help to bring up and evaluate new ideas about the town through intensive interaction among 8 to 12 individuals. Such sessions could also be used to uncover marketable aspects of the town's uniqueness that may not otherwise surface.

Focus groups can be important because they gather input from townspeople in an environment of free discussion. The flexibility of these groups allows them to probe various subjects as they arise—even subjects that weren't considered important before the discussion started. Because of the interaction of participants, the focus groups uncover more detail than individual interviews do.

The group must be run by someone who has experience with focus group techniques. A discussion run by an untrained moderator will likely be no more than an interesting (or perhaps chaotic) coffee klatch that yields little or no usable information. Likewise, improper makeup of the group (a poor cross section, or one participant who is loud or short-tempered) can drastically affect the results.

The session, which should last about an hour, is tape-recorded and transcribed later. This allows the moderator to reflect on every detail of the group discussion, and it provides the town with a detailed summary of participants' key statements. Participants should be informed that community leaders will only see the transcript, not hear the tape, and that no names will be used. The tape itself will become the property of the moderator, who will be responsible for protecting the anonymity of the participants.

If your town decides that it would like to conduct a focus group, there are two sources to contact for help. You could contact a marketing research firm or an advertising agency that has the expertise to conduct focus groups. (Not all firms can offer this service.) It would be helpful to get a list of references for whom the company has conducted focus groups, and call these references. Choose a firm only after you establish that they have performed satisfactorily in the past. As a less expensive alternative, you can contact the community development specialists with your Cooperative Extension Service. They will use the resources available to them to help you get your focus group underway. (Also see the list of references at the end of this publication.)

School Essay Contest

Another inexpensive method of uncovering your town's differential advantage is a school essay contest. Such a contest is most easily run where the community has its own school, but with proper coordination it can also be run in a school that serves several different communities.

Contact school officials to determine the feasibility of such a contest, The contest could be announced in English classes as an assignment (optional or otherwise) to write a 200-word essay entitled "What Is Unique about My Town." All age groups should be encouraged to participate.

When the papers are handed in, they should first be graded by the English teachers for style and grammar, then sent to the sponsoring organization for judging. Essays should be divided by grade level and judged on content.

Ideally, winners should be awarded prizes by representatives of the community at an assembly of the student body, Scholarships or savings bonds make excellent prizes, but they should be given in addition to, not instead of, small plaques or trophies. The essay contest would be healthy competition for the students, and it would help community leaders acquire yet another perspective of what is unique about their town.

Professional Visitation

Those who live in and drive through your town can provide you with some insight into its differential advantage, but a team of visiting professionals can give you information you might not get from any other source.

Your Extension community development specialist is in contact with university and other resources that you might put to work for your town, Through your community development specialist, you might arrange for, say, an urban planner, a geographer, a historian, a marketer, and a business executive to visit your community and report on their observations. The visit is not difficult to arrange. The outsiders can come to town in the morning and can be given a guided tour for orientation purposes. They need to know what you believe is important about your town. The tour can finish with lunch at a local restaurant. At lunch, the visitors will have an opportunity to ask questions and talk with community leaders about the town. After lunch, the professionals should be free to look around on their own to become as familiar as possible with your community. Some of them may wish to arrange special interviews with business representatives, utility managers, city officials, the industrial development authority, or the planning commission for more in-depth questioning in their specialty areas.

The professionals will have been instructed to write summary reports describing what they liked about your community and what they believe to be the marketable uniqueness of your town. They will also be invited to comment on any conditions they feel need improvement. This is all valuable marketing information and it can be obtained for a relatively modest cost. It is a good opportunity for you to get input on what your town is doing right, what it may be doing wrong, and where it could improve.

Promotion

Once your town has identified its differential advantage, you must successfully promote this uniqueness to prospective customers. Community marketers have four distinct areas from which to create a promotional mix. As mentioned earlier in this publication, these elements are advertising, personal selling, sales promotion, and publicity.

Advertising

Advertising is the promotional medium that communities use most often. It includes paid presentations in brochures, trade publications, magazines and newspapers, billboards, and other advertising media. Information on the community's uniqueness and its potential customers, gained through the techniques outlined in this publication, can help the community fine-tune its advertising to make it more efficient than before.

For example, let's say that a town is trying to attract tourist trade. Its visitor questionnaire has revealed that many of the town's guests are vacationers from large cities in the same state who are en route to a nearby resort area. This would suggest that the town buy ads in advertising media that will be seen by these prospective customers.

There are many advertising alternatives available. Use common sense in deciding how to spend your advertising dollar to communicate your message as efficiently as possible.

Personal Selling

The next element of the promotional mix, personal selling, consists of verbal conversation with prospective customers. Community residents are using personal selling every time they speak with others about their town. It is important for community leaders to realize that employees in contact with the public must conduct themselves as the town's sales representatives-because that is really what they are.

Another type of personal selling happens away from home. For example, if your town were to find that it had the ideal conditions and labor force to support electrical assembly operation, it could seek out a trade association serving this industry. Since most such organizations hold conventions, it might be possible for the town to rent a small booth in a trade mail at the association's next convention. If community salespeople were armed with good sales presentations, their personal selling efforts at the convention could pay off.

Likewise, a weekend booth at a shopping center in one of the larger cities in the state may be effective in attracting in-state visitors to your town.

Sales Promotion

The third element of the promotional mix is called sales promotion. It consists of coupons, trading stamps, balloons, bumper stickers, free entertainment, and other promotional items paid for by the marketer. Many towns already use some form of sales promotion, but these promotions are often not well-planned. Many communities hastily jump into a general advertising and promotion campaign before they have identified unique marketable products, and before they have identified their best potential customers.

When deciding to use a sales promotion, ask yourself two questions:

1) Will this promotion reach our prospective customers? 2) Will this promotion make a lasting impression upon our prospective customers—or will it soon be forgotten?

There is no specific formula for promotional success, but if you screen your activities in this fashion, you will probably eliminate most unwise sales promotions before they become unwise expenditures.

Publicity

Publicity differs from the first three elements of the promotional mix in a very important way—it's free. For small towns with small budgets, publicity can be an effective way to reach prospective customers who could never be reached through paid promotion.

Publicity usually materializes when some event or characteristic of a town becomes "newsworthy" in the eyes of the media-radio, television, magazine, or newspaper. Smart marketers know that many news stories exist only because someone put forth the effort to write a press release. A press release can often tie in with some of the town's other promotional activities. But the story won't be run if nobody writes it!

Familiarize yourself with techniques for writing good, concise press releases. This can greatly increase the chances of your press release resulting in a story on the front page of the newspaper's community section rather than in the editor's wastebasket. Make sure your town has a well managed publicity program to take advantage of this least expensive element of your promotional mix.

Most towns know that promotion is essential for growth to occur. By knowing who your customers are, and by knowing the unique features of your town, you can design a promotional message that can have a far greater impact than one designed on guesswork. By utilizing all four elements of the promotional mix to push your differential advantage, your town will be assured of running the most successful marketing campaign possible.

13

Packaging: a Tourism Marketing Tool

RURAL ECONOMIC DEVELOPMENT THROUGH TOURISM

Time is a valuable commodity for today's travelers. Dual-income families find it difficult to schedule vacation time; family members often have jobs or activities that conflict; or an individual's job makes long vacations impractical. As a result, more families and individuals are taking long weekend or holiday vacations, or extending business trips into short getaway vacations. Packaging is a popular technique used for attracting these customers, because packages make travel easier and more convenient.

In the hospitality and tourism industry, "packaging" is the process of combining two or more related and complementary offerings into a single-price offering. A package may include a wide variety of services such as lodging, meals, entrance fees to attractions, entertainment, transportation costs (air, auto, train, cab or bus), guide services, or other similar activities.

Packaging can also create a variety of benefits for participating businesses. This publication will:

Identify reasons for the increased popularity of packaging.

Address issues a business should consider when developing a package.

Describe the components of successful packages.

Discuss the process of pricing a package.

Why Packages Are Popular

Travel packages have become increasingly popular over the years. They are attractive because they benefit both the customer and participating businesses; packaging provides convenience and value to the customer, and added revenue for participating businesses.

Benefits to the Customer

Packaging can be an effective marketing tool to provide several customer benefits. These may include:

Ability to budget for trips. Packages include most of the components a customer must pay for during a trip. The customer pays at one time and has a good idea of the trip's total cost.

Increased convenience. Trips can be time consuming and difficult to arrange. Several telephone calls and letters may be required to arrange for tickets, accommodations, reservations, and other components of a trip. A package allows a customer to arrange many components of a trip with one call or letter and one payment, saving the customer time and aggravation.

Greater economy. Businesses that package can frequently purchase tickets, meals, and other package components at wholesale prices. The business can add in the cost of packaging and still provide a competitive price to the customer. Thus, the cost to the customer is usually more economical than purchasing the package components individually.

Popular programs and activities. Visitors and travelers are often unfamiliar with many of the activities and attractions in an area: a package can help customers find them easily.

Specialized interests. Packaging provides a unique opportunity to design components of a package for specialized interests. These so-called "benefit bundles" can include a package component not readily available to individual customers. For example, a package weekend may feature a cooking demonstration by a well-known chef or a lecture by a well-known author. Benefits to Participating Businesses

Packaging can be used by businesses to help improve profitability and build customer volume. Examples include:

Improved profitability. During peak or high-demand periods, use packaging to add value to an existing product. Purchasers may be required to stay a prescribed period or purchase a combination of goods and services. Packaging may also allow a business to price its product at a premium by adding special goods and services.

Smooth business patterns. Use packaging during low demand periods to add attractive features to the business's service or product, thus generating additional business. Other businesses may also be willing, to discount their services during this time. Adding these services to the existing product mix may generate new business.

Joint marketing opportunities. Packaging can allow the business to reduce marketing costs or start a new program one could not normally afford by joining with one or more businesses to conduct a marketing or advertising program. This strategy can be especially effective if the businesses involved have similar customers.

Improved target marketing. Packaging can be an effective tool to tailor tourism and travel products for specific target markets. Examples can be ski, sports, or theater weekends. Good market research is needed so an appropriate mix of tourism and travel services will meet the needs and desires of a target group of customers.

Greater holiday weekend business. Packaging can be used to highlight special holiday weekends by developing services appropriate to the theme of the weekend. New Year's, Valentine's Day, or Mother's Day are just a few of the holidays that can be used to develop special programs for parties, couples, or family gifts.

Unique recurring events. Businesses can create their own events that can occur throughout the year. Events could be tournaments such as chess or bridge or crime re-enactments that let guests do the detective work. Events of this type will require imagination and inventiveness to take advantage of the wide variety of activities that take place in the community. This technique is often called "programming."

Redirected traffic to lesser-known attractions. Directing visitors to often overlooked attractions can help in two ways: heavily visited attractions may be offered some relief, while newly discovered attractions may thrive and prosper.

Businesses can use many different strategies in designing a package product. Success will depend on good market research, an understanding of existing customers, research, an understanding of existing customers, and a good knowledge of the community and its activities.

Items to Consider in Developing a Package

Before developing a tourism packaging program, the business should devise a marketing plan through practical marketing research. The business owner should ask him/herself the following questions:

Are you willing to do market research to determine who your customers are and what they want?

What are the potential attractions, businesses, or marketing service firms that could provide a part of the package? Meet with the managers of these businesses and public attractions to discuss their interests and ideas.

What are potential marketing and promotional networks that will help spread the word about your product?

Convention and visitors bureaus, chambers of commerce, retail travel agents, clubs and organizations, state offices of tourism, and other attractions or travel businesses all have the potential to play an important role in merchandising your package.

Will the physical appearance and service skills of your business match the target audience?

Does your business have the ability to manage and service the customers you generate through your packaging program?

Are you prepared for a risk? Because you will be including customer service activities that are not under your direct control, you will be required to develop formal, written agreements between the cooperating businesses.

Elements of a Successful Package

Putting together a successful package is not easy. However, by following the suggestions listed below, the chances of success will be greater. Include attractions or demand generators. Every package needs one or more core attractions. These could be tickets to a special event, specialized programming, or reduced prices. Provide value to the customer. Many travelers buy packages because they perceive they will receive greater value for the travel dollars they spend. For some, this translates into a package that costs less than the sum of the regular prices of individual elements. Almost everybody is interested in getting something for nothing or next to nothing. Be well planned and coordinated. A successful package must be well planned and coordinated. Each element should flow naturally from one to the next. Use a theme to hold the package together and create a positive experience for the tourist.

Offer consistent quality and compatibility among elements. Many customers buy packages because they expect consistency in quality. Combine only package components that are compatible and enhance the overall quality of the traveler's experience. Customer dissatisfaction with one part of the package will often spoil the entire experience. Provide a distinctive customer benefit. The best packages provide customers something they would not get if they purchased package elements separately. Sometimes this benefit is the offer of value, but in other cases, it is a component that is not readily available to individual customers. This might involve incorporating special lectures or appearances, unique dining experiences, or other activities.

Cover all the details. The temptation might be to throw a package together, but the close attention to detail makes some packages more successful than others. Remember, it is often the little things a business does for guests that matter the most. Some things to consider include a policy on refunds and cancellations and complete information on all package elements included in the price, as well as items not included.

Generate a profit. Clearly, packages offer a unique way to satisfy traveler needs and wants. Of course, the package should also be designed to generate a profit. The ideal time to effer packages is when demand is low and when the package will not displace customers who may generate higher revenues.

Pricing a Package

Lodging or transportation—the most expensive parts of a package product-are usually the first contact points for customers who purchase a packaged vacation or travel product. Lodging operations or travel agents are usually the key to organizing a packaging program, even though an area's attractions may bring visitors to a community.

Although accommodations and transportation are the basic ingredients of a package, tickets to attractions, dining, and other services are other key parts of the product mix that make the package marketable. It is necessary for a business to understand its target market and conduct basic practical market research in order to develop a successful package. Experimenting with a set of packages can also help you identify which sets of activities are most attractive to your customers.

Issues to consider when pricing a package include:

The package must be a good value and competitive in the market. Customers should not be able to purchase separate items in the package for less than the package price. A large user of package components should be able to receive discounts from businesses that provide them. Evaluate the role packaging can play in the business's marketing program. While packaging can be used to implement many different strategies, the basic intent is to generate additional business.

Determine if the package is feasible by applying a break-even analysis to help determine how many packages a business must sell before earning a profit.

Break-Even Analysis

Break-even analysis is a tool used to determine total sales needed to recoup costs, hence the name "break-even." This analysis technique can also be used to evaluate alternative pricing levels.

14

Tourism and the Pub Culture

A pub that offers lodging may be called an inn or (more recently) hotel in the UK. Today many pubs in the UK, Canada and Australia with the word "inn" or "hotel" in their name no longer offer accommodation, or in some cases have never done so. Some pubs bear the name of "hotel" because they are in countries where stringent anti-drinking laws were once in force. In Scotland until 1976, only hotels could serve alcohol on Sundays.

Overview

There are approximately 57,500 public houses in the United Kingdom, with at least one in almost every city, town and village. In many places, especially in villages, a pub can be the focal point of the community, playing a complementary role to the local church in this respect. The writings of Samuel Pepys describe the pub as the heart of England and the church as its soul.

Public houses are culturally and socially different from places such as cafés, bars, bierkellers and brewpubs.

Pubs are social places based on the sale and consumption of alcoholic beverages, and most public houses offer a range of beers, wines, spirits, alcopops and soft drinks. Many pubs are controlled by breweries, so beer is often better value than wines and spirits, while soft drinks can be almost as expensive. Beer served in a pub may be cask ale or keg beer. All pubs also have a range of non-alcoholic beverages available. Traditionally the windows of town pubs are of smoked or frosted glass so that the clientèle is obscured from the street. In the last twenty years in the UK and other countries there has been a move away from frosted glass towards clear glass, a trend that fits in with brighter interior décors.

The owner, tenant or manager (licensee) of a public house is known as the publican or landlord. Each pub generally has "locals" or *regulars*; people who drink there regularly. The pub that people visit most often is called their *local*. In many cases, this will be the pub nearest to their home, but some people choose their *local* for other reasons: proximity to work, a venue for their friends, the availability of a particular cask ale, non-smoking or formerly as a place to smoke freely, or maybe a darts team or pool table.

Until the 1970s most of the larger public houses also featured an off-sales counter or attached shop for the sales of beers, wines and spirits for home consumption. In the 1970s the newly built supermarkets and high street chain stores or off-licences undercut the pub prices to such a degree that within ten short years all but a handful of pubs had closed their off-sale counters.

A society with a particular interest in British beers, ales and the preservation of the 'integrity' of the public house is Campaign for Real Ale, (CAMRA).

Another organisation, lauched in Dorset (initially) in 2009 is Community Alert on Pubs which seeks to prevent the closure of pubs which form part of the rural social fabric. A particular concern has been the practice of closing a pub and leaving it derelict as an eyesore until such time as the local authority may (or may not) grant a change of use e.g. for residential property development.

History

The inhabitants of the UK have been drinking ale since the Bronze Age, but it was with the arrival of the Romans and the establishment of the Roman road network that the first Inns called tabernae, in which the traveller could obtain refreshment, began to appear. By the time the Romans had left, the Anglo-Saxons had formed alehouses that grew out of domestic dwellings. The Saxon alewife would put a green bush up on a pole to let people know her brew was ready. These alehouses formed meeting houses for the locals to meet and gossip and arrange mutual help within their communities. Here lies the beginnings of the modern pub. They became so commonplace that in 965 King Edgar decreed that there should be no more than one alehouse per village.

A traveller in the early Middle Ages could obtain overnight accommodation in monasteries, but later a demand for hostelries grew with the popularity of pilgrimages and travel. The Hostellers of London were granted guild status in 1446 and in 1514 the guild became the Worshipful Company of Innholders.

Traditional English ale was made solely from fermented malt. The practice of adding hops to produce beer was introduced from the Netherlands in the early 15th century. Alehouses would each brew their own distinctive ale, but independent breweries began to appear in the late 17th century. By the end of the century almost all beer was brewed by commercial breweries.

The 18th century saw a huge growth in the number of drinking establishments, primarily due to the introduction of gin. Gin was brought to England by the Dutch after the Glorious Revolution of 1688 and started to become very popular after the government created a market for grain that was unfit to be used in brewing by allowing unlicensed gin production, whilst imposing a heavy duty on all imported spirits. As thousands of gin-shops sprang up all over England, brewers fought back by increasing the number of alehouses. By 1740 the production of gin had increased to six times that of beer and because of its cheapness it became popular with the poor, leading to the so-called Gin Craze. Over half of the 15,000 drinking establishments in London were gin-shops.

The drunkenness and lawlessness created by gin was seen to lead to ruination and degradation of the working classes. The distinction was illustrated by William Hogarth in his engravings *Beer Street* and *Gin Lane*. The Gin Act (1736) imposed high taxes on retailers but led to riots in the streets. The prohibitive duty was gradually reduced and finally abolished in 1742. The

1751 Gin Act however was more successful. It forced distillers to sell only to licensed retailers and brought gin-shops under the jurisdiction of local magistrates.

Beer Houses and the 1830 Beer Act

By the early 1800s and encouraged by a lowering of duties on gin, the gin houses or "Gin Palaces" had spread from London to most major cities and towns in Britain, with most of the new establishments illegal and unlicensed. These bawdy, loud and unruly drinking dens so often described by Charles Dickens in his Sketches by Boz (published 1835–6) increasingly came to be held as unbridled cesspits of immorality or crime and the source of much ill-health and alcoholism among the working classes.

The British government's eventual response to the problem seems strange now to modern eyes. Under a banner of "reducing public drunkenness" the Beer Act of 1830 introduced a new lower tier of premises permitted to sell alcohol, the **Beer Houses**. At the time beer was viewed as harmless, nutritious and even healthy. Young children were often given what was described as small beer, which was brewed to have a low alcohol content, to drink, as the local water was often unsafe. Even the evangelical church and temperance movements of the day viewed the drinking of beer very much as a secondary evil and a normal accompaniment to a meal. The freely available beer was thus intended to wean the drinkers off the evils of gin, or so the thinking went.

Under the 1830 Act any householder who paid rates could apply, with a one-off payment of two guineas, to sell beer or cider in his home (usually the front parlour) and even brew his own on his premises. The permission did not extend to the sale of spirits and fortified wines and any beer house discovered selling those items were closed down and the owner heavily fined. Beer houses were not permitted to open on Sundays. The beer was usually served in jugs or dispensed direct from tapped wooden barrels lying on a table in the corner of the room. Often profits were so high the owners were able to buy the house next door to live in, turning every room in their former home into bars and lounges for customers. In the first year four hundred beer houses opened but within eight years there were 46,000 opened across the country, far outnumbering the combined total of long established taverns, public houses, inns and hotels. Because it was so easy to obtain permission and the profits could be huge compared to the low cost of gaining permission, the number of beer houses was continuing to rise and in some towns nearly every other house in a street could be a Beer House. Finally in 1869 the growth had to be checked by magisterial control and new licensing laws were introduced. Only then was the ease by which permission could be obtained reduced and the licensing laws which operate today formulated.

Although the new licensing laws prevented any new beer houses from being created, those already in existence were allowed to continue and many did not fully die out until nearly the end of the 19th century. A vast majority of the beer houses applied for the new licences and became full public houses. These usually small establishments can still be identified in many towns, seemingly oddly located in the middle of otherwise terraced housing part way up a street, unlike purpose built pubs that are usually found on corners or road junctions. Many of today's respected real ale micro-brewers in the UK started as home based Beer House brewers under the 1830 Act.

The beer houses also tended to avoid the traditional public house names like *The Crown*, *The Red Lion*, *The Royal Oak* etc and, if they didn't simply name their place *Smith's Beer House*, they would apply topical pub names in an effort to reflect the mood of the times.

Licensing Laws

From the middle of the 19th century restrictions were placed on the opening hours of licensed premises in the UK. However licensing was gradually liberalised after the 1960s, until contested licensing applications became very rare, and the remaining administrative function was transferred to Local Authorities in 2005.

The Wine and Beerhouse Act 1869 reintroduced the stricter controls of the previous century. The sale of beers, wines or spirits required a licence for the premises from the local magistrates. Further provisions regulated gaming, drunkenness, prostitution and undesirable conduct on licensed premises, enforceable by prosecution or more effectively by the landlord under threat of forfeiting his licence. Licences were only granted, transferred or renewed at special Licensing Sessions courts, and were limited to respectable individuals. Often these were ex-servicemen or ex-policemen; retiring to run a pub was popular amongst military officers at the end of their service. Licence conditions varied widely, according to local practice. They would specify permitted hours, which might require Sunday closing, or conversely permit all-night opening near a market. Typically they might require opening throughout the permitted hours, and the provision of food or lavatories. Once obtained, licences were jealously protected by the licensees (always individuals expected to be generally present, not a remote owner or company), and even "Occasional Licences" to serve drinks at temporary premises such as fêtes would usually be granted only to existing licensees. Objections might be made by the police, rival landlords or anyone else on the grounds of infractions such as serving drunks, disorderly or dirty premises, or ignoring permitted hours.

Detailed records were kept on licensing, giving the Public House, its address, owner, licensee and misdemeanours of the licensees for periods often going back for hundreds of years. Many of these records survive and can be viewed, for example, at the London Metropolitan Archives centre.

These culminated in the Defence of the Realm Act of August 1914, which, along with the introduction of rationing and the censorship of the press for wartime purposes, also restricted the opening hours of public houses to 12noon–2.30pm and 6.30pm–9.30pm. Opening for the full licensed hours was compulsory, and closing time was equally firmly enforced by the police; a landlord might lose his licence for infractions. There was a special case established under the State Management Scheme where the brewery and licensed premises were bought and run by the state until 1973, most notably in the Carlisle District. During the 20th century elsewhere, both the licensing laws and enforcement were progressively relaxed, and there were differences between parishes; in the 1960s, at closing time in Kensington at 10.30 pm, drinkers would rush over the parish boundary to be in good time for "Last Orders" in Knightsbridge before 11 pm, a practice observed in many pubs adjoining licensing area boundaries. Some Scottish and Welsh parishes remained officially "dry" on Sundays (although often this merely required knocking at the back door of the pub).

However, closing times were increasingly disregarded in the country pubs. In England and Wales by 2000 pubs could legally open from 11am (12 noon on Sundays) through to 11pm (10.30pm on Sundays). That year was also the first to allow continuous opening for 36 hours from 11am on New Year's Eve to 11pm on New Year's Day. In addition, many cities had by-laws to allow some pubs to extend opening hours to midnight or 1am, whilst nightclubs had long been granted late licences to serve alcohol into the morning. Pubs in the immediate vicinity of London's Smithfield market, Billingsgate fish market and Covent Garden fruit and flower market were permitted to stay open 24 hours a day since Victorian era times to provide a service to the shift working employees of the markets. These restricted opening hours led to the tradition of lock-ins.

Scotland's and Northern Ireland's licensing laws have long been more flexible, allowing local authorities to set pub opening and closing times. In Scotland, this stemmed out of a late repeal of the wartime licensing laws, which stayed in force until 1976.

The Licensing Act 2003, which came into force on November 24, 2005, aimed to consolidate the many laws into a single act. This now allows pubs in England and Wales to apply to the local authority for opening hours of their choice. Supporters at the time argued that it would end the concentration of violence around half past 11, when people had to leave the pub, making policing easier. In practice, alcohol-related hospital admissions rose following the change in the law, with alcohol involved in 207,800 admissions in 2006/7. Critics claimed that these laws will lead to '24-hour drinking'. By the day before the law came into force, 60,326 establishments had applied for longer hours, and 1,121 had applied for a licence to sell alcohol 24 hours a day. However, nine months after the act many pubs had not changed their hours, although there is a growing tendency for some to be open longer at the weekend but rarely beyond 1:00 am.

Indoor Smoking Ban

In July 2007, a law was introduced to forbid smoking in all enclosed public places in England and Wales. Scotland had introduced the ban in April 2006. Concerns by publicans prior to the ban that a smoking ban would have a negative impact on sales appear to have come true with Wetherspoons reporting a 16% fall in profits, and Scottish & Newcastle's take over by Carlsberg and Heineken being reported as partly the result of its weakness following falling sales due to the ban.

To accommodate the remaining smokers most pubs, that have the space, have provided outdoor facilities. These can range from a simple picnic bench table with a parasol umbrella in the garden or carpark, to a purpose built brick lean-to with a tiled roof. The law states that the facility must be open on at least one side and cannot be in an area where nonsmokers have to pass while entering or leaving the pub premises. Country pubs with plenty of space and beer gardens have adapted to the changes reasonably easily, but smaller city centre pubs on the pavement edge and with no rear gardens have suffered significant losses of custom by not being able to provide a suitable smoking area.

PUB ARCHITECTURE

The Saloon or Lounge

By the end of the 18th century a new room in the pub was established: the saloon. Beer establishments had always provided entertainment of some sort — singing, gaming or a sport. Balls Pond Road in Islington was named after an establishment run by a Mr. Ball that had a pond at the rear filled with ducks, where drinkers could, for a certain fee, go out and take a potshot at shooting the fowl. More common, however, was a card room or a billiards room. The saloon was a room where for an admission fee or a higher price of drinks, singing, dancing, drama or comedy was performed and drinks would be served at your table. From this came the popular music hall form of entertainment—a show consisting of a variety of acts. A most famous London saloon was the Grecian Saloon in *The Eagle*, City Road, which is still famous these days because of an English nursery rhyme: "Up and down the City Road / In and out The Eagle / That's the way the money goes / Pop goes the weasel.". The implication being that, having frequented the Eagle public house, the customer spent all his money, and thus needed to 'pawn' his 'weasel' to get some more. The exact definition of the 'weasel' is unclear but the two most likely definitions are: that a weasel is a flat iron used for finishing clothing; or that 'weasel' is rhyming slang for a coat (*weasel and stoat*).

A few pubs have stage performances, such as serious drama, stand-up comedians, a musical band or striptease; however juke boxes and other forms pre-recorded music have otherwise replaced the musical tradition of a piano and singing.

The Public Bar

By the 20th century, the saloon, or lounge bar, had settled into a middle-class room — carpets on the floor, cushions on the seats, and a penny or two on the prices, while the public bar, or tap room, remained working class with bare boards, sometimes with sawdust to absorb the spitting and spillages, hard bench seats, and cheap beer.

Later, the public bars gradually improved until sometimes almost the only difference was in the prices, so that customers could choose between economy and exclusivity (or youth and age, or a jukebox or dartboard). During the blurring of the class divisions in the 1960s and 1970s, the distinction between the saloon and the public bar was often seen as archaic, and was frequently abolished, usually by the removal of the dividing wall or partition itself. While the names of saloon and public bar may still be seen on the doors of pubs, the prices (and often the standard of furnishings and decoration) are the same throughout the premises, and many pubs now comprise one large room. However, the modern importance of dining in pubs encourages some establishments to maintain distinct rooms or areas, especially where the building has the right characteristics for this. Yet, in a few pubs there still remain rooms or seats that, by local custom, "belong" to particular customers.

However there still remain a few, mainly city centre pubs, that retain a public bar mainly for working men that call in for a drink while still dressed in working clothes and dirty boots. They are now very much in a minority, but some landlords prefer to separate the manual workers from the more smartly dressed businessmen or diners in the lounge or restaurant.

The Snug

The "snug", also sometimes called the *Smoke room*, was typically a small, very private room with access to the bar that had a frosted glass external window, set above head height. You paid a higher price for your beer in the Snug, but nobody could look in and see you. It was not only the well off visitors who would use these rooms. The snug was for patrons who preferred not to be seen in the public bar. Ladies would often enjoy a private drink in the snug in a time when it was frowned upon for ladies to be in a pub. The local police officer would nip in for a quiet pint, the parish priest for his evening whisky, and lovers would use the snug for their clandestine visits.

The Counter

It was the public house that first introduced the concept of the bar counter being used to serve the beer. Until that time beer establishments used to bring the beer out to the table or benches. A bar might be provided for the manager to do his paperwork whilst keeping an eye on his customers, but the casks of ale were kept in a separate taproom. When the first public houses were built, the main room was the public room with a large serving bar copied from the gin houses, the idea being to serve the maximum amount of people in the shortest possible time. It became known as the public bar. The other, more private, rooms had no serving bar - they had the beer brought to them from the public bar. There are a number of pubs in the Midlands or the North which still retain this set up. But these days you fetch the beer yourself from the taproom or public bar. The most famous of these is The Vine, known locally as The Bull & Bladder, in Brierley Hill near Birmingham.

Isambard Kingdom Brunel, the British engineer and railway builder, introduced the idea of a circular bar into the Swindon station pub in order that customers were served quickly and didn't delay his trains. These island bars quickly became popular as they also allowed staff to serve customers in several different rooms surrounding the bar. In a modern renovated pub, where the partitions between rooms have been removed, the island can be clearly seen.

Beer engine

A "beer engine" is a device for pumping beer, originally manually operated and typically used to dispense beer from a cask or container in a pub's basement or cellar. It was invented by the locksmith and hydraulic engineer Joseph Bramah. Strictly the term refers to the pump itself, which is normally manually operated, though electrically powered and gas powered pumps are occasionally used; when manually powered, the term "handpump" is often used to refer to both the pump and the associated handle.

ENTERTAINMENT

Games and Sports

Traditional games are played in pubs, ranging from the well-known darts, skittles, dominoes, cards and bar billiards, to the more obscure Aunt Sally, Nine Men's Morris and ringing the bull. Betting is legally limited to certain games such as cribbage or dominoes, but these are now rarely seen. In recent decades the game of pool (both the British and American versions) has increased in popularity, other table based games such as snooker, Table Football are also common.

Increasingly, more modern games such as video games and slot machines are provided. Many pubs also hold special events, from tournaments of the aforementioned games to karaoke nights to pub quizzes. Some play pop music and hip-hop (dance bar), or show football and rugby union on big screen televisions (sports bar). Shove ha'penny and Bat and trap was also popular in pubs south of London.

Many pubs in the UK also have football teams composed of regular customers. Many of these teams are in leagues that play matches on Sundays, hence the term "Sunday League Football".

Music

While many pubs play piped pop music, the pub is often a venue for live song and live music. See:

- Pub rock - bands such as Kilburn and the High Roads, Dr. Feelgood or The Kursaal Flyers
- Pub songs from Skiffle to Danny Boy
- Folk music

The pub has also been celebrated in popular music. Examples are "Hurry Up Harry" by the 1970s punk rock act Sham 69, the chorus of which was the chant "We're going down the pub" repeated several times. Another such song is "Two Pints Of Lager and a Packet of Crisps Please!" by UK punk band Splodgenessabounds.

As a reaction against piped music, the Quiet Pub Guide was written, telling its readers where to go to avoid piped music.

Food

Traditionally pubs in England were drinking establishments and little emphasis was placed on the serving of food, usually called 'bar snacks', of which the usual fare consisted of specialised English snack food such as pork scratchings, pickled eggs, along with crisps and peanuts — salted snacks sold or given away to increase customers' thirst. If a pub served meals they were usually basic cold dishes such as a ploughman's lunch. In South East England (especially London) it was common until recent times for vendors selling cockles, whelks, mussels and other shellfish, to sell to customers during the evening and at closing time. Many mobile shellfish stalls would set up near to popular pubs, a practice that continues in London's East End.

In the 1950s most British pubs would offer "a pie and a pint", with hot individual steak and ale pies made easily on the premises by the landlord's wife. In the 1960s and 1970s this developed into the then fashionable and universal "chicken in a basket", a portion of roast chicken with chips, served on a napkin, in a small wicker basket.

The offering in Irish pubs has always been a hearty experience, with fresh local food being offered. In less well-off times this would have been a stew and some fresh soda bread but today all over the world you can enjoy the best of food locally supplied.

Since the 1990s food has become more important as part of a pub's trade and today most pubs serve lunches and dinners at the table (colloquially this is known in England as *pub grub*) in addition to (or instead of) snacks consumed at the bar. They may have a separate dining room. Some pubs serve excellent meals that can rival a good restaurant's. A pub that claims to focus on quality food (perhaps rather than necessarily on good beer) will now call itself a gastropub. The growth in importance of food, and the appeal of eating informally in a pub rather than with the formality expected in a restaurant, has led to some establishments giving all tables over to food and removing the bar stools (even though a visitor expecting a quick drink and a conversation at the bar is likely to receive short shrift at such places, there is no legal bar to such a licensed restaurant calling itself a pub).

PUB GRUB

"Pub grub" is food that is typically found in a pub. A British pub menu tends to include items such as beef and ale pie, steak and kidney pie, shepherd's pie, fish and chips, bangers and mash, hot pot, Sunday roast, ploughman's lunch, pasties. Some dishes that are quite specific to pubs include chicken or scampi in a basket, and meals served in plate-sized Yorkshire puddings. In addition, international dishes such as burgers, curry, lasagne and chilli con carne are often served.

Typically pub food is ordered at the bar and paid for in advance. Customers traditionally seat themselves, and are often given a number, or a unique table marker, to assist the barstaff in delivering their food.

Gastropub

A gastropub is a pub which specialises in high-quality food a step above the more basic "pub grub." The name is a combination of pub and gastronomy and was coined in 1991 when David Eyre and Mike Belben opened a pub called The Eagle in Clerkenwell, London. They placed emphasis on the quality of food served.

In 1393 King Richard II compelled landlords to erect signs outside their premises. The legislation stated "Whosoever shall brew ale in the town with intention of selling it must hang out a sign, otherwise he shall forfeit his ale." This was in order to make them easily visible to passing inspectors, borough ale tasters, who would decide the quality of the ale they provided. William Shakespeare's father, John Shakespeare was one such inspector. Another important factor was that during the Middle Ages a large percentage of the population would have been illiterate and so pictures on a sign were more useful than words as a means of identifying a public house. For this reason there was often no reason to write the establishment's name on the sign and inns opened without a formal written name—the name being derived later from the illustration on the public house's sign.

The earliest signs were often not painted but consisted, for example, of paraphernalia connected with the brewing process such as bunches of hops or brewing implements, which were suspended above the door of the public house. In some cases local nicknames, farming terms and puns were also used. Local events were also often commemorated in pub signs. Simple natural or religious symbols such as the 'The Sun', 'The Star' and 'The Cross' were also incorporated into pub signs, sometimes being adapted to incorporate elements of the heraldry (e.g. the coat of arms) of the local lords who owned the lands upon which the public house stood. Some pubs also have Latin inscriptions.

Other subjects that lent themselves to visual depiction included the name of battles (e.g. Trafalgar), explorers, local notables, discoveries, sporting heroes and members of the royal family. Some pub signs are in the form of a pictorial pun or rebus. For example, a pub in Crowborough, East Sussex called *The Crow and Gate* has an image of a crow with gates as wings.

Most British pubs still have decorated signs hanging over their doors, and these retain their original function of enabling the identification of the public house. Today's pub signs almost always bear the name of the pub, both in words and in pictorial representation. The more remote country pubs often have stand-alone signs directing potential customers to their door.

Names

Pubs often have traditional names. A very common name is the "Marquis of Granby". These pubs were named after John Manners, Marquess of Granby, who was the son of John Manners, 3rd Duke of Rutland) and a general in the 18th century British Army. He showed a great concern for the welfare of his men, and on their retirement, provided funds for many of them to establish taverns, which were subsequently named after him. The name may also have gained popularity because of the novel The Pickwick Papers. In that much-loved book, Charles Dickens depicted a character, Tony Weller, who was owner (by marriage) of a pub named The Marquis of Granby.

Many names for pubs that appear nonsensical may have come from corruptions of old slogans or phrases, or of certain nobles' or politicians' names. Often, these corruptions evoke a visual image which comes to signify the pub; these images had particular importance for identifying a pub on signs and other media before literacy became widespread. An example is the pub name *The Goat and Compasses*, which is said to be a corruption of the phrase "God encompasseth us". Another example of a mistaken pub name is the Oyster Reach pub in Ipswich, England. This pub spent several decades being called the Ostrich, before historians informed the owners of the original name. More possible but uncorroborated corruptions include "The Bag o'Nails" (Bacchanals), "Elephant and Castle", (Infanta de Castile), "The Cat and the Fiddle" (Caton Fidele) and "The Bull and Bush", which purportedly celebrates the victory of Henry VIII at "Boulogne Bouche" or Boulogne-sur-Mer Harbour. While these corruptions are amusing there are usually more substantiated explanations available.

A too-obviously humorous name is likely to be a recent coining of a marketing executive, rather than traditional. This is especially true for names with unsubtle double-entendres or names that have elements common to all the pubs in a particular chain (eg "XXXX and Firkin").

TYPES OF PUBS

After the development of the large London Porter breweries in the 18th century, the trend grew for pubs to become tied houses which could only sell beer from one brewery (a pub not tied in this way was called a Free house). The usual arrangement for a tied house was that the pub was owned by the brewery but rented out to a private individual (landlord) who ran it as a separate business (even though contracted to buy the beer from the brewery). Another very common arrangement was (and is) for the landlord to own the premises (whether freehold or leasehold) independently of the brewer, but then to take a mortgage loan from a brewery, either to finance the purchase of the pub initially, or to refurbish it, and be required as a term of the loan to observe the solus tie. A growing trend in the late 20th century was for the brewery to run their pubs directly, employing a salaried manager (who perhaps could make extra money by commission, or by selling food).

Most such breweries, such as the regional brewery Shepherd Neame in Kent and Young's in London, control hundreds of pubs in a particular region of the UK, whilst a few, such as Greene King, are spread nationally. The landlord of a tied pub may be an employee of the brewery—in which case he would be a manager of a managed house, or a self-employed tenant who has entered into a lease agreement with a brewery, a condition of which is the legal obligation (trade tie) only to purchase that brewery's beer. This tied agreement provides tenants with trade premises at a below market rent providing people with a low-cost entry into self-employment. The beer selection is mainly limited to beers brewed by that particular company. A Supply of Beer law, passed in 1989, was aimed at getting tied houses to offer at least one alternative beer, known as a guest beer, from another brewery.This law has now been repealed but while in force it dramatically altered the industry.

The period since the 1980s saw many breweries absorbed by, or becoming by take-overs, larger companies in the food, hotel or property sectors. The low returns of a pub-owning business led to many breweries selling their pub estates, especially those in cities, often to a new generation of small chains, many of which have now grown considerably and have a national presence. Other pub chains, such as *All Bar One* and *Slug and Lettuce* offer youth-oriented atmospheres, often in premises larger than traditional pubs.

A free house is a pub that is free of the control of any one particular brewery. "Free" in this context does not necessarily mean "independent", and the view that "free house" on a pub sign is a guarantee of a quality, range or type of beer available is a mistake. Many free houses are *not* independent family businesses but are owned by large pub companies. In fact, these days there are very few *truly free* houses, either because a private pub owner has had to come to a financial arrangement with a brewer or other company in order to fund the purchase of the pub, or simply because the pub is owned by one of the large pub chains and pub companies (PubCos) which have sprung up in recent years. Some chains have rather uniform pubs and products, some allow managers some freedom. Wetherspoons, one of the largest pub chains does sell large amounts of a wide variety of real ale at low prices - but its pubs are not *specifically* "real ale pubs", being in the city centre to attract the Saturday night crowds and so also selling large quantities of alcopops and big-brand lager to large groups of young people.

Companies and Chains

Organisations such as Wetherspoons and the Eerie Pub Company, were formed in the UK since changes in legislation in the 1980s necessitated the break-up of many larger tied estates. A PubCo is a company involved in the retailing but not the manufacture of beverages, while a Pub chain may be run either by a PubCo or by a brewery. If the owning company is not a brewery, then the pub is technically a 'free house', however limited the manager is in his/her beer-buying choice.

Pubs within a chain will usually have items in common, such as fittings, promotions, ambience and range of food and drink on offer. A pub chain will position itself in the marketplace for a target audience. One company may run several pub chains aimed at different segments of the market. Pubs for use in a chain are bought and sold in large units, often from regional breweries which are then closed down. Newly acquired pubs are often renamed by the new owners, and many people resent the loss of traditional names, especially if their favourite regional beer disappears at the same time. A small number of pub chains (usually small ones) are noted for the independence they grant their managers, and hence the wide range of beers available.

Theme Pubs

Pubs that cater for a niche audience, such as sports fans or people of certain nationalities are known as **theme pubs**. Examples of theme pubs include sports bars, rock pubs, biker pubs, Goth pubs, strip pubs, and Irish pubs (see below).

In Canada the majority of theme pubs are referred to as bars, such as 'biker bar', 'sports bar', 'gay bar', 'strip bar', etc. Pubs centred on dance floors featuring DJ's or less often, live music, are usually referred to as 'dance clubs'.

In the U.S., almost all drinking establishments called "pubs" are simply bars with an Irish or British theme.

Country Pub

A "country pub" by tradition is a rural public house. However, the distinctive culture surrounding country pubs, that of functioning as a social centre for a village and countryside community, has been changing over the last thirty or so years. In the past, many rural pubs provided opportunities for country folk to meet and exchange (often local) news, while others - especially those away from village centres - existed for the general purpose, before the advent of motor transport, of serving travellers as coaching inns.

In more recent years, however, many country pubs have either closed down, or have been converted to establishments more intent on providing seating facilities for the consumption of food, than that of the local community meeting and convivially drinking.

Organisations such as CAMRA (Campaign for Real Ale) show real concern that these trends be reverted before the inevitable disappearance of the country pub.

UK Pubs of Interest

Contenders for the smallest pub in the UK include:

- The Nutshell in Bury St Edmunds
- The Lakeside Inn, Southport
- The Little Gem, in Aylesford, Kent.

The largest pub in the UK is The Regal, Cambridge, converted from a former cinema.

Oldest pub contenders include:

- The Bingley Arms, Leeds
- Ye Olde Trip To Jerusalem, Nottingham
- Ye Olde Fighting Cocks, St Albans

PUBS OUTSIDE BRITAIN

Although "British" or "Irish" pubs found outside of Britain and its former areas of influence are, as previously mentioned, often themed bars owing little to the original British public house, a number of "true" pubs may be found around the world. In Denmark - a country, like Britain, with a long tradition of brewing - a number of pubs have opened which eschew "theming", and who instead focus on the business of providing carefully conditioned beer, often independent of any particular brewery or chain, in an environment which would not be unfamiliar to a British pub-goer. Some go to the considerable trouble of importing British cask ale, rather than kegs, in order to provide the full British real ale experience to their customers. This newly-established Danish interest in British cask beer and the British pub tradition is reflected by the fact that some 56 British cask beers were available at the 2008 European Beer Festival in Copenhagen, which was attended by more than 21,000 people.

In Popular Culture

Inns and taverns feature throughout English literature and poetry, from Chaucer onwards. All the major soap operas on British television feature a pub, with their 'pub' becoming a household name. The Rovers Return is the pub on *Coronation Street*, the British soap broadcast on ITV. The Queen Vic (short for the Queen Victoria) is the pub on *EastEnders*, the major soap on BBC One, while The Bull in *The Archers* and the Woolpack on *Emmerdale* are also central meeting points. The sets of each of the three major television soap operas have been visited by royalty, including Queen Elizabeth II. The centrepiece of each visit was a trip into the Rovers, the Vic or the Woolpack to be offered a drink.

Much of the plot-line in British film *Shaun of the Dead* involves the characters trying to reach their local public house, The Winchester, to escape a zombie invasion.

Another famous fictional pub is The Nag's Head featured in the BBC sitcom Only Fools and Horses.

British comedian Al Murray's best-known character is a comic right-wing pub-owner, "The Pub Landlord", not necessarily a representation of the southern-English pub landlord.

US president George W. Bush fulfilled his ambition of visiting a 'genuine English pub' during his November 2003 state visit to the UK when he had lunch and a pint of non-alcoholic lager with British Prime Minister Tony Blair at the Dun Cow pub in Sedgefield, County Durham.

Lock-in

A "lock-in'" is when the owner of a public house allows a number of patrons to continue staying in the pub after the legal closing time. The origin of the lock-in was a reaction to changes in the licensing laws in England and Wales in 1915, which curtailed opening hours to stop factory workers turning up drunk and harming the war effort. Since 1915 the licensing laws changed very little, leaving the United Kingdom with comparatively early closing times. The tradition of the lock in therefore remained and is on the whole a peculiarly British concept.

The attraction for many was that lock-ins were secret, a conspiracy between publican and patron. Also, they were exclusive, usually with only a few select regulars. The lock-in became a tradition. While publicans risked losing their licences by allowing them, police often turned a blind eye if things were kept low key.

As a result of the Licensing Act 2003 premises in England and Wales may apply to extend their opening hours beyond 11 pm, allowing round-the-clock drinking and removing much of the need for lock-ins.

In other areas, a "lock-in" occurs when a violent, or potentially-violent patron is removed from the premises, and the doors are deadlocked to prevent the individual(s) from re-entering, and to prevent patrons inside from leaving for a short duration so as to prevent contact with aggressors (as a measure of duty of care). During the lock-in period, it is often a traditional courtesy of the venue to provide free drinks and snacks. This practice depends on the local public liability laws and is far less common where bouncers are used.

Ireland

Irish pubs are known for their atmosphere or "craic". In Irish, a pub is referred to as *teach tábhairne* ("tavern-house") or *teach an óil* ("house of drink").

The general history and tradition of the Irish pub mirrors that of the UK.

15

Tourism and Restaurant

A **restaurant** prepares and serves food and drink to customers. Meals are generally served and eaten on premises, but many restaurants also offer take-out and food delivery services. Restaurants vary greatly in appearance and offerings, including a wide variety of cuisines and service models.

A restaurant owner is called a *restaurateur*; both words derive from the French verb *restaurer*, meaning "to restore". Professional artisans of cooking are called chefs, while prep staff and line cooks prepare food items in a more systematic and less artistic fashion.

HISTORY

Islamic World

Restaurants came into existence throughout the medieval Islamic world before doing so in China. The Islamic world had "restaurants where one could purchase all sorts of prepared dishes." These restaurants were mentioned by Al-Muqaddasi (born 945) in the late 10th century.

Restaurants in medieval Islamic Spain served three-course meals, which was earlier introduced in the 9th century by Ziryab, who insisted that meals should be served in three separate courses consisting of soup, the main course, and dessert.

The concept of the take-away restaurant was later developed by the Bengali Muslim entrepreneur Sake Dean Mahomed (1759–1851). After migrating to England, he founded the Hindoostanee Coffee House in 1810. It was an Indian curry house that operated on George Street, Central London.

China

Food catering establishments which may be described as restaurants were known since the 11th century in Kaifeng, China's northern capital during the first half of the Song Dynasty (960–1279). With a population of over 1 million people, a culture of hospitality and a paper currency, Kaifeng was ripe for the development of restaurants. Probably growing out of the tea houses and taverns that catered to travellers, Kaifeng's restaurants blossomed into an industry catering to locals as well as people from other regions of China. Stephen H. West argues that there was a direct correlation between the growth of restaurant businesses and institutions of theatrical stage drama, gambling, and prostitution which served the burgeoning merchant middle class during the Song.

Restaurants catered to different styles of cuisine, price brackets, and religious requirements. Even within a single restaurant much choice was available, and people ordered the entree they wanted from written menus. An account from 1275 writes of Hangzhou, the capital city for the last half of the dynasty:

> *"The people of Hangzhou are very difficult to please. Hundreds of orders are given on all sides: this person wants something hot, another something cold, a third something tepid, a fourth something chilled; one wants cooked food, another raw, another chooses roast, another grill".*

The restaurants in Hangzhou also catered to many northern Chinese who had fled south from Kaifeng during the Jurchen invasion of the 1120s, while it is also known that many restaurants were run by families formerly from Kaifeng.

Ma Yu Ching's Bucket Chicken House was established in Kaifeng in 1153 AD during the Jurchen-controlled Jin Dynasty (though documentation does not exist to prove continuous service) and is still serving meals today.

Western World

In the West, while inns and taverns were known from antiquity, these were establishments aimed at travellers, and in general locals would rarely eat there. Restaurants, as businesses dedicated to the serving of food, and where specific dishes are ordered by the guest and generally prepared according to this order, emerged only in the 18th century. According to the Guinness Book of Records, the Sobrino de Botin in Madrid, Spain, is the oldest restaurant in existence today. It opened in 1725. Another claim to be the world's oldest restaurant is made by Stiftskeller St. Peter in Salzburg, which has been in existence since 803 AD, since the time of emperor Charlemagne.

The term *restaurant* (from the French *restaurer*, to restore) first appeared in the 16th century, meaning "a food which restores", and referred specifically to a rich, highly flavoured soup. It was first applied to an eating establishment in around 1765 founded by a Parisian soup-seller named Boulanger. The first restaurant in the form that became standard (customers sitting down with individual portions at individual tables, selecting food from menus, during fixed opening hours) was the Grand Taverne de Londres (the "Great Tavern of London"), founded in Paris in 1782 by a man named Antoine Beauvilliers, a leading culinary writer and gastronomic authority who achieved a reputation as a successful restaurateur. He later wrote what became a standard cookbook, *L'Art du cuisinier* (1814).

Restaurants became commonplace in France after the French Revolution broke up catering guilds and forced the aristocracy to flee, leaving a retinue of servants with the skills to cook excellent food; whilst at the same time numerous provincials arrived in Paris with no family to cook for them. Restaurants were the means by which these two could be brought together — and the French tradition of dining out was born.

A leading restaurant of the Napoleonic era was the Véry, which was lavishly decorated and boasted a menu with extensive choices of soups, fish and meat dishes, and scores of side dishes. Balzac often dined there. Although absorbed by a neighboring business in 1869, the resulting establishment Le Grand Véfour is still in business. The restaurant described by Britannica as the most illustrious of all those in Paris in the 19th century was the Café Anglais (the "English coffee-shop") on the Boulevard des Italiens, showing for a second time the high regard that Parisians evidently had for London, England, and the English — at least when it came to naming their restaurants.

Restaurants then spread rapidly across the world, with the first in the United States (*Jullien's Restarator*) opening in Boston in 1794. The oldest restaurant with contiguous operation in the United States, Union Oyster House is also in Boston and has been open since 1826. Most restaurants continued on the standard approach of providing a shared meal on the table to which customers would then help themselves (*Service à la française*, commonly called "family style" restaurants), something which encouraged them to eat rather quickly. Another formal style of dining, where waiters carry platters of food around the table and diners serve themselves, is known as *Service à la russe*, as it is said to have been introduced to France by the Russian Prince Kurakin in the 1810s, from where it spread rapidly to England and beyond. The familiar pattern of service where customers are given a plate with the food already arranged on it is called "American Service," though it surely did not originate in America...

TYPES OF RESTAURANTS

Restaurants range from unpretentious lunching or dining places catering to people working nearby, with simple food served in simple settings at low prices, to expensive establishments serving refined food and wines in a formal setting. In the former case, customers usually wear casual clothing. In the latter case, depending on culture and local traditions, customers might wear semi-casual, semi-formal, or even in rare cases formal wear.

Typically, customers sit at tables, their orders are taken by a waiter, who brings the food when it is ready, and the customers pay the bill before leaving. In finer restaurants there will be a host or hostess or even a maître d'hôtel to welcome customers and to seat them. Other staff waiting on customers include busboys and sommeliers. Restaurants often specialize in certain types of food or present a certain unifying, and often entertaining, theme. For example, there are seafood restaurants, vegetarian restaurants or ethnic restaurants. Generally speaking, restaurants selling "local" food are simply called restaurants, while restaurants selling food of foreign origin are called accordingly, for example, a *Chinese restaurant* and a *French restaurant*.

Restaurant Regulations

Depending on local customs and the establishment, restaurants may or may not serve alcohol. Restaurants are often prohibited from selling alcohol without a meal by alcohol sale laws; such sale is considered to be activity for bars, which are meant to have more severe restrictions. Some restaurants are licensed to serve alcohol ("fully licensed"), and/or permit customers to "bring your own" alcohol (BYO / BYOB). In some places restaurant licenses may restrict service to beer, or wine and beer.

Restaurant Guides

Restaurant guides review restaurants, often ranking them or providing information for consumer decisions (type of food, handicap accessibility, facilities, etc). In 12th century Hanzhou (mentioned above as the location of the first restaurant,) signs could often be found posted in the city square listing the restaurants in the area and local customer's opinions of the quality of their food. This was an occasion for bribery and even violence. Today, restaurant review is carried out in a more civilized manner. One of the most famous contemporary guides, in Western Europe, is the Michelin series of guides which accord from 1 to 3 stars to restaurants they perceive to be of high culinary merit.

Restaurants with stars in the Michelin guide are formal, expensive establishments; in general the more stars awarded, the higher the prices. The main competitor to the Michelin guide in Europe is the guidebook series published by Gault Millau. Unlike the Michelin guide which takes the restaurant décor and service into consideration with its rating, Gault Millau only judges the quality of the food. Its ratings are on a scale of 1 to 20, with 20 being the highest.

In the United States, the Mobil Travel Guides and the AAA rate restaurants on a similar 1 to 5 star (Mobil) or diamond (AAA) scale. Three, four, and five star/diamond ratings are roughly equivalent to the Michelin one, two, and three star ratings while one and two star ratings typically indicate more casual places to eat. In 2005, Michelin released a New York City guide, its first for the United States. The popular Zagat Survey compiles individuals' comments about restaurants but does not pass an "official" critical assessment. In the United States Gault Millau is published as the *Gayot* guide, after founder Andre Gayot. Its restaurant ratings use the same 20 point system, and are all published online.

The Good Food Guide, published by the Fairfax Newspaper Group in Australia, is the Australian guide listing the best places to eat. Chefs Hats are awarded for outstanding restaurants and range from one hat through three hats. The Good Food Guide also incorporates guides to bars, cafes and providers. *The Good Restaurant Guide* is another Australian restaurant guide that has reviews on the restaurants as experienced by the public and provides information on locations and contact details. Any member of the public can submit a review. Nearly all major American newspapers employ restaurant critics and publish online dining guides for the cities they serve. A few papers maintain a reputation for thorough and thoughtful review of restaurants to the standard of the good published guides, but others provide more of a listings service. More recently Internet sites have started up that publish both food critic reviews and popular reviews by the general public. This is a growing area and the market is still immature with no sites yet gaining dominant public or critical support. Several are gaining traction including Zagat.com, chowhound.com, and Fodors.com. Their major competition comes from bloggers and search engines since search engines often favor active bloggers over large somewhat static websites.

Economics

As of 2006, there are approximately 215,000 full-service restaurants in the United States, accounting for $298 billion, and approximately 250,000 limited-service (fast food) restaurants, accounting for $260 billion. There are 86,915 commercial foodservice units in Canada, or 26.4 units per 10,000 Canadians. By segment, there are:

- 38,797 full-service restaurants
- 34,629 limited-service restaurants
- 741 contract and social caterers
- 6,749 drinking places

Fully 63% of restaurants in Canada are independent brands. Chain restaurants account for the remaining 37%, and many of these are locally owned and operated franchises.

One study of new Cleveland, Ohio restaurants found that 1 in 4 changed ownership or went out of business after one year, and 6 out of 10 did so after three years. (Not all changes in ownership are indicative of financial failure.) The three-year failure rate for franchises was nearly the same.

INN

Inns are generally establishments or buildings where travelers can seek lodging and, usually, food and drink. They are typically located in the country or along a highway.

History & Origins

Found in Europe, they possibly first sprang up when the Romans built their system of Roman roads two millennia ago. Some inns in Europe are several centuries old. In addition to providing for the needs of travellers, inns traditionally acted as community gathering places.

"Inn" in more recent times has often come to denote a business serving alcoholic beverages, especially in North America, where they are usually alcohol-serving restaurants that have never provided lodging or serviced the needs of travellers.

In Europe, it is the provision of accommodation, if anything, that now differentiates inns from taverns, alehouses and pubs. The latter tend only to supply alcohol (although in the UK the conditions of their licence sometimes require them to have a nominal supply of food and soft drinks). Inns tend to be grander and more long-lived establishments. Famous London examples include the George and The Tabard. There is however no longer a formal distinction between an inn and other kinds of establishment, and many pubs will use the name "inn", either simply because they are long established and maybe were once a Coaching inn, or to summon up a particular kind of image; however, originally an *Inn* had to provide not only food and lodging, but also stabling and fodder for the traveller's horse(s) and for fresh horses for the Mail coach.

The original functions of an inn are now usually split among separate establishments, such as hotels, lodges, and motels, all of which might provide the traditional functions of an inn but which focus more on lodging customers than on other services; public houses, which are primarily alcohol-serving establishments; and restaurants and taverns, which serve food and drink. (Hotels often contain restaurants and also often serve complimentary breakfast and meals, thus providing all of the functions of traditional inns.) In North America, the lodging aspect of the word "**inn**" lives on in hotel brand names like Holiday Inn, and in some state laws that refer to lodging operators as innkeepers.

German Language

The German words for "inn", "innkeeper", and "innkeeping" illustrate the historical importance of inns. An innkeeper is **Wirt** (a host), the inn itself is a **Wirtshaus** (a host's house), and innkeeping is **Wirtschaft**. This last word, *Wirtschaft*, has departed from its meaning as simple hospitality and is now the German term for business and the economy; the latter usage may have derived by analogy, as the word "economy" itself is the Greek term for housekeeping (from *oikos*, "house," and *nomos*, "law"). Taken one step further, economics is *Wirtschaftswissenschaft*, literally the "science of the economy," or (still more literally) the "science of innkeeping."

Inns of Court

The Inns of Court were originally ordinary inns where lawyers met to do business, but have become institutions of the legal profession in London.

HOTEL TOILET-PAPER FOLDING

Hotel toilet-paper folding is a common practice performed by hotels worldwide as a way of assuring guests that the bathroom has been cleaned, and sometimes, with more elaborate foldings, to impress or delight guests with the management's creativity and attention to detail.

The common fold normally involves creating an inverted triangle▽ or "V" shape out of the first sheet or square on a toilet paper roll. Commonly, the two corners of the final sheet are tucked behind the paper symmetrically, forming a point at the end of the roll. More elaborate folding results in shapes like fans, sailboats, and even flowers.

Toilet-paper folding (also known as "Toilet paper origami") has attracted the attention of observers within the hotel industry and beyond it, involving both sober discussion of the practice as a marketing move as well as wry commentary with various degrees of seriousness.

Extent of Hotel Toilet-paper Folding

The practice is followed by hotels "the world over", according to Stephen Gill, a British photographer who published a book of pictures of folded hotel toilet paper from various nations.

Dr. Susan Blackmore, who uses the example of hotel toilet-paper folding to illustrate the use of "memes", pointed out in the 2006 Darwin Day Lecture before the British Humanist Association that even a remote guesthouse she visited in rural Assam in India folded the first sheet on its rolls of toilet paper.

Hotel toilet-paper folding is such an institution that in the horror movie *1408* it is used as one of the eerie happenings noticed by the main character — after using the toilet paper, he finds it mysteriously has been freshly folded over.

Reasons for Hotel Toilet-paper Folding

The practice is meant to assure customers that their hotel room has been cleaned, according to David Feldman, in his "Imponderables" syndicated newspaper column. Feldman reported that he had contacted "most of the largest chains of innkeepers in the country", asked why the toilet paper was folded, "and received the same answer from all". He quoted James P. McCauley, executive director of the International Association of Holiday Inns:

Hotels want to give their guests the confidence that the bathroom has been cleaned since the last guest has used the room. To accomplish this, the maid will fold over the last piece of toilet paper to assure that no one has used the toilet paper since the room was cleaned. It is subtle but effective.

Gill believes the practice is meant to please or impress customers: "But the neatly made bed, the folded toilet paper — all these things symbolise attention and love. Perhaps such finishing touches are also an attempt to suggest flawlessness or excellence, and so distract you from whatever failings the room may have. They create a moment of stillness."

Variations in Hotel Toilet-paper Folding

Gill found differences in the style and care of folding between hotels. One example from Tokyo, "with its tiny pleats, really stands out", according to the photographer. "Only in Japan did I find such minute attention to detail. ... The New York City example, on the other hand, is very poor quality, asymmetrical on rough, thin paper. And the Romania example is a great slab with a small, right-hand fold."

"Toilet Paper Origami" (also called "toilegami"), involves folding toilet paper, often in more elaborate shapes.

According to one hotel industry website, "Housekeepers at luxe lairs around the world are neatly folding the loose end of a partially used roll of toilet paper into a neat little bow or fan." Some hotels provide more elaborate flourishes: some apply a sticker attaching the folded end to the roll; others wrap spare rolls with a ribbon; Thompson Hotels imprint their logo on the first square. The Eldorado Hotel in Santa Fe, New Mexico, also imprints its name and logo on the ends of its toilet paper — a practice done by supervisors checking the work of the housekeepers.

As part of a $1 billion renovation of the Fountainebleau Hotel in Miami Beach, Florida in 2006, the typical triangular fold practice was stopped as one of a number of changes in order to give customers an impression that the hotel was special. Other changes included setting policy in the way linen cocktail napkins would be folded and the shape of glass tumblers.

"We're not going to do the little pointy thing," rooms division chief Charlotte Rosenau told the *Miami Herald*. "Every hotel does that." The change in toilet-paper policy was made after Rosenau and several housekeepers crowded into a bathroom to experiment with different methods. They settled on "folding the first square in half, then resting the crease midway down the roll", according to the newspaper. "It just looks nice and clean," Rosenau explained.

The Tickle Pink Inn, a motel in Carmel Highlands, California, folds the ends of its toilet paper into fan-like designs, mirroring the folds of its bathroom washcloths. A review in the San Francisco Chronicle noted the practice as "a fancy touch".

One travel writer noted seeing toilet paper folded into flowers and sailboats at hotels in Costa Rica.

Elaborate Toilet-paper Folding Beyond Hotels

An automated toilet paper folding machine called "Meruboa" was invented in Japan. With the push of a lever, the device folds the first sheet of toilet paper into a triangle.

Elaborate wedding dresses have been made from folded toilet paper (also using glue).

Opinions on and Humor about Hotel Toilet-paper Folding

In a humorous opinion article at the Hotel Online website, Larry Mundy wrote in his "Room With a View" column, perhaps partly with seriousness: "In my experience, there are two basic types of hotels: those that have the housekeeper fold a cute little triangle into the unused end of the toilet paper, and those that don't. Call it silly, call it pointless, I call it a sure indicator of the service levels I can anticipate at the property." Mundy continued: "That tiny detail of carefully triangulated tissue tells me that someone cared, that another member of my own species was here, in this very room, within the past few hours and spared no effort to make the end of the roll both presentable and easier to grip in my time of need. I don't need to engage in frustrating roll-rotation exercises just to find the loose end. I don't need to contemplate the jagged tear-line from the last user's haste — in fact, it doesn't occur to me there was a 'last user' at all, because the roll looks neat and new." Comedian John Cleese has commented on the practice in a humorous speech: "Why? What is it for? Is it proof that your house-maid has studied origami? ... If you're a Mason, are you supposed to fold it again into some sort of rhomboid?"

A reviewer writing about the Walden Country Inn & Stables, a hotel in Aurora, Ohio, noted a "horsey theme" reflected throughout the hotel's decoration, "never overdone (except, perhaps, for the Walden horse-head logo crimped into the end of the toilet paper)".

An anonymous commentator at the Hotel Chatter website pooh-poohed the idea of elaborate toilet-paper folding, "Certainly, this is an experience that should give anyone pause. At least a moment or two to wonder what hotel industry executive dreamed up this idea (and if his colleagues laughed in the meeting where he presented it). We'd also like to know if they couldn't find something better for the housekeepers to do besides fold the toilet paper ends into clever little forms? Were they not happy with the existing hotel towel origami art?"

NIGHT AUDITOR

A **night auditor** is a hotel employee who typically handles both the duties of the front desk agent and some of the duties of the accounting department. This is necessitated by the fact that most fiscal days close at or around midnight, and the normal workday of the employees in the accounting department does not extend to cover this time of day.

In larger hotels, night auditors may work alongside other nighttime employees, such as security officers, telephone attendants, room service attendants, and bellhops. In smaller hotels and motels, the night auditor may work alone, and may even only be "on-call", meaning that once he or she completes running the daily reports, the auditor retires to an area away from the desk while remaining available to attend to unexpected requests from guests.

Qualifications

In the United States, applicants to the position of night auditor are usually required to be high school graduates who are able to communicate effectively in English. Formal training in accounting or bookkeeping is not necessary. The successful night audit candidate will be detail-oriented, have a good grasp of basic arithmetic, and have a customer service focus.

Compensation

In the United States, night auditors are usually hourly employees. The salary ranges from $7 to $20 per hour. A night auditor typically makes $0.50 to $1.00 more per hour than a front desk agent with similar experience. This pay differential is due to the shift worked (11PM-7AM) and the additional responsibilities if there is no manager on site during the shift.

Accounting Function

The night audit itself is an audit of the guest ledger. The guest ledger (or front office ledger or transient ledger) is the collection of all accounts receivable for currently registered guests. It can also be defined as the collection of all guest folios. A folio is the account of an individual guest who is currently registered. The guest ledger is distinct from the city ledger, which a the collection of accounts receivable for non-registered guests (such as crcard companies).

One task of the night auditor is posting the day's room rate and room tax to each guest folio at the close of business (which usually occurs from midnight to 2AM).

Second, the night auditor must ensure the accuracy of the charges to the guest folios. Ensuring that the sum of revenues due to .accounts receivable from the various departments (ie. Food & Beverage, Rooms, gift shop) found on the department control sheets equals the sum of the charges made to the guest folios.

The closing balance of the guest folios is calculated using the night audit formula:

TODAY'S CLOSING GUEST LEDGER BALANCE = TODAY'S OPENING GUEST LEDGER BALANCE + TODAY'S

CHARGES (ie. room rates, Food & Beverage, etc.) - TODAY'S CREDITS (ie. payments from guests in cash, or transfers to the city ledger)

The folios for guests who are scheduled to leave the next morning may be printed and delivered to the guests' rooms.

Most hotels currently use computerized property management systems (PMS) to help perform the night audit. This has significantly reduced the amount of time required to perform the audit, as well as the arithmetic skill required of the auditor. An audit for a 1,000 room hotel can be completed in an hour with a PMS, whereas it would have taken an eight hour shift using previous generation of technology (the NCR 4200 mechanical system). Another duty of night auditors is to run daily management reports off of the PMS. These include occupancy reports and calculations of average daily rate (ADR) and revenue per available room (Revpar).

Front Desk Function

In addition to the accounting function, night auditors may also be required to perform the typical front desk functions during the graveyard shift. These functions include check-in, check-out, reservations, responding to guest complaints, coordinating housekeeping requests, and handling any emergencies that may arise.

Due to the nighttime shift, the clientele that the night auditor must deal with may be different than that of a typical front desk agent. At some properties, night auditors are known for frequent interactions with prostitutes, who tend to visit hotels at late hours for rendezvous with guests and the graveyard shift staff.

Night Auditors usually work alongside a Security Officer to maintain a level of security during late-night hours for both night staff and guests.

APARTMENT HOTEL

An **Apartment Hotel** (also **ApartHotel**, **Apart Hotel** and **Apart-Hotel**) is a type of accommodation, described as "a serviced apartment complex that uses a hotel style booking system". It is similar to renting an apartment, but with no fixed contracts and occupants can 'check-out' whenever they wish.

Apartment hotels are flexible types of accommodation; instead of the rigid format of a hotel room, an apartment hotel complex usually offers a complete fully fitted apartment. These complexes are usually custom built, and similar to a hotel complex containing a varied amount of apartments. The length of stay in these apartment hotels is varied with anywhere from a few days to months or even years. Prices tend to be cheaper than hotels. The people that stay in apartment hotels use them as a home away from home, therefore they are usually fitted with everything the average home would require.

Origins

Apartment hotels were first created in holiday destinations as accommodation for families that needed to 'live' in an apartment rather than 'stay' as they would in a hotel. The apartments would provide a 'holiday home' but generally be serviced. Later on these apartments evolved to be complete homes, allowing occupants to do everything they would at home, such as cleaning, washing and cooking.

Services and Facilities

Essentially the apartment hotel combines the flexibility of apartment living with the service of a hotel. Many of the apartments take advantage of prime locations with panoramic views of cities seen through wall to ceiling windows. Suites usually include high quality finishes, broadband connection & interactive TV, servicing and integrated kitchen and bathroom. High quality leather sofas in the living area and king size beds bring the hotel experience to a whole new level. Those are the luxuries, they also come with the basics: satellite or cable TV, washer, dryer, dishwasher, cooker, oven, fridge, freezer, sink, shower, bath, wardrobes, all the furnishings to be expected in a luxury home.

Extended Stay Hotels

Extended stay hotels are a type of lodging with features unavailable at standard hotels. These features are intended to provide more home-like amenities. There are currently 27 extended stay chains in North America with at least 7 hotels, representing over 2,000 properties. There is substantial variation among extended stay hotels with respect to quality and the amenities that are available. Some of the economy chains attract clientele who use the hotels as semi-permanent lodging.

Extended-stay hotels typically have self-serve laundry facilities and offer discounts for extended stays, beginning at 5 or 7 days. They also have guestrooms (or "suites") with kitchens. The kitchens include at a minimum usually: a sink, a refrigerator (usually full size), a microwave oven, and a stovetop. Some kitchens also have dishwashers and conventional ovens.

Extended stay hotels are popular with business travelers on extended assignments, families in the midst of a relocation, and anyone else in need of temporary housing. Extended stay hotels are also used by travelers who appreciate the larger space a typical suite provides.

Residence Inn is credited with popularizing the "extended stay" concept. The chain was launched in 1975 in Wichita, Kansas by Jack DeBoer, and acquired by Marriott Corporation in 1987. As of April 2005, there were over 450 Residence Inn hotels in the United States, Canada and Mexico. Jack DeBoer has jumped back in the Extended Stay market developing a concept called Value Place.

Other upscale brands of extended-stay hotels, such as Staybridge Suites which is part of the InterContinental Hotels Group, have made this segment of the lodging industry one of the fastest-growing.

One of today's most popular long term lodging brands came from the merger of Extended Stay America and Homestead Hotels. Both these chains were already well established when they combined in 2004 to become Extended Stay Hotels with over 670 owned and operated properties nationwide.

Another worldwide hotel chain, Choice Hotels International, franchisor for name brands such as Comfort Inn, Comfort Suites, Sleep Inn and Quality Inn, entered the extended stay market with their MainStay Suites brand. They proceeded to acquire the Suburban Extended Stay hotel chain in 2005, making them a sizeable extended stay system with over 150 hotels open and under development.

In the United States, a popular low-budget extended stay chain is Intown Suites. The chain, which was founded in 1988, now has nearly 140 locations in 21 states, and is distinguised for offering weekly rates much lower than many other chain lodging companies in North America. The company, however, has been criticized by many of its guests and reviewers for providing a sub-standard quality of service, poorly maintaining its properties, and treating its guests poorly.

Extended stay concept is steadily spreading throughout Europe due to increase in the number of travelers and business people visiting every year. The concept was organized by Belgium Housing and the chain of hotels covers 42 countries of Europe including all the major cities of the continent.

BOUTIQUE HOTEL

Boutique hotel is a term popularised in North America and the United Kingdom to describe intimate, usually luxurious or quirky hotel environments. Boutique hotels differentiate themselves from larger chain/branded hotels and motels by providing personalized accommodation and services / facilities. Sometimes known as "design hotels" or "lifestyle hotels", boutique hotels began appearing in the 1980s in major cities like London, New York, and San Francisco. Typically boutique hotels are furnished in a themed, stylish and/or aspirational manner. They usually are considerably smaller than mainstream hotels, often ranging from 3 to 50 guest rooms. Boutique hotels are always individual and are therefore extremely unlikely to be found amongst the homogeneity of large chain hotel groups. Guest rooms and suites may be fitted with telephony and Wi-Fi Internet, air-conditioning, honesty bars and often cable/pay TV, but equally may have none of these, focusing on quiet and comfort rather than gadgetry. Guest services are often attended to by 24-hour hotel staff. Many boutique hotels have on-site dining facilities, and the majority offer bars and lounges which may also be open to the general public. Despite this definition, the popularity of the boutique term and concept has led to some confusion about the term. Boutique hotels have typically been unique properties operated by individuals or companies with a small collection. However, their successes have prompted established multi-national hotel companies to usurp the term and/or try to establish their own brands in order to capture a market share. The most notable example is Starwood Hotels and Resorts Worldwide's W Hotels, ranging from large boutique hotels like the W Union Square NY to the W 'boutique resorts' in the Maldives to true luxury boutique hotel collections like the Bulgari collection, SLS Hotels, Thompson Hotels, Joie De Vie hotels, and The Keating Hotel, among many others.

There is some overlap between the concept of a small boutique hotel and a bed and breakfast.

In the United States, New York remains the centre of the boutique hotel phenomenon, as the original Schrager-era boutique hotels remain relevant and are joined by scores of independent and small-chain competitors, mainly clustered about Midtown and downtown Manhattan. The French Quarter and Garden District, New Orleans have several dozen boutique hotels, most of which are located in old homes or inns. These usually provide an ambience based on 19th-century antiques, artwork with New Orleans themes, vintage or reproduction furniture and decor and/or interesting historical associations. Miami and Miami Beach also have a large number of boutique hotels, mostly found along the beachfront streets Ocean Drive and Collins Drive. Most of these are in buildings from the heyday of the Art Deco period. Their attractions include the Art Deco ambiance, beach access, nouvelle and Latin cuisines and tropical-themes interior decor. Spain have boutique hotels distributed all around its geography.

The concept of boutique or design hotels has spread elsewhere outside the US. A good example is Thailand where many boutique or design hotels are sprouting, especially in resort locations, such as Phuket and Hua Hin. Boutique hotels are even now appearing in such places as Indonesia, Shanghai, Iceland, Peru and Turkey. Boutique and design hotels are becoming increasingly popular in Far Eastern cities such as Bangkok, Singapore, Hong Kong and even Beijing. Currently, there are a few publications dedicated to boutique hotels. One is boutique DESIGN magazine, which is published quarterly. Another is Deluxe Traveller Magazine, which is available in print and online. The online version can be downloaded for free at their website, www.deluxetraveller.com. Boutique hotel resources are more commonly available online. A number of sites are dedicated to boutique hotels such as Avantgarde Hotels, Chic Retreats, Epoque Hotels, Escapio, Tablet Hotels, and TemptingPlaces.com though some are purely a collection of online brochures with limited editorial content and review. There are also a number of stylized design and coffee table books highlighting various properties throughout the world.

An increasing number of hotels label themselves "boutique" nowadays forcing true boutique hotels to make focused choices to differentiate themselves. They typically promote local culture, ecology, cultural heritage, and art and choose to provide real experiences to their visitors. For example : swimming amidst Singapore's skyline (the Naumi in Singapore), sleeping in Francis Ford Coppola's villa in Belize (the Turtle Inn), releasing baby turtles in Malaysia's South-East China (Gem Island in Malaysia) sea, choosing the colour of your room in Hong Kong (the Cosmo), experiencing a carbon neutral hotel in Shanghai (the URBN), or taking Mexican cooking lessons in Peubla (Meson Sacristia de la Compania in Mexico)...

ECO HOTEL

Eco hotel is a term used to describe a hotel or accommodation that has made important environmental improvements to its structure in order to minimize its impact on the environment. Traditionally these hotels were mostly presented as Eco Lodges because of their location, often in jungles, and their design inspired by the use of traditional building methods applied by skilled local craftsmen in areas such as Costa Rica and Indonesia. Today the term has developed to include properties in less "natural" locations that have invested in improving their "green" credentials.

An eco hotel should meet the following criteria1:

- Dependence on the natural environment
- Ecological sustainability
- Proven contribution to conservation
- Provision of environmental training programs
- Incorporation of cultural considerations
- Provision of an economic return to the local community

The term is being used on a more regular basis as new websites devoted to the subject become more prominent and hotel owners are more interested in protecting the areas their guests have come to visit.

New properties are being built from sustainable resources – tropical hardwoods, local stone – and designed to better blend in with their environment. In addition they are also being run on eco-friendly principles, such as serving organic or locally grown food or using natural cooling as opposed to air conditioning, all of which is doing far more good than just asking guests to reuse their towels.

There are many ways of establishing the "green" credentials of your hotel and as there are more than 100 certification programs worldwide there is a certain amount of confusion on the subject. It is up to guests to check whether the hotel is being run on environmental principles and the best way of doing this is to research your hotel before booking.

Ecolabelling of hotels in Europe

Any tourism accommodation operator in the EU - from a large hotel chain to a small farmhouse has been able to apply for the European Eco-label since 2003. The operators must meet strict minimum standards with regard to environmental performance and health standards. These should include the use of renewable energy sources, an overall reduction in energy and water consumption, measures to reduce waste, environmental policy setting and the provision of non-smoking areas.

The first eco-labelled hotel in the European Union was the Sunwing Resort Kallithea, Rhodes Greece in 2003. **The**

first eco-labelled hotel on the Iberian Peninsula (Spain and Portugal) was the Hotel Jardim Atlântico on the Portuguese island of Madeira. This hotel was built with major ecological concern and it was integrated with the landscape in order to minimize the impact of the infrastructure on the natural environment. For example, it has a biological wastewater treatment station. To build the hotel and meet the standards for eco-labelling certification was more than a challenge as the hotel is located on clifftops 480m above the Atlantic Ocean and surrounded by mountains in The Laurissilva forest which is UNESCO World Natural Heritage.

HOMESTAY

Homestay is a form of tourism and/or study abroad program that allows the visitor to rent a room from a local family to better learn the local lifestyle as well as improve their language ability. While homestays can occur in any destination worldwide, some countries do more to encourage homestay than others as a means of developing their tourism industry. Hosting a homestay participant also allows the local family to earn some additional, needed income. Having low profitability, as it is, homestay can not be regarded as strictly commercial activity, but more of cross cultural exchange. Students generally arrange a homestay with their school or educational institution, but can also informally arrange to stay with a family through social connections, and through a variety of private agencies. There are a number of online homestay agencies that connect students with hosts all over the world (usually for a nominal fee).

Types of Homestays

Homestay scenarios can range from a completely immersive family experience, to a very basic room rental.

In the immersive family experience a homestay student lives, eats, and shares the majoritiy of their time in the host country with the hosts and their family. Family events such as dining out, amusement parks, camping, travel, etc. usually involve the host student who may or may not be expected to pay a portion for the participation (tickets, parking, gas, travel expenses, et al.) The student is invited to participate in Holiday festivities (Thanksgiving, Christmas, etc.) and family events (weddings, birthdays, etc.)

At the other end of the spectrum, students may simply be renting a room within a private home with minimal supervision from a host or family. Additionally, there are a working homestay agreements where a student is expected to perform duties such as yard work, farm work, babysitting, maid services - usually in exchange for accommodation fees or as part of.

Typical Contracts and Agreements

A clash of cultures can sometimes result between a homestay student and the host family. To mitigate any issues, most homestay arrangements involve a contract or written agreement between the host and student. A contract will outline what is expected of the homestay student and may include items such as;

- Chores to perform (cleaning, laundering)
- Curfews
- Use of the Internet, television
- Use of the telephone
- Guest visits
- Smoking/drinking rules

as well as the details of what is being provided by the host in terms of:

- Accommodations
- Furniture/facilities
- Meal provisions
- Transportation
- Communications (Internet, telephone)
- Entertainment (TV, radio)

Generally, a host must provide a private room for sleep and study that has a lock and a washroom must be available that is convenient for the student to use. Most other items are negotiable in terms of availability and price.

Risks for the Host

Typically, hosting a homestay student is a rich and rewarding experience that allows the sharing of cultures, information, and experience. However, studying abroad is often the first time the homestay student is away from the parents and home country. This may result in adjustment issues for the student. The host must be able to deal with separation issues, anxiety, and the like.

Scams on the internet are becoming fairly commonplace - when engaging in financial transactions that may require international payments, cheques, and money orders being sent there is always the possibility of making oneself vulnerable to scams and fraud. The host family is best to educate themselves on the issues, and protect themselves adequately through the use of a good contract.

A recent and common example of a scam perpetrated on host families plays as follows;

- Parents of a student email the host family to request a room - usually claiming to be from Europe/Asia.
- The host replies with availability and costs etc.
- The parent agrees to the fees, and offers to pay the fees up front.
- Usually some sort of family crisis arises, and the transaction must be handled with urgency.
- The parent sends payment with an overage, and aks the host to refund the excess payment.
- The host family refunds the payment.
- The initial payment (cheque, money order, etc.) bounces or is fraudulent.
- The host family has lost the money it has sent as a refund.

This scam can happen in any situation any time payment is required in the form of cheque/money order/cashiers cheque, etc. In-depth discussion on frauds of this type is beyond the scope of this article, but the host family is encouraged to exercise caution when dealing with overseas payments and transactions.

Risks for the Student/guest

There are two basic motivations for a family to engage in the operation of a homestay:

1. The family is looking to assist students, inject culture, and better understand the world and its people through a mutual exchange of traditions, knowledge and culture.
2. The family is looking to augment their income.

Usually, a family bears a healthy mix of these two reasons in opening their home to students and international visitors.

Occasionally, however, there are instances where a family, or individual, is looking only to capitalize on the financial opportunity and has little or no concern for the interests of the student. A student is encouraged to look at the history of students and guests that the family has hosted, and to ask for a reference from a student who has recently attended their homestay. If a family refuses to give a reference, a student is advised to stay away. Also, look for a contract that not only protects the interests of the homestay host, but also the interests of the student. There should be a clear listing of the obligations of both the student and host family.

VACATION RENTAL

Vacation rental is a term in the travel industry meaning renting out a furnished apartment or house on a temporary basis to tourists as an alternative to a hotel. Vacation rentals have long been a popular travel option in Europe (especially in the UK) as well as in Canada and are becoming increasingly popular across the world. They are often referred to as self-catering rentals or villa rentals. In some cities, like Barcelona, local authorities determined that vacation rentals were becoming a threat to the hotel industry and passed some legislation placing regulations and limits on the industry, while in others, such as England, Ireland, France and Spain, the government promotes and certifies holiday rentals, even offering its own program of holiday/vacation rentals.

A **vacation rental** is a fully furnished property, such as a condominium, townhome or single-family-style home, often referred to as villa rentals in Europe. The client/traveler arranges to rent the vacation rental property for a designated period of time, many rent on nightly basis similar to hotel rooms, although the more prevalent vacation rental industry practice is typically weekly rentals. A true vacation rental is not for sale to the guest; rather, the owner of the vacation rental merely allows the guest to rent the property for a predetermined length of time.

Differences between Villa/vacation Rentals and Timeshares

Consumers unfamiliar with the concept of a vacation rental may confuse it with the seemingly similar, but distinctly different, timeshare. A timeshare can still be rented as a vacation rental should an owner decide to put his owned week(s) on a vacation rental program. Many timeshare resorts offer quarter-ownership which offers the owner 13-weeks of ownership and, therefore, more weeks to offer for rental.

A timeshare is a piece of real estate—often a fully furnished condominium—that is jointly shared by multiple owners. While different types of timeshare ownerships exist, in general, each owner bears a portion of the responsibility, along with the right to a segment of time in which he or she is granted sole use of the property. Timeshare resorts allow financially qualified guests to rent and tour their unowned properties and then make those properties available to the guest for purchase. Timeshare owners can also choose to bank their week with and exchange company such as RCI, or rent the unit

Although lower rents for vacation rentals by owner were once the norm, this is not always the primary benefit. Quite often a vacation rental will feature more amenities and features, such as more space, fully-equipped kitchens, sports and beach equipment, games, DVD libraries, books, etc. Owners managing their own properties tend to be more aware of wear and tear and have better cash flow to use to maintain and upgrade the property. Perhaps the primary difference is that vacation rentals tend to offer more space and the advantage of sampling what life in one's destination is truly like for the locals.

Pros and Cons of Vacation Rentals

Vacation and villa rentals are generally appealing for many reasons, some of the foremost being cost savings, more space, and no tips, taxes or service charges that are associated with hotel rooms. Villa and vacation rentals have kitchens for cooking, living rooms for gathering together and offer the appeal of living in a real neighborhood and soaking up the rhythm of the locals. In the United States, hotels often enjoy the advantages of brand recognition, familiar reservation processes, and on-site staff for problem resolution. For a guest, booking a vacation rental may mean stepping out of that comfort zone in order to garner some of the advantages they offer. Perceived cons of vacation rentals can include having to communicate directly with the property owner, being unfamiliar with the property, lack of on-site staff, and concerns about quality or cleanliness — however, these are most often mitigated by dealing with villa or vacation rental agencies that manage vacation properties for owners and they offer many of the same services hotels offer to their guests, e.g., front desk check-in, 24-hour maintenance, in-house housekeeping, concierge service.

The benefits generally outweigh the potential negatives, with many vacation rentals offering more space (multiple bedrooms and bathrooms, separate living areas), more amenities (fully equipped kitchens, fireplaces, private hot tubs), convenient locations (on the beach, ski-in/ski-out, city centers in real neighborhoods) and greater privacy than a hotel, including the fact that many villa/vacation rentals give travelers the option of inhabiting real neighborhoods in their destination and living like the locals. As of 2006, vacation rental management has become a $10 billion industry and continues to become more popular. Vacation rentals can range from budget studio apartments to lavish, expensive private villas in the world's most desirable locations, some with pricetags of many thousands per night and all the amenities you would find in any luxury accommodation (fully staffed, private beaches, boats, chefs, cooking lessons, etc) to cater to the guests.

Vacation rentals are available in most states of the US and very prevalent in major tourist areas such as Hawaii, California, and Florida. The vacation rental market is much larger in Europe than it is in the United States as it has long been a common travel option for European travellers.

Management Companies

Many property owners contract a vacation rental management company to manage the business of their vacation rentals. These management companies market the vacation rental property, providing information and photos to guests and handling reservations and billing in the homeowner's stead. These companies also handle details such as guest check-in, housekeeping and property maintenance.

The largest vacation rental property management company in the United States represents nearly 17,000 vacation rental properties and there are many such specialty agencies throughout the world. Guests who book through vacation rental management companies may experience benefits including quality control, housekeeping services, professional reservations agents and on-site or on-call staff.

Many such companies are members of the Vacation Rental Managers Association and there are additionally many rental property management companies that deal only with vacation rental brokers/agencies that specialize in the villa/vacation rental industry.

Listing Services and Aggregators

There are numerous agencies that specialize in villa/ vacation rentals and most can be booked via the internet. Reputable vacation rental agencies will have familiarity with the regions and properties they represent as well as official booking/rental agreements and generally standardized booking procedures, cancellation policies, key collection, etc.

Additionally, vacation rentals may be offered through aggregation portals. Aggregators typically display property information and photos provided by the homeowner, however the listing services bear no legal responsibility for the accuracy of the information. Also, because the listing services do not verify the information guests are encouraged to request references from past renters and to procure a lease agreement prior to sending money directly to a homeowner.

A vacation rental may not be booked directly with a listing service. Because each property owner has his or her own deposit and payment requirements, cancellation policies, key-pick-up procedures, etc., a guest must contact the property owner or owner's agent directly in order to book. A guest who books through a listing service or direct from owner may experience the benefit of lower rental rates.

CONCIERGE

A **concierge** is an employee who lives on the premises of apartment buildings and serves as a general property caretaker; while the phenomenon and the term are most common in France, they can be seen elsewhere, for example in the French-influenced neighborhood of Heliopolis in Cairo, Egypt. A similar position, known as the *portera*, exists in Spanish-speaking regions. In medieval times, the concierge was an officer of the King who was charged with executing justice, with the help of his bailiffs. The term concierge evolved from the French *Comte Des Cierges*, The Keeper of the Candles, who tended to visiting nobles in castles of the medieval era.

In 19th century and early 20th century apartment buildings, particularly in Paris, the concierge often had a small apartment on the ground floor and was able to monitor all comings and goings. However, such settings are now extremely rare; most concierges in small or middle-sized buildings have been replaced by the part-time services of door-staff. These are less costly and less intrusive. Some larger apartment buildings or groups of buildings retain the use of a concierge. The concierge may, for instance, keep the mail of absented dwellers; be entrusted with the keys of apartments in cases of emergencies in the absence of the inhabitant; and perform other tasks.

In hotels, a concierge assists guests with various tasks like making restaurant reservations, arranging for spa services, recommending nightclubs, finding escorts, procurement of tickets to special events and assisting with various travel arrangements and tours of interesting places to visit. In upscale establishments, a concierge is often expected to "achieve the impossible", dealing with any request a guest may have, no matter how strange, relying on an extensive list of personal contacts with various local merchants and service providers.

Hotel concierge staff have their own professional association, called Les Clefs d'Or ("The Golden Keys"). It was formed in France in October 1929. It now reaches over 3000 members in over 50 countries. Members can be distinguished by the gold keys they display on their lapels.

In hospitals, concierge services are becoming more and more available. A concierge in hospital will provide similar services to those of a concierge in a hotel, however rather than just serving a guest, they are serving patients and employees as well. This adds a huge benefit to the employees of hospitals who work long shifts, and helps to provide work-life balance.

Personal concierge services are also available that allow clients to "buy back" their precious time. A personal concierge works on the most basic of premise: people want things done and just don't have the time to do them.

Today there are numerous independently owned and operated concierge companies. Many of these companies provide errand services, as well as informational services for their members. Services include informational requests, setting dinner reservations, making telephone calls, researching travel arrangements and more.

Typically, concierge companies will bill on an hourly rate, and depending upon the type of task at hand fees can fluctuate drastically. Other companies bill a flat monthly fee based upon the number of requests a member is allowed to place each month. This service offering is also know as lifestyle management. The number of independently owned concierge companies has skyrocketed as the start up costs and barriers of entry are quite feasible for many entrepreneurs. Concierges also entertain their clients.

The owners and operators of concierge and errand service businesses are supported and advocated by the non-profit International Concierge and Errand Association and the

National Concierge Association. These associations serve their members through essential resources, continuing education, networking opportunities and other professional endeavors.

RECEPTIONIST

A **receptionist** is a person in an office/administrative support position. The work is usually performed in a waiting area such as a lobby or front office desk of an organization or business. The title "receptionist" is attributed to the person who is specifically employed by an organization to greet any visitors, patients, or clients.

A receptionist is usually expected to have a high school diploma or the equivalent, but a receptionist may also possess a vocational certificate/diploma in business and office administration. Although a post secondary degree is not normally required for this position, some receptionists may hold four year university degrees in a variety of majors. Some receptionists may even hold advanced degrees.

The business duties of a receptionist may include: answering visitor inquiries about a company and its products or services, directing visitors to their destinations, sorting mail, answering incoming calls on multi-line telephones or, earlier in the 20th century, a switchboard, setting appointments, filing, records keeping, keyboarding/data entry and performing a variety of other office tasks, such as faxing or emailing. Some receptionists may also perform bookkeeping or cashiering duties. Some, but not all, offices may expect the receptionist to serve coffee or tea to guests, and to keep the lobby area tidy.

A receptionist may also assume some security guard access control functions for an organization by verifying employee identification, issuing visitor passes, and by observing and reporting any unusual or suspicious persons or activities.

A receptionist is often the first business contact a person will meet at any organization. It is an expectation of most organizations that the receptionist maintain a calm, courteous and professional demeanor at all times regardless of the visitor's behavior. Some personal qualities that a receptionist is expected to have in order to do the job successfully include: attentiveness, a well groomed appearance, initiative, loyalty, maturity, respect for confidentiality and discretion, a positive attitude and dependability. At times, the job may be stressful due to interaction with many different people with different types of personalities, and being expected to perform multiple tasks quickly.

Depending upon the industry, a receptionist position can be considered a low-ranking, dead end or servile position, or it could be perceived as having a certain veneer of glamor with opportunities for networking in order to advance to other positions within a specific field. Some people may use this type of job as a way to familiarize oneself with office work, or to learn of other functions or positions within a corporation. Some people use receptionist work as a way to earn money while pursuing further educational opportunities or other career interests such as in the performing arts or as writers.

While many persons working as receptionists continue in that position throughout their careers, some receptionists may advance to other administrative jobs such as customer service representative, dispatcher, interviewers, secretary, production assistant, personal assistant, Marketing and executive assistant. In smaller businesses, such as doctor's or lawyer's office, a receptionist may also be the office manager who is charged with a diversity of middle management level business operations. When receptionists leave the job, they often enter other career fields such as sales and marketing, public relations or other media occupations.

A few famous people were receptionists in the beginning, such as Betty Williams, a co-recipient of the 1976 Nobel Peace Prize. A number of celebrities had worked as receptionists before they became famous, such as singer/songwriter Naomi Judd and the late entrepreneur/Beatle wife Linda McCartney1. Other famous people who began their careers as receptionists or worked in the field include civil rights activist Rosa Parks and former Hewlett Packard CEO Carly Fiorina.

The advancement of office automation has eliminated some receptionists' jobs. For example, a telephone call could be answered by an Automated attendant. However, a receptionist who possesses strong office/technical skills and who is also adept in courtesy, tact and diplomacy is still considered an asset to a company's business image, and is still very much in demand in the business world.

CATERING

Catering is the business of providing foodservice at a remote site.

Mobile Catering

A mobile caterer serves food directly from a vehicle or cart that is designed for the purpose. Mobile catering is common at outdoor events (such as concerts), workplaces, and downtown business districts.

Event Catering

Event ranges from box-lunch drop-off to full-service catering. Caterers and their staff are part of the food service industry.

When most people refer to a "caterer", they are referring to an event caterer who serves food with waiting staff at dining tables or sets up a self-serve buffet. The food may be prepared on site, i.e., made completely at the event, or the caterer may choose to bring prepared food and put the finishing touches on once it arrives.

The event caterer staff are not responsible for preparing the food but often help set up the dining area. This service is typically provided at banquets, conventions, and weddings. Any event where all who attend are provided with food and drinks or sometimes only hors d'oeuvres is often called a *catered event*.

Many events require working with an entire theme or color scheme. A catering company or specialist is expected to know how to prepare food and to make it attractive. As such, certain catering companies have moved toward a full-service business model commonly associated with event planners. They take charge of not only food preparation but also decorations, such as table settings and lighting.

The trend is towards satisfying all the clients senses with food as a focal point. With the correct atmosphere, professional event caterers with experience can make an event special and memorable.

Beautifully prepared food alone can appeal to the senses of taste, smell, and sight - perhaps even touch, but the decorations and ambiance can play a significant part in a successfully catered event.

Catering is often sold on a per-person basis, meaning that there is a flat price for each additional person. However, things like lighting and fire permits are not scaled with the guest count, so per-person pricing is not always appropriate. It is necessary to keep the cost of the food and supplies below a price margin in order to make a profit on the catering.

As many others in the food service industry, caterers and their staff work long hours. It is not uncommon for them to work on holidays or 7 days a week during holiday event seasons.

A comprehensive, formal full-service catering proposal is likely to include the following elements:

- Time-line matters: rental arrival time, staff arrival time, bar open time, meal serve time, bar close time, rental pickup, out-of-venue time. Each of these factors affects the catering price.

For example, a rental quote for an "anytime" weekday delivery is usually much more economical than an "exact-time" delivery.

- General menu considerations: Clients may have specific dietary or religious needs to consider. these include Halal, Kosher, Vegetarian, Vegan and food allergy requests. Increasingly, clients are interested in food sustainability and food safety.
- Hors d'oeuvres: it should be clear if these are passed or stationary. Most caterers agree that three or four passed items are appropriate for the one-hour period prior to a meal.
- Meal Rentals: May include tables, chairs, dance floor, plants, tabletop (china, flatware, glassware, linens,

chargers), bar glassware, serving equipment, salt/ peppers, etc. It should be clear whether table and chair setup and take-down is included. Most rental companies do not automatically include setup and take-down in the rental charges.

- Labor: Verbiage varies from caterer to caterer, but generally speaking, an event will have a Lead/Captain/ Event Manager, a Chef, perhaps a Sous Chef or Kitchen Assistant, Wait staff and Bartenders. The labor on a plated dinner is generally much higher than the labor on a buffet, because a plated dinner involves double the china, and usually a minimum of three served courses, plus served coffee. Simply put, there's a lot more to do. To do it properly requires roughly 10 to 50% more staff. On a large event, this can be substantial, especially if overtime or doubletime applies.
- Service Charge: Sales TaxSome quotes will include lighting, fire permits, draping, florals, valet and coat check.Many venues discreetly get a "cut" of the catering bill. Caterers are contractually committed to not disclose this fee specifically in their contracts with the clients. Therefore, catering will sometimes cost substantially more at one venue versus another.Also, caterers must compete with illegal operators. A legitimate caterer will have a business license and a health permit both showing the address of the place from which they do business.

Catering Officers on Ships

Merchant ships often carry Catering Officers - especially ferries, cruise liners and large cargo ships. In fact, the term "catering" was in use in the world of the merchant marine long before it became established as a land-bound business. The "Careers Scotland" website 1 gives the following definition of a Catering Officer's duties:

Merchant Navy catering officers oversee the purchase, preparation and serving of food and drink to crew members and passengers. They are also responsible for accommodation services, including the provision of linen, bedding and laundry.

They may be in overall charge of administration, organising record keeping, wage payment, and the interpretation of customs and immigration records that apply while the ship is in port.

On larger ships, responsibilities may be shared with the purser, who looks after passengers' comfort and facilities such as banking and shopping, while the catering officer concentrates on organising stores, overseeing the preparation of menus and meals and generally managing dining rooms and services. On a cruise liner, catering officers may be known as 'hotel services managers'.

Merchant Navy officers sometimes work in difficult and uncomfortable conditions. They spend long periods of time away from family and friends.

Bibliography

Berry, A., Jarvis, R.: *Business Accounting for Hospitality and Tourism*, London, Chapman and Hall, 1995.

Black, Wendy: *Elegant Hotels of Europe*, Glen Cove, PBC International, 1994.

Boissevain, J.: *Coping withTourists*, Oxford, Berghahn Books, 1996.

Bryson, McDowell: *Concierge: Key to Hospitality: A Training Manual*, New York, Wiley, 1992.

Clark, Mona: *Interpersonal Skills for Hospitality Managers*, London, Chapman Hill, 1995.

Dennis, J.: *How Consumers Pick a Hotel: Strategic Segmentation and Target Marketing*, New York, Haworth Press, 1997.

Donald, M.: *Customer Service in the Hospitality and Tourism Industry*, Englewood Cliffs, Prentice Hall, 1994.

Eberts, Marjorie: *Careers in Travel, Tourism, and Hospitality*, Lincolnwood, VGM Career Horizons, 1997.

Elio, C.: *The Hospitality Law Desk Reference*, Miami, Southern Beverage Journal, 1994.

Hubert, B.: *A Host of Opportunities: An Introduction to Hospitality Management*, Chicago, Irwin, 1996.

James, M. : *The Meeting Planner's Legal Handbook*, Washington, D.C.: Goldberg & Associates, 1996.

Koontz, H.: *Management: A Global Perspective*, New York, McGraw Hill, 1993.

Medlik, S.: *Managing Tourism*, Oxford, Butterworth-Heinemann Ltd., 1991.

Michael, John: *Principles of Hospitality Law*, London, Cassell, 1999.

Nancy, N.: *Choosing a Career in Hotels, Motels, and Resorts,* New York, Rosen Pub. Group, 1997.

Norman, G.: *Hotel, Restaurant, and Travel Law: A Preventive Approach,* Albany, Delmar Publishers, 1993.

Pender, Lesley: *Marketing Management for Travel and Tourism,* Cheltenham, Stanley Thornes Publishers, 1999.

Robert, H.: *Managing Hospitality Human Resources,* East Lansing, Educational Institute of the American Hotel & Motel Association, 1997.

Rocco, M.: *An Introduction to Hospitality Today,* Orlando, Educational Institute, 1998.

Rosemary, E.: *Managing Employee Relations in the Hotel and Catering Industry,* London, Cassell, 1995.

Swarbrooke, J.: *Marketing Tourism, Hospitality and Leisure in Europe,* London, International Thomson Business Press, 1996.

Thomas, F. : *Introduction to the Hospitality Industry,* New York, Wiley, 1995.

Thomas, F.: *Introduction to Management in the Hospitality Industry,* New York, Wiley, 1995.

Timothy, R.: *Cases in Hospitality Management: A Critical Incident Approach,* New York, Wiley, 1995.

Waller, Keith: *Improving Food and Beverage Performance,* Oxford, Butterworth-Heinemann, 1996.

Ware, Richard: *How to Open Your Own Restaurant: A Guide for Entrepreneurs,* New York, Penguin Books, 1991.

Zaccarelli, Herman E. : *Food Service Management by Checklist: A Handbook of Control Techniques,* New York, Wiley, 1991.

Index

Cyber 575
01/09/10